Future *of* Governance

FROM INDIA TO BHARAT

Future *of* Governance

FROM INDIA TO BHARAT

N Vittal, IAS (Retd)
Former Central Vigilance Commissioner (CVC)
Government of India

Manas Publications
(We Convert Fighters into Writers)
New Delhi - 110 002 (INDIA)

MANAS PUBLICATIONS
(We Convert Fighters into Writers)
(Publishers, Library Suppliers, Importers & Exporters)
4402/5-A, Ansari Road (Opp. HDFC Bank)
Darya Ganj, New Delhi - 110 002 (India)
Phones : Off.: 011-23260783, 23265523, Res.: 011-23842660
E-mail : manaspublications@gmail.com
manaspublications@yahoo.com
Website : www.manaspublications.in

ISBN 978-81-7049-526-0
₹ 995.00

Designed at
Manas Publications

Printed in India at
R.K. Printers, Delhi
and published by Mrs Suman Lata for
Manas Publications, 4402/5-A,
Ansari Road (Opp HDFC Bank),
Darya Ganj, New Delhi - 110002 (INDIA)

PREFACE

I have been blessed by Lord Venkatachalapathy with a good life. As I look back, I find that my life has been in three parts ie good, better and best. In a way, it was the reversion of Lord Curzon's life as summarised by Winston Churchill in his book *The Great Contemporaries*. For Lord Curzon, Churchill wrote, "Morning was gold, noon was silver and evening was bronze. But each was perfect in its own way." In my case, morning was bronze, noon was silver and evening is gold, and each was not only perfect in its own way but had seeds for transmutation for the next metallic state.

As it will be clear from this book, this has all been due to the grace of Lord Venkatachalapathy. I have realised that I am only an instrument in His hands. In fact, my friend and colleague in the IAS, PVRK Prasad (IAS, 1966 Andhra Pradesh cadre), in his partial autobiography describing his experiences in Tirupati titled *Na Hum Karta, Hari Karta* (I am not doing anything, the real author is Lord Narayána).

Many of my friends and colleagues had been urging me to write my autobiography for the sake of posterity. Like PVRK Prasad, I also came to realise that recalling one's career and life will only be an exercise in vanity, if we do not realise the fact *sic transit gloria* (so transient is our life). This realisation made me very hesitant to write my autobiography at all.

The second reason which held me back was that I have read great biographies like that of Mahatma Gandhi's *The Story of My*

Experiments with Truth and more elaborate autobiographies like the autobiography of Jawaharlal Nehru – *An Autobiography*. Gandhiji particularly has been forthright even in highlighting his failures at a very personal level, which I think many other men would have kept silent. After all, this is what distinguishes Gandhiji from lesser mortals. One of the questions I asked myself is, "Will I be able to be as frank and transparent as Gandhiji?", and the answer is a decisive 'NO'. Hence, I thought undertaking an autobiography exercise will be really less than perfect because I would not be leaving an honest record. But then there was a third argument, I found about the need for a policy-maker in governance to leave a record. This gained strength after I read in December 2013, the autobiography of one of the great icons of IAS, Mr G Ramachandran (1949 Tamil Nadu cadre). As he describes, his autobiography written practically in the last 9 months of his life, which in itself was an exercise in public service. G Ramachandran had been a very important player in various historical events in the development of democracy in India, particularly post-independence; being close to the revolutionary changes brought about by Indira Gandhi. The Government of India did not have the original records to find out how the 'stray thoughts' of Indira Gandhi, which led to the nationalisation of banks in 1969, came about. This is indeed, the key document in that policy. It was drafted by G Ramachandran. As an upright civil servant with a great sense of propriety, he had kept quiet and the whole information remained secret. All these would have been lost to the future historians but for Montek Singh Ahluwalia (former Deputy Chairman of the Planning Commission), who had requested him to leave a record. As I read it, I realised that I was also blessed by God to play a key role in the evolution of right policies, in two critical sunrise areas of the Indian economy today, namely Telecommunications and Information Technology.

I realised, dramatically, how fickle public memory could be when on 21st December 2013, I responded to a last minute call from Hyderabad from my dear friend and colleague JA Chowdary, who operated the Software Technology Park in Hyderabad in 1990, when we were experimenting with the concept of Software Technology Parks for boosting software exports from India. The technique was a great success. Today's icons and veterans in the Indian IT sector, like NR Narayana Murthy (Infosys), Nandan Nilekani (Infosys), Faqir Chand Kohli (founder of TCS), Azim Premji (Wipro) and others freely recognise this fact. It has become an Indian fashion to decry the government and the bureaucracy in the media, the government departments and bureaucrats (*babus*) are usually perceived as whipping boys who are responsible for the lack of progress in our country. While I was the Secretary, Department of Electronics for five and a half years, India had started to make a name for herself in the software sector. It was a time when Indian girls like Aishwarya Rai and Sushmita Sen overcame global competition and made us proud by winning beauty pageants like 'Miss Universe', 'Miss World', and so on. That was also the time when the Narasimha Rao government had opened up the economy by way of the economic liberalisation policies introduced in 1991. The joke going around was that Indian girls were able to beat the global competition because the Government of India did not operate a 'Ministry of Beauty'. Indian software industry was also beating the world because the government encouraged the whole industry by benign neglect.

In fact, the positive role the Department of Electronics (DOE) played by way of strategic alliance with the industry has been repeatedly acknowledged and emphasised by the icons of the IT industry. I thought that the memory will be lost if I did not document my memories.

I had a great humbling experience in the meeting I attended in Hyderabad on 21st December 2013. This was the programme called Test which was supposed to be a TiE (Global Entrepreneurship Organization) entrepreneurship services. TiE in itself is a venture capital fund promoted by NRIs in the Silicon Valley and elsewhere. TiE stands for Indus entrepreneurs, another concept of TED (Technology, Entertainment and Design) which specialised in short presentations not exceeding 18 minutes of those who have achieved success through entrepreneurship, imagination and vision in various fields conducted from the early part of the 21st century. I must confess that I was totally unaware of what was expected. I had earlier participated in TED programmes in Chennai. Knowing TiE and the other TED, I thought I will be able to pull it off by communicating to the youngsters of today; the excitement of how the software industry (IT) grew in India. My two other panelists in the session were well-known internationally recognised sportsmen of Hyderabad itself, like cricketer VVS Laxman and badminton player Pullela Gopichand. Whereas, the audience knew them, this was an audience of, may be, about 800 people, with a small section of about 20 from the IT sector. When the question was asked by the compere, do they know the name N Vittal, unlike many hands went up when the other two names were mentioned, only two hands went up when my name was mentioned. That itself was a humbling experience to realise that I have already become a part of the forgotten history. Thereafter, when I started talking within my allotted time of 15 minutes, I was booed twice and clapped out so much so that I had to drastically cut down my talk. I realised that I made a terrible mistake by not budgeting for the total ignorance of the sector by the youngsters of today and also the fact that the major difference between my generation in their 70s and the current generation of teens and youngsters is that the younger generation brought up today, in the era of the internet and Google, have very little patience to go deep into any particular subject. They may collect a vast amount of data based on mass of information available in sources like Google, and so on. But the old capacity of thinking through and original thinking is greatly affected. Perhaps, as an old person of the bygone era, I may be harsh in judging. But in the context of what G Ramachandran's book, *Walking with Giants – A Memoir* was written, I also felt that this was the time when I, still not a victim of generative ailments, should put down in a readable form my experiences in government.

In fact, soon after the disastrous meeting I addressed on 21st December 2013 at Hyderabad, I had a quiet dinner with some of my old colleagues from the industry. One of them, Praveen Gandhi reminded me that the current generation have no idea about how IT came to India. It will be useful if I write in a chatty and readable form my experiences. That gave me a shock because, I have written 15 books of my experiences in various government departments with quite a few of them from a purely management point of view and some from the point of view of governance.

In fact, once Macmillan Publishers asked me to write a book on 'How to Get Things Done in India?' and it was a time in early 2000 when India was getting the first wave of investments in the post-liberalisation period and the investors in India had to face problems compared to the easy time they were having in China which was everybody's favourite at that time. Macmillan did not publish my book. Ultimately it was published as *Roots of Effective Governance* by ICFAI (Institute of Chartered Financial Analysts of India) based in Hyderabad promoted by Dr Yasaswy and Dr Besant Raj. Unfortunately, ICFAI had closed its publication division. While I am today happy that there are serious students in public administration and governance and IT sector who are preparing their doctorates based on my writings, they complain that my books are not easily available. Secondly, my books are written in a language which is not in the popular form of being very chatty, simple and of general interest. So, I realised this lacuna in my thinking and writing after Praveen Gandhi made this suggestion to me. That night itself I resolved that I should write a book of this type. In fact, coming to think of it, I had realised even earlier in 2012 when I wrote a book, as requested by Penguin, on fighting corruption. That book, *Ending Corruption: How to Clean up India?* had a good reception and one of the perceptive comments made by one of my dearest friends, YV Pai made me realise the defect in my style of writing. He has been my close senior and right from the time I joined the Gujarat cadre as one year junior to him, our families are very close to each other and he has been one of the few lifelong friends my family has. He has been religiously reading whatever books I have been publishing. He said, "of all the books you have written, this is perhaps, the most readable." That made me realise that while my earlier books would have been a shade better than the notes of the government files, the Penguin book really was meant for the general audience and has really done well and it has gone into reprints and the company has also entered into deals for bringing out Marathi, Gujarati, Hindi and Tamil versions. I do not know when these books will see the light of day. But the Penguin experience made me realise that there is no point in just writing a book, there has to be readers to read it. The value of a book increases if more people read it. More people will not read it unless it is readable. It is said that human beings are rational and they will do the rational thing only after trying everything else. Perhaps, I being a true human being, I am also following the same path. At least I am happy that I came to the right path when my faculties are not totally gone. I hope you enjoy this book.

N Vittal

CONTENTS

CHAPTER 1

WHY THE TITLE?

I have been an extremely fortunate person, blessed by Lord Venkateswara, the benign, the all powerful Lord of the universe. When I look back at my life, I am amazed at how I have been particularly blessed by Him. I was fortunate to be born on 31st January 1938, just a decade before our ancient rich nation became independent and after nearly a thousand years started governing itself. India has always been a rich country. As the legendary Nani Palkhivala had pointed out, "India is a rich country but we have managed to keep it poor." It has perhaps, the best of the natural resources but there has been a perception that India is a poor developing country. Nani Palkhivala represented the best of one of the rare races in the world, the Zoroastrians, though persecuted in their own country and had to seek refugee elsewhere, brought sweetness and light wherever they landed. When more than thousand years ago, forefathers of the Parsis, landed in Sanjan on the west coast of India in Gujarat, the local ruler sent him an overflowing bowl of milk, to politely indicate that there was hardly any space to accommodate the immigrants. The leader of the Parsis is believed to have added sugar to the milk and sent it back in an equally polite way with a sweeter message that like the sugar they would merge with the population and would not cause any tension. The history of the Parsis in the last 1,000 years had shown how although they are perhaps a microscopic minority, they have produced brilliant individuals in every field, be it music, law, painting, culture, science and what have you, and their contributions to the social capital as well as the financial capital of the country has been stupendous.

Right from my younger days, I have been moved by noble examples like that of Mr Palkhivala, who apart from carving a unique position for himself in the horizon of constitutional law in our country, also demonstrated his large heart by donating a substantial part of his wealth to another noble enterprise like Dr Badrinath's 'Shankara Netralaya' in Chennai. These gestures show that, as we become old and look at our own life, and if we have been successful, we realise that it is the grace of God that helped us all along and it will be totally wrong and egoistic on our part to presume that we achieved all that we did in our life mainly through our own efforts. In the *Bhagavad Gita*, Lord Krishna, towards the end, highlights this basic point. We are all only instruments in the hands of the Lord. *Nimitta matram bhava savya sachin*, he says. We are only an instrument.

I started realising it increasingly, as I went on in my life and towards the end when I look back, I find that by some curious design, I have been present at the right place in the right moment and as a result, I have been able to make a positive contribution, introduced policies or at least catalysed policies which helped India in realising its unique potential in the evolving knowledge economy. The two sunrise sectors in technology today are the Telecommunication Sector and the Information Technology Sector. It looks unbelievable that as a single individual, I was the Secretary in the Department of Electronics from June 1990 to January 1996, with a short break of 6 months between July 1993 and January 1994, for five and a half years. I was connected with the Telecom Commission of India for all these six years and was fortunate to become the Chairman of the Telecom Commission from 1st October 1993 to 4th September 1994. It was just less than a year but what a year it was.

That was the year when the century-old monopoly of the Department of Telecommunications (DoT), established by the

British government and governed by the Indian Telegraphic Act of 1885, was drastically modified to throw open the entire telecom sector of India to collaborations from the private sector. In one stroke, by the policy announced by the government headed by Prime Minister PV Narasimha Rao, the century old Telecom Department's monopoly was given a shock treatment by throwing open the sector to the private sector and also to global competition. This aspect of economic liberalisation, both in the general economy and particularly in telecommunication and the realisation of the Government of India about the importance of electronics and information technology in the emerging knowledge economy, gave a flying start to India and totally changed the perception of India as a poor, over-populated, developing country. Population which was once considered in the period of 1947 till 1997 a problem, became an opportunity.

Sanjay Gandhi, the stormy petrel flourishing during the Emergency (1975) introduced by his mother Indira Gandhi, focused on compulsory sterilisation as a weapon and as a ready solution to the problem of over population and poverty. All these changed overnight, once the world economic paradigm changed from the old model of the industrial revolution of more than 300 years, to the 21st century model of knowledge being the driving force for not only economic breakthroughs but also for adding value to the economy. Steel was typical of the old economy. If one kilo of steel costs ₹1,000, 95% of that value is thanks to material contents like iron, cobalt, nickel, manganese and chromium, and so on, and the remaining 5% was steel technology. On the other hand, in softwares like Lotus 1-2-3 or Microsoft Office software, 95% of the price was for the technology and hardly 5% for the material content. The contributions to the economy, therefore, came from not metal and physical resources but from brain power. Hence, suddenly, human beings were valued as human capital, even though it appears to be degrading the worth of the individual as special and one can never equate pure material resources like physical resources with brain power of human beings. After all, the brain is a unique gift to humanity by God.

It was the unique blessing of God that I was the Secretary in both these key departments which were typical Government of India organisations bound in yards of red tape. I recall, in 1991 when PV Narasimha Rao became the Prime Minister of the country, the Indian economy was considered to be a basket case and with an ideologically leftist and socialistic stance, displayed by great leaders of independence like Jawaharlal Nehru, realised that in the process of planning for the whole economy and adopting the Soviet model, they themselves landed in a mess. After more than 70 years of their experiments in communism, which was dramatically launched in Russia with the October 1917 Revolution, ultimately imploded and collapsed in 1990, dramatically symbolised by the fall of the Berlin Wall which divided the vanquished nation of Germany into East and West Germany and the capital was also divided into East and West Berlin with a wall to emphasis the separation. The coming down of the wall because of the explosion of people's anger and frustration against the dehumanised system of communism, which killed the spirit of enterprise of the people, led to a chain reaction throughout the world.

Till then, the world was divided into three parts. First World was a developed economy depending on the market oriented economies lead by the United States and Western Europe. The Second World was the Communist world where the Soviet Union and its allies of nearly 60 countries following the totalitarian centralised planned model and the third was the other countries who as a huge population, although rich with natural resources, hardly making any progress to build their wealth. The Third World countries were all earlier colonies or very poor countries and the two major powers, the United States and the West and the Soviet Union, tried to spread their influences on them. The world appeared to a bipolar world in which there was a strong battle of ideologies between two opposite philosophies, should the State intervene in the economy and control the commanding heights or should it allow the spirit of enterprise to flourish, and ensure level playing fields so that there is no large jungle in the market place when economic competition for goods and services takes place.

The collapse of the Soviet model in 1990 lead to a re-orientation of the world order of governance and many of the erstwhile communist countries adopted different forms of the market oriented liberalism demonstrated by the United States and the European countries. In fact, when I look back at my life, I find that I joined the Indian Administrative Service in 1960 and the motivation for joining the IAS came from my father Nagarajan. He was the only son of my grandfather Narayan Rao Nagarajan and being the only son, he was too precious for his parents and there were lot of restrictions on the choice of career, and so on. My father had told me that he wanted to appear for the ICS which in those days involved going to England and competing. But my grandfather, who at the prime of his life as a Class I government officer, being a District Munsiff (Civil Judge, Senior Division) would not permit him to undertake a trip abroad and cross the border, even though from the financial point of view, he did not have any restrictions.

My father, being a very sincere and dutiful son, obeyed him and stayed back and chose a career in law. He became a lawyer with the State government in Madras and ended up as Assistant Public Prosecutor in Trichy. Fortunately, even though he was in a transferrable job, he could continue for nearly 40 years in Trichy itself, even though later in his life, nearing his retirement age, which was 55 years in those days, he was transferred outside Trichy as a First Class Magistrate. This long tenure helped him to bring up his children, five of us, four brothers, Raghavendran, Mohan, Ranganathan and my sister Prema, and see them settled in life. As a college student, he also nourished the dream of studying French which unfortunately he could not materialise. Therefore, as I was growing up, my father wanted to realise apparently, his dreams through me. Persuaded by him to take French in intermediate class in St Joseph College, I studied French and when I finished my degree BSc (Hons) in Chemistry, which was equivalent to the post-graduate at the age of 20, my desire was to go for a career in research in Chemistry. But my father advised that I must try for the IAS and if I failed, I could go for research.

In those days, the minimum age for competing for the IAS was 21 and one can avail a maximum of three attempts as the maximum age limit was 24. If you are able to write from the age of 21 but if you lose, you lose a chance. I got into the IAS in my first attempt itself, thanks mainly to the blessing of Lord Venkateswara and my father. In those days, the age of retirement was 56 and it was increased to 58 and I retired at the age of 58 in 1996. I got into the IAS at the age of 22 in the 1960 batch. After I retired on 1st January 1996, the retirement age was further increased to 60. But I was not eligible to get that advantage. Nevertheless, the Government of India appointed me as the Chairman, Public Enterprises Selection Board, and before that could be over in another 3 years in January 1999, on September 3, 1998, I was selected to be the first Central Vigilance Commissioner to be appointed by the selection process recommended by Justice JS Verma, in the Vineet Narain case, also popularly known as the Hawala Case.

This led to the wide perception that I was the first Central Vigilance Commissioner. In fact, I was the eleventh Central Vigilance Commissioner starting with Justice Nittoor Srinivasa Rao, the only judge who ever occupied the position of the Central Vigilance Commissioner. Justice Nittoor Srinivasa Rao was the Chief Justice of the then Mysore High Court later on known as the Karnataka High Court. He was the only Judge ever to occupy the position of CVC. He was succeeded by ICS officers like MG Pimputkar and others. ICS officers in turn were succeeded by IAS officers like CG Somaiah and TU Vijayasekharan. The 10th CVC was my own batchmate, SV Giri of the Andhra Pradesh cadre, who was selected by then Prime Minister PV Narasimha Rao and approved by his Cabinet. The then President Dr Shankar Dayal Sharma did not fully go along and the earlier practice of the Prime Minister recommending the name of the CVC and the President approving it was given up.

It was during the tenure of SV Giri that Justice Verma, the Chief Justice, delivered the judgement on 18th December 1997 in the Vineet Narain case popularly known as the Hawala Case. It was in that judgement that the Supreme Court laid down the guideline that the selection of a person to be the CVC must be made by a High Power Committee consisting of the Prime Minister, the Home Minister and the Leader of the Opposition in the Lok Sabha. The conditions of service of the post of CVC are unique, so far as the Government of India is concerned. The President administers the Oath of Office to the CVC, whose term is limited to a single term of four years. After completing the term, the person occupying the post of CVC is debarred for life from occupying any office of profit under the Central Government, any State Government and even constitutional positions like Governor, Vice-President, President of India. The last condition does not apply to any other top post in India.

The notification of an Ordinance to implement the Supreme Court's judgement of December 1997 was issued much later in 1998 and unless that Ordinance, I was the first Central Vigilance Commissioner to be selected. Therefore, general impression aroused in the public that I was the first CVC to be appointed. In fact, as mentioned earlier, I was the 11th and the only major difference was that I was selected by a process prescribed by the Supreme Court and the independence of the CVC was to be guaranteed by enacting a special legislation as directed by the Supreme Court, the CVC Act, 2003. The CVC thus, became an authority, not merely based on a government order or office memorandum of 11th February 1964, which was in force, and giving the position of the CVC a statutory position by enacting the CVC Act, which Parliament did in late 2003.

I was therefore, appointed when the Ordinance was in force as the first Central Vigilance Commissioner under the new system. This came as a total surprise to me and more so to my wife. She thought that I have had a career in which I was mostly connected with industrial development and the public sector and a post like CVC which has a judicial flavour was totally different from the type of work I have been doing so far. Of course, this impression was not correct. IAS by nature of its service is called generalist and there is no concept of specialisation unlike other services of the Government of India, dedicated to special sectors like Police, Law and Order, revenue collection, finance, forest and environment, and so on.

Nevertheless, the career of an IAS officer generally has a basic theme when one reaches the end of one's career, some have spent their career mostly in the state and some have their career partly in the state and partly in Government of India which is what is expected of the IAS as an All India Service. They are supposed to be a link in the basic concept of a Federation and the Constitution reflecting India as a Union of States. While several powers are still with the Central Government, the advantage of an All India dedicated cadre of administrators, who occupy positions at policy making levels in the State as well as at the Central Secretariat is with the idea that the Government of India's policy-makers have hands-on experience of running the government, governing the states also so that the policies framed are in tune with the basic tenets of the Constitution as well as reflect a pragmatic common ground and philosophy of administration. In that sense, I have handled not only departments connected with industries and economic development, but also maintenance of law and order and regulatory administration. For instance, my last posting in Gujarat itself was as Additional Chief Secretary, Home. I was also in charge of the Civil Supplies Department as well as managing Public Sector enterprises like Gujarat Narmada Valley Fertilisers Corporation. I therefore, handled both economic development departments and the departments of regulations. Majority of the posts I held were connected with industry. The following will indicate the time I have spent in state and the centre and the sectors where I was able to act and contribute for a long time in my career.

So far as the industries and economic development is concerned, in the state and at the centre, I occupied the following positions:

1. Director of Geology and Mining, Gujarat (1970-1974)
2. Managing Director, Gujarat Narmada Valley Fertilizers & Chemicals Limited (GNFC), Bharuch (1982-1987)
3. Additional Secretary, Department of Atomic Energy, Government of India (1988-1990)
4. Secretary, Department of Electronics (later on renamed as Ministry of Information Technology) (1990-1996)
5. Member, Telecom Commission (1990-1996)
6. Officer on Special Duty, Department of Telecommunications (July 1993–October 1993)
7. Chairman, Telecom Commission and Secretary, Department of Telecommunications (October 1993–September 1994)
8. Secretary, Department of Electronics (September 1994–January 1996)
9. Chairman, Public Enterprises Selection Board (January 1996–September 1998)

Government of Gujarat

1. Collector, District Magistrate, Sabarkantha district, Gujarat (1964-1965)
2. Secretary, Civil Supplies, Government of Gujarat (February 1980)
3. Additional Chief Secretary, Home, Gujarat (June 1987–June 1988)

It will be obvious that I spent more time in departments, connected with industrial development rather than regulations. I sometimes used to describe my entire career with tongue in cheek as all that I did in my career was to run industries or run after industries or after retirement from service, select people to run public sector industries and finally, I ended up with a very strong regulatory function of checking corruption, the most flourishing industry. One can look at corruption itself as perhaps the most flourishing industry in India because, after all, running business is an intelligent exercise in assessing the risk and reward and choosing the activities that give the best rewards. Any industry requires some capital and clever imaginative and visionary management to create more wealth. Corruption is one industry where there is zero investment by way of money, so long as one manages to get an influential position in government and one can exploit it to the full. The conviction rate in Indian courts is hardly 6% and viewed from this point of view, this is the one industry, where the risk is only 6% and the chance of escape from punishment is 94%. No wonder, corruption flourishes in our country. My wife asked me, as soon as we got the message in September 1998 that I was going to be selected as Central Vigilance Commissioner, why has the government chosen you, who has spent most of his career in industrial promotion function, to head a very important regulatory function of checking corruption, that too under the more empowered directions given by the Supreme Court? I tried to convince her by saying how, if we take a slightly different view, my entire career also connected with industry in some form or other and corruption was the most widespread industry in India?

That apart, as I look back at my career and the role I was able to play in development of two sunrise industries in India, namely, Telecommunications and Information Technology, I can only attribute this to Lord Venkatachalapathy's grace. I was placed in the right departments in the right position at the right time. I therefore, realise the significance and the depth of meaning that is there in the famous advice given by Lord Krishna in the eighteenth chapter of the *Bhagavad Gita*:

sarva-dharman parityajya mam ekam saranam vraja aham tvam sarva-papebhyo moksayisyami ma sucah.

(Leave all religious practices and surrender to me; I guarantee that I will protect you from all past, present and future sins and I guarantee *moksha* to you.)

Such a clear articulation of what one should do and such an assurance for liberation may hardly be seen in perhaps any other religion or any other belief.

Hence, when I started writing my autobiography, I thought *nimitta matram* (Chapter 11, *Bhagavad Gita*) should be the one phrase which will express, in the pithiest manner, a summary of my entire life. I find that I have been able to journey through the entire spectrum of governance. I have been in the public administration in governments in the states and at the centre. I have been in business enterprises by way of joint sector enterprises and finally after completing my tenure today, I am connected with many educational activities and this in turn has blossomed into an imaginative and visionary combination between education and industry by way of special economic zones like the Vittal Innovation City and the Reserve Water Foundation.

CHAPTER 2

A PRE-BIOGRAPHICAL NOTE ON THIS AUTOBIOGRAPHY

An autobiography is the record of a person written by himself, this note is a short biography of the autobiography itself.

As explained in the Preface, this autobiography was written as a reaction to two key developments of my fiasco in the Hyderabad conference of 23rd December 2013 and the impact it had on me when I read the autobiography of one of my most ideal seniors, G Ramachandran, published a month before his death.

The choice before me was how to frame the autobiography. I have been writing and keeping notes depending upon my mood from time to time, for many years. These notes were written as and when I had spare time, like the three months at the MIT in 1989, or in the early days of my training in 1961 at Godhra as a supernumerary assistant collector. Some were written in 1981, when I tried to emulate Ram K Vepa (IAS, 1958 Andhra Pradesh cadre), some in 1999, not to speak of all the subsequent writings I have been doing more or less continuously from 1996 till today.

The choice I made was instead of trying to *de novo* write a coherent autobiography, I will make my autobiography into sort of an album of my writings, which in itself has the advantage of reflecting my change in style of expression, my values, especially my judgements about events and above all, retain the freshness of the impressions that I must have had when I wrote the pieces.

A certain degree of repetition becomes unavoidable in such a situation. However, I have tried my best to avoid reader unfriendliness. At the same time, one additional benefit is that, I can myself see, as the reader will, how my ideas have evolved over a period of time. For example, when it comes to the issue of corruption, I have been writing continuously and extensively and these writings reflect the evolution of my thoughts. Perhaps, the most cohesive and comprehensive book I have written on corruption is *Ending Corruption: How to Clean-Up India*, published by Penguin in 2012. Nevertheless, the major issue of tackling black money on the basis of the formula promoted by Fali Nariman was an important development, which I did not elaborate in that book. At the same time, I thought that there is a valuc, so far as my earlier writings on corruption are concerned, as they reflect the intellectual search of an administrator with hands-on experience in searching for an effective solution to the most important problem, ensuring good governance, in the context of an orthodox Hindu and an inheritor of the Sanatana Dharma of this country.

CHAPTER 3

TURNING POINTS IN MY LIFE: COINCIDENCE OF INTELLIGENT DESIGN?

As I look back through the spectrum of governance and the life I have led, I am really amazed the way my life has evolved. From an astrological point of view, the prediction of Demai Maharaja, the venerable old astrologer Agnihotri, whom I met soon after my marriage with Gita in 1964, turned out to be an accurate map of the path my life followed. The astrologer told me, "Sir, your luck has hardly started blossoming. You will have a life which can be classified as good, better and best. The first third of life will be good, the second better and the final part of your life would be the best." As you read this biography, you will find that what venerable old Agnihotri had told me has turned out to be very accurate.

But if you go a step deeper into my life, you will find that there were so many coincidences and my life took turns, each phase turning out to be better in the long run, even though some of them at the moment when they occurred, appeared to be setbacks. I have always wondered, how does this happen, may be it is something natural, I being a very optimistic person.

I was asked by Dr Pradip Khandwalla, Professor at IIMA in the 1980s while delivering a talk at the IIMA about "My Philosophy, My Action". I summed it up by saying that my philosophy is basically this: be positive, be creative and have sound common sense, and above all, have faith in God and keep your personal life clean.

This realisation, about keeping one's personal life clean, came to me much later when I became the CVC in 1998 and when I was able to draw national and international attention by being the first in the world to utilise Information Technology of the Internet, in 2000, to expose corruption and possibly check corruption. That was when as CVC, I published on the website of the CVC, the list of senior corrupt public servants belonging to the All India Services and Central Services in the Government of India and the top executives of Banks, particularly officers of revenue departments like Income Tax, Customs and Excise.

The manner in which, I was selected for each of my posts, made me realise that there is a divine power which guides all of us and that power, to me, is Lord Venkateswara, who gave me the strength of the mind and the fortitude to face health problems like becoming diabetic at the age of 25 or breaking the IAS barrier with hardly any experience of meeting any of the IAS officers on a personal level. In fact, my father had only suggested three services – IAS, IPS and IFS (Indian Foreign Service). Only after I became familiar with the exam procedures, I realised that for the effort I put in to appear for these three services, I could have as well appeared in all the 14 services of the Government of India for which the examination was common. In the case of the IAS, of course, and the IFS, in addition to the three papers which are called optional papers, one had to take two advance papers. In fact, in the IAS interview I was asked, "why have you restricted your options only to three services?" I got away by merely saying, "I have deliberately restricted my choice so that my attention would be focused on these specific services and it was for me like crossing the Rubicon for Julius Caesar." When I analysed the marks I got, both in the written paper and in the interview, I realised that I could have made only to the IAS considering my rank. I ranked 40 in the all India list and in those days, only the top 10 or 15 ranks managed to get into the IFS (Indian Foreign

Service). So far as the IPS is concerned, I had to get more marks in the two papers which were only considered for the IPS and I am afraid I did not make it. In retrospective it appears as if God tailor made the results in such a way that, I had no option but to join the IAS. This is just one example of coincidence in my life and throughout my life I have constantly come across such coincidences which are really uncanny.

Dr Eddington, one of the eminent atheists of the early 20th century, in his book defined God as 'anti-chance'. Einstein, one of the greatest scientists and original minds of all time, speculated the most ennobling experience of human life is the sense of the mysterious. He later on, also made other comments, pointing out that there is a design and pattern in the laws of science. God does not play dice with mankind or an equivalent word he had adopted. There are others who claim, those were not the exact words used by Einstein but the common perception is that even the most scientific advanced analytical mind of the 20th century like Einstein recognised that there was a greater power ruling over our destiny, than what can be explained only by pure physical sciences. Perhaps, another great thinker of the 20th century, namely Stephen Hawking, does not accept the presence of God. But when we read his speculations about multiple dimensions, we find that his assumptions border very much on the borderlines of physics and metaphysics. Those who are not scientists but rationalists and atheists believe themselves to be acting on scientific logic.

But in the domain of science, this goes as the principle of what is known as the provability of fallibility, unlike religion where "Rome is spoken. The case is closed", for Catholics. Any theory starts with fundamental assumptions on which they erect their hypotheses. Any hypothesis when empirically tested and proved becomes a scientific law of theory. If we look at some of the advanced concepts today in astronomy and cosmology, we find that we are in an area where physics and metaphysics seem to combine, where science and religion seem to come together or science and spiritualism seem to merge. In fact, the irony of human life is that in spite of living 70 years or more, one still does not have definite answers to the questions, where we came from, what is conscience, is there a soul, and so on. Many of the concepts cannot be empirically proved but they have to be realised. This has been the eternal conflict between the materialistic approach or scientific and rational approach to life and its spiritual and religious approaches. But a traditional set of beliefs like in our Hindu religion gives us a lot of peace of mind and provides an excellent guide, both in terms of living, a happy and healthy life and also in developing the courage to live through the crises and tragedies in one's life and above all; towards the end of one's life, one achieves a sense of peace and a sense of detachment, thereby being able to meet one's physical end without being in too much of terror and worry about where we will go after this world. Tiruvalluvar, the great Tamil poet, who some claim to be a Jain, put it very simply, "death is like going to sleep, birth is like waking up from sleep." But between birth and death, a most interesting thing happens, which is our human lives. All this is my attempt to capture the particular life I have had in the hope that people who read my experiences may find them worth learning about.

CHAPTER 4

MY ROOTS

FATHER

We are all shaped by our parents. Parents not only bring us to this world but literally script our life. At a physical level, we inherit their genes and feature. What is more, they decide and script our character and personality. There is a Tamil proverb *"thaayai pol pillai noolai pol selai"* (as the mother so the child, as the yarn so the sari).

I have inherited perhaps more of my features from my mother Padma Bai than my father Nagarajan. There is a proverb *"matha mukhi sada sukhi!"* The son who looks like his mother and has her face is bound to be prosperous all the time.

That proverb has proved to be correct in my life. Looking back at this distance of 76 years of my life, it has been a remarkable smooth and even life. Is that because I inherited my mother's feature?

My mother lived up to the ripe old age of 79. My father died relatively young by today's standards. On 28th July 1975 when he breathed his last in my sister Prema Seshagiri's house at Karaikudi, he was just two weeks short of 66.

Thoughts about my father always make me quietly happy. He was the most humane and pleasant person I have come across in my life. I have never seen him shout or lose his temper. He never preached about virtue of the need to be polite and honest.

Children learn their most valuable lessons in life and imbibe values, I think, through a process of silent osmosis.

Even today if I close my eyes, I can picture my father as he was. He was just 5'6" and always somewhat roly-poly. He was not dark but not very fair either. He had a kind round smiling face and was always gentle. He had pock marks on his face, the legacy of the small pox, he suffered from when he was a boy. He had curly hair which none of us inherited, except my son Sharad.

My father had tonnes of patience and was a very good listener too. I do not remember any occasion when he would cut short anyone in mid-sentence. He spread a sense of quiet cheerfulness wherever he was around.

He was a lawyer, the Assistant Public Prosecutor who handled the prosecution side in government cases. Throughout his life, he was mostly in Tiruchirapalli. This element of stability helped our family and complete our education without much disturbance or change of place or schools.

He was popular amongst his colleagues and had an excellent reputation. He used to handle some very independent and sensitive cases. I remember the Udayarpalayam murder case, the Communist Conspiracy case, the anti-Hindi agitation and the Vanoli agitation cases. The last three cases had political implications. SA Dange, the Communist leader was examined in the Communist conspiracy case and EV Ramasamy Naicker (EVR), popularly known as 'Periyar' who was the founder of the Dravidar Kazhagam, was the accused in the Vanoli agitation case. The Dravidar Kazhagam wanted All India Radio to be renamed in Tamil as 'Vanoli' instead of the Hindi 'Akash Vani'.

At the end of the long gruelling trial, I was told by my father that EVR, the bearded octogenarian leader of the movement came to my father and said, "Thanks, Sir. You treated me with great dignity." That was my father. He was always a gentleman.

We lived in a small house at 24, Viswappa Pet, Puthur, Tiruchirapalli from 1949 to 1967. The front part of the house was the office. This would have been the main hall to be used as a drawing room.

A small passage from the office led to a smaller hall which was used as a dining room. Adjacent to this was a dark room which was mainly a storeroom.

Beyond the dining hall was a verandah which was used as a kitchen. In the backyard was a 'dry toilet' and a small room which was the bathroom.

There was a first floor with the steps leading from the drawing room. For children, this was the main living area. We studied, played and slept here.

Most of the time, father remained busy with the policemen (mainly inspectors) discussing cases in the drawing room.

I do not know, when he went through all the case papers and prepared his arguments. He had to travel at least once or twice a week to the talukas of the district where cases were heard. There were days when he used to come late. I was always worried about him and prayed that he comes home safely.

Money was always a problem. I do not think my father earned more than ₹500 a month when he was in service. It was only after retirement in 1964, at the age of 55 that he started earning a little more. He was appointed as a Special Prosecutor in the anti-Hindi agitation case in 1964, when in Coimbatore, a couple of police officers were burnt alive by the agitators. He shifted base to Coimbatore during that period.

Another case which he handled was the counterfeit currency case. He had to work in Chennai (Madras) for this case. Perhaps, he earned at the rate of ₹100 per day in this case.

But money or lack of it, never held him back in taking vital decisions. We were four brothers and one sister. I was the eldest followed by Prema (1939), Raghavendran (1941), Mohan (1942) and Ranganathan (1945). We had another sister Radha (1946) who died at the age of 11 months on 1st August 1947.

The year India became independent was a year that tested my father in the prime of his life. It was a year of deaths in our family. My grandmother died on 10th March 1947. Six weeks later, my grandfather died on 17th April 1947. The merciless hat trick of deaths was completed on 1st August 1947 when my infant sister died of dehydration.

These deaths were not only a great emotional strain for my father, they also caused a severe financial strain. We are Madhwa Deshastha and among the Brahmins who constitute a minority in Tamil Nadu. We were a minority within a minority, a micro-minority. There are only 75,045 people of my caste in the 6 crore population of Tamil Nadu.

We Madhwas are very conservative and orthodox. Rituals become very important in our life. (At least, it was so during my youth.) My father was particular that all the rituals must be strictly and completely observed for his dead parents.

My father, who never had much money or property, went into debt, thanks to the triple deaths of 1947. But the same deaths, brought out another starling dimension of his character. This was his capacity to face the slings and arrows of outrageous failure. He was indeed an outstanding example for unflappability. He was never ruffled. He could bear any misfortune silently.

In fact, this aspect of his character used to irritate me sometimes. When it comes to catching a train, I always wanted to go with sufficient margin of time and be at the station at least one hour ahead of schedule. My father was just the opposite. He would always plan to be there at the last possible moment. The funny thing was most of the time, he was able to get away with it.

Even Homer nods, it is said. I remember at least one occasion when he missed a train. My brother Ranganathan had to be escorted by him for an interview at Chennai and they reached the station that day, just as the train was steaming away from the platform. My father, of course, remained calm. He took Ranganathan by bus to Chennai the next day. He was very religious and used to worship Lord Vinayaka at Teppakulam Rock Fort Temple before catching any train. He told us that he could not go to temple that evening since he returned late from the court. Hence, he missed the train!

The net result was that many a time when I will be worrying about keeping an appointment with the college during admission time, my father would be taking his own time, keeping me on pins and needles.

Our parents influence our character in curious ways. If I imbibed his faith in God and integrity, when it comes to matters like time management, I took the opposite trait. I am an anxiety ridden person and I always provide a safe margin of time for every activity.

The bedrock of my father's unflappability was his unshaken faith in God. Every Friday, whatever the time and however late it was, he would take his bicycle and go to Thiruvanaikoil to worship Goddess Akilandeswari. He must have *darshan* of the deity every Friday. That was the iron discipline.

My father's life was a life of struggle. He never had it easy. But at the end of it all, he could perhaps look back on his life with satisfaction. We, the four sons of his; went on to become professionals in four different areas. I joined the IAS, Raghavendran became an engineer, Mohan a surgeon and Ranganathan, following family traditions, became a lawyer. (Incidentally, my paternal grandfather Narayana Rao was a lawyer and retired as a District Munsiff). My sister Prema did her BSc and married my cousin Seshagiri, who retired as a professor from the Engineering College at Karaikudi.

In retrospect, it may appear that my father had a plan and a vision to bring up his children to become successful professionals. In fact, he never forced his views on us.

Each one of us, chose the subject of our study according to our perception and desire. I did well in the intermediate examination in 1955 and stood second in the university.

Engineering was a popular choice in those days, but of all things, I wanted to study chemistry. I learnt from my neighbour who was an executive in the All India Radio that BSc (Honours) Chemistry was an exclusive course and there were only 20 seats, 10 each of Presidency College and Loyola College at Madras.

My father did not have much money. He could easily have asked me to take up BSc (Honours) Physics which was available in St Joseph's College at Tiruchirapalli itself. Without a word of criticism, my father quietly arranged for my studies at Loyola College, Madras. I stayed in the hostel for three years. All this added to the cost.

Mine was not only the case. My sister and brothers had also to be educated in professional courses. All this added a great financial strain on him. Never once had I heard him complain.

I had a glimpse of what all this meant in 1957. I was in the final year of my course and my mother's jewels and family jewels had to be sold. It all came to 55 sovereigns and fetched hardly ₹1,600! It was one of the saddest days in my life. My mother's view was that the financial crisis was more due to the death ceremonies of 1947 and not due to educational expenses.

It seems that my maternal grandfather C Balakrishna Rao asked my father how he was going to finance the education of all of us. My father expressed his intense faith in God and said that education was the one asset he could give to his children. His faith in God and in us were borne out.

My father had rock-like faith in God. He faced a lot of disappointments in life and financially he was always in trouble. He had debts all the time and used to share his worries with us when we became adults. He used to quote Kamban who described the mental agony of Ravana as comparable to the one who has a huge debt. He would quote from *Hamlet*, Polonius advice to Laertes, "Neither a borrower nor a lender be." One of the embarrassing and, for him, the most painful moments was when my uncle Chandru mama (C Ramachandra Rao) suddenly demanded the return of a loan as he had to book a flat in Mumbai. Somehow my father managed that situation.

In later life, he repaid most of the loans. In 1975 June, just before my youngest brother's (Ranganathan's) marriage, we found he still had debts of ₹7,000. We brothers shared the burden and returned the loan. Our father was at last free from debt but alas! He did not live long. He died within three months. We at least had the satisfaction that his trust in us was vindicated.

The continuous mental tension on the financial front had taken its toll on him. He always felt that our relatives, particularly his sisters did not appreciate the help, he had given them umpteen times in times of trouble through physical means and in human terms. He always had an element of self pity.

But he was not the constantly moaning type. He counted his blessings. He was proud of our achievements in school and college. A proud moment was when he was invited to be the Chief Guest in the Silver Jubilee Celebrations of our school – Bishop Heber High School, Puthur. All of us, four brothers had studied there and all of us had done well. It was indeed very gracious of the school management to have invited my father, who was not a Christian, to be the Chief Guest on such an important occasion.

My father had a positive approach to life. He dreamt for all of us. After finishing my education, BSc (Honours) in 1958, I wanted to go for research. My father said, "Try the competitive exams for the IAS. If you fail go for research." I think that was the best advice I ever had in life. I have been very happy in my career as an IAS officer.

My getting into the IAS was definitely a turning point in my life. Earlier when I was 7, I had a more serious turning point. When I was a student in the IVth standard.

I went to school only at the age of 7. I started from the IVth standard in the All Sair's Middle School at Puthur. We were living then at 67, Pattabhirama Pillai Street at Tennur. My cousins

Venkata and Chummi (Janaki) were also studying in the same school. A horse-drawn vehicle driven by one Ghulambhai used to take all of us to school. It was a day in August 1945, I heard in the school from my classmates that in the airport at Chembhat, there was a display of planes. It was just after the Second World War.

I do not still know why or what or who created a desire in me that I must go to see the display. I had no idea how far the airport was. Therefore, after the school, I went along with my friends to the airport. I do not recall the display but all that I recall is that it was a very long walk (may be more than 5 kilometres and while returning, it had become dark.

It was my class teacher John who saved me. He found me alone and crying and started escorting me home. While we were crossing the bridge near the District Court, my cousin's cousin Ranga (Raghavendran) met me and took me home.

On reaching home, I realised the havoc I had caused. My parents and grandfather were shocked and extremely worried at my absence. It was also a day, when the famous Kulumai Amman festival was being celebrated at Puthur. This had attracted a lot of crowd. All at home were worried that I might have been kidnapped or lost.

My mother and all at home were greatly relieved when I came home, may be at 9 PM. Surprisingly, no one, not my father, mother or grandfather, shouted at me. Perhaps, they were so greatly relieved. My mother, a typical symbol of all forgiving love, gave me coffee with a lot of milk which I used to like very much. Even today, I wonder, if I had been lost, my life would have been totally different. That day in 1945 was certainly a very important turning point in life.

My father had intense faith not only in God but also on us, his children. He used to tell me that I was born on the Amavasya day of the month of Thai which is considered special. It was called *'mahodaya'*. It seems, I was born on that day in the evening, so that the *shraddha* of my great grandfather was not disturbed. Because of the date and time of birth, my father said that I would succeed in everything that I touched. If I was on the right path, I will be successful in society. If I took to a life of crime, I will become a great don in the underworld! Incidentally, I was lost and found, he never had any words of reprimand.

My father had very sensitive tastes. He was very fond of Carnatic music. He used to regale us with the stories about the legends of Carnatic music like Ariyakudi, Maharajapuram Vishwanatha Iyer, Madurai Mani, and so on. He used to fondly recall the various concerts he had attended. The great GNB (GN Balasubramaniam) was his classmate in college and he would recall how GNB used to sing for his friends on the Marina Beach.

Unfortunately, I was not able to appreciate classical music till that point in time. I used to call classical music as classickly music. I was all for Hindi film music, particularly, Mukesh. We used to listen actually to the 'Binaca Geetmala' for years.

When I was 38 in 1976, I saw the film 'Sankarabharanam', a Telugu film highlighting the grace of Carnatic music. Overnight, I became a fan of Carnatic music and have remained so all my life thereon. Now I wish that I had become a fan of this divine music when my father was alive!

My father was fond of recalling the major incidents in his life. One such was how he donated blood to his father Narayana Rao when he was down with dropsy. He would describe in detail how the young British doctor Alexander treated my grandfather who was entitled to a special ward in the hospital because he was a Gazetted officer. Blood transfusions were perhaps not so common those days. It seems that the doctor asked my father, "your father gave you life. Can you partly return that debt, by giving some blood to him?" Of course, my father agreed and the operation was a success. My grandfather developed some reaction post the operation. It seems that the doctor was more worried about the donor than the done.

Of course, another memorable incident was how my father went to see my mother before marriage. The tradition is that the girl's parents arrange for a formal meeting between the boy and the girl with all possible relatives being present. My mother was in Thiruvananthapuram (Trivendrum), and she was brought all the way to Chennai (Madras) for the bride viewing function.

My father and my uncle, Krishnaswamy Rao, my aunt's husband, wanted to be sure that they must get a view of the girl without make-up. So, early in the morning, when the train steamed into the Central Station, they were loafing on the platform and had a view of my mother without her having any idea that the bride viewing was already getting over!

Years later my father used to tease my mother over this and remark that even after 30 years and more of marriage, she had not changed. Now that I am married for 40 years and more, I can appreciate the sentiments of my father.

My father was a great Anglophile. In cricket, he used to always support England while we all rooted for Australia. My father would point out how graceful and gentlemanly were players like Jack Hobbs and how unsupportive were the Australian players. After all, he would say, Australia was a criminal settlement! One of his heroes was Douglas Jardine who captained the MCC during the controversial bodyline bowling days of Harold Larwood.

My father also had a lovely voice and when he was in the mood, he would sing classical songs. I have a cassette of Seshagopalan and sometimes, when I hear him sing, he reminds me of my father's voice.

My father led an active life and was generally quite healthy. He appreciated good food. For many years, he would eat only rice with milk and not curd as we used to.

All the tension and struggle he faced in life had their toll on his health. The first serious illness, I recall was in May 1954. He had pleurisy and had to be hospitalised. The fever would not come down and the situation was quite serious. Then one day, he told us he had a dream. In the dream, he saw a saint, may be Raghavendra Swami, our revered saint, who came in a *'Mena'* (palanquin), get down and bless him. My father perhaps thought that his end was near. On the contrary, from that night his health improved. He was discharged after a few days. Till that illness, he would not wear vests (*baniyan*). After this illness, he started wearing vests.

A few years later, another issue worried him. He found that his legs would swell. He had to be on his legs for most of the time and perhaps his heart was beginning to give way or that he was going to suffer from elephantiasis. Fortunately, neither happened.

His next serious illness was in January 1960. I had appeared for the IAS and had to go to Delhi for the UPSC interview. I left on 14th January 1960. My father was down with typhoid and was running a high temperature. He had started talking incoherently. I had to leave that day because the interview was on 18th January 1960 and with a prayer in my heart, I left. God was merciful. I got selected for the IAS and by the time I returned, father was free from his illness.

Again in 1973, he fell sick. This time in August 1973, he had a heart attack in myocardial infection. He was hospitalised and my brother Raghavendra and I were with him. He made a steady recovery.

This attack brought a dramatic change in him. He could no longer practice independently at Tiruchirapalli. We had to close our establishment and shift base to Chennai (Madras). Our elder aunt Tulsibai (Sita Rama Rao) was at Madras in Nanganallur. That house became our base.

My father became a broken man after August 1973. Even after retirement, he had started feeling that he was becoming a nobody – a 'mere old man' (*verum periyavar*). The fact that my youngest brother Ranganathan had not yet settled in life was hurting him.

In 1974 he came with my mother to Gandhidham (Kutch) where I was posted as Development Commissioner of Kandla Free Trade Zone. He used to go for a morning walk, always taking care to take 'Sorbitrate' with him.

I used to take my parents with me for any programme where I was a Chief Guest. There was one such programme at Adipur. We got down and before entering the hall, we had to remove our shoes. I got down and removed my father's shoes and after the programme was over, I helped him to put his shoes on. I had absolutely forgotten this incident. Later on, sometime in 1975, after my father's death, my mother told me that my father was much touched by the fact that I did not mind the presence of others and attended to my father. "Vittal is a good son", it seems my father said. This certificate from my father moved me and has remained ever fresh in my memory.

When he came to Gandhidham, his last worry was about Ranganathan. Fortunately, his marriage was also settled and celebrated in June 1975. It was on the day of that marriage, I had a glimpse of how fast my father's health was deteriorating and how delicate and frail, he had become. I was sitting next to him at dinner and he held me. His hands had become cold and he was obviously in discomfort. My brother Mohan got some medicines and attended to him. The next day, we left for Chennai by train. My sister Prema was in an advanced stage of pregnancy. We were a large group and reached Chennai safely.

I think it was on 28th May 1975 we left Chennai for Kandla Gandhidham. As usual, I paid my respects to him and left. I never knew that was the last time I will be seeing him alive.

There can be two views about whether a son should be at the bedside of a dying parent. Perhaps it is desirable, but, there is also a positive side of one not being present at the time of death. In such cases, one always remembers the parent as being alive. The final denial of life in death is not part of one's memory.

My father died just 14 days short of his 67th birthday (11 August 1909 – 28 July 1975). In retrospect, I think his life was one of struggle and although not much of a success in terms of wealth accumulation, he brought up a family of four sons and one daughter. He helped each of us to succeed in life and inculcated the values of integrity and humanism. He was a very kind and gentle person and was very considerate about other's feelings. He never uttered a harsh word or shouted at anyone. Most of the time, he had his charm and tremendous skills of persuasion.

He was sensitive and self-wounded if anyone insulted him. One person who hurt him most, was my cousin Parthu (Raghavendran), my aunt's son (my father's younger sister's son), Unfortunately or fortunately, Parthu played a great part in shaping my life. It was he who introduced me to the exciting world of books. Soon after I finished my BSc (Honours), I went with him on a trip to Madurai and Tiruchendur. It was a lovely trip for me but my father felt, I think, very bad about it.

He was at times in a blue mood. He felt that he has been unlucky. One of his friends, it seems told him that when Brahma was writing people's fate on their foreheads, he was using an excellent pen, when my father's turn came, the pen developed some trouble. Brahma therefore, seized what was readily available, namely a broomstick and wrote his fate on his forehead!

He used to mourn the disappointments, he had in life. He wanted to study French in college. He could not. Instead, I took French in Intermediate.

It seems he wanted to appear for the ICS. He had even taken the money to pay the fees. In those days, the exams were held in London. Being the only son, his parents did not agree and he gave up the ICS option.

He was therefore, keen that I must appear for the IAS. I think, God was very kind and I got through the exam in my first attempt itself. My success gave my father a lot of delight.

At the same time, he had a lot of reservations. He used to tell me stories about ICS officers, who insulted their fathers after getting into the service. He used to quote the case of SY Krishnaswamy (ICS), who apparently dared to smoke in front of his father!

My uncle, Parthu's father KK Krishnaswamy Rao, added to my father's fears about me. It seems he told him that I would not care for my father in the future.

I am afraid, my father had this slight feeling of reservation throughout his life. I used to write to him regularly, but he always felt that I did not write more frequently. In fact, when I went to England for the first time in 1972, I brought for my teacher Azariah, the *Scofield Reference Bible*. It seems that my father wanted an Oxford Dictionary. I never knew it and the fact that I did fulfil the desire of my teacher led to the misunderstanding that I did not meet his needs. The whole thing was cleared when it came out that he had never written to me or told me about the dictionary!

That is why, I think when the shoelace tying incident took place in Gandhidham, and he was so happy and reassured.

Rock-like faith in God and particularly Lord Venkateswara, Rama, Raghavendra Swami and Goddess Akilandeswari was his hallmark. It is this which helped him to pull through his life. This also gave him a positive outlook in life.

What is it that I have inherited from my father? Certainly, not his looks. He had lovely curly hair, a round face and a flopping kindly appearance. I do not have any of these features. I think I have internalised the value of integrity (intellectual, financial and moral) and faith in God. I have discovered a later stage love for Carnatic music. Unfortunately, I have not been able to learn his kindly and persuasive skills.

One negative feature of his was an element of self-pity. This I have avoided. Another trait of his was to reach the railway station at the last moment. This trait also I have consciously avoided. Above all, I thank God that he blessed me with such a good father.

I was not at his bedside when he breathed his last. I got the message by telegram that evening from my cousin and brother-in-law Seshagiri. We rushed to Madras for the 10-day ceremony. The most moving and avoidable part of the ritual was removing from mother's neck the sacred Mangalyam which my father tied around her neck in July 1935 when they got married. The Purohit got the golden Mangalyam.

It was I think 5th August 1975, all we had was the ashes and bones of my late father. We brothers took them in a bag, went by bus to the Marina Beach and immersed the remains into the sea.

My father's life was over. "An honest man is the noblest work of God," says the poet Alexander Pope. My father was one of the noble works of God.

MOTHER

As I look back, perhaps the most important and long lasting impact on my personality and character, and approach to life was from my parents, particularly from my mother. The two great things about her, I always cherish – first is the boundless and limitless love, she showered on me in arise that I can never do anything wrong and the second aspect, went beyond this 100% support and affection for everything I did. It being her supreme confidence that I will succeed in whatever I undertake. I do not know whether it is because, as father used to say that I was born on the auspicious day of *'mahodaya'* which was a no-moon day (*amavasya*) and that too in the month of 'Thai'. I was born in the evening which also happened to be the day of my great grandfather's *'shraddha'*. My father used to say that I was born conveniently for everyone after the *'shraddha'* function was over and someone who was knowledgeable in astrology said that I was born on such a day, *'mahodaya'*, that if I chose to become a wise person, I will do very well in life and become great. If I chose the opposite, of let us say, becoming a robber, then I will become a great Robin Hood. I do not know whether it is the effect of this prediction of some elder in the family (in those days in most orthodox Hindu Brahmin families like ours, elders were all familiar with astrology). My family, the Dvaithas, being followers of Madhavacharya, is supposed to be the most visual minded and hence, conservative and making a great virtue about strictly observing all codes regarding the rituals to be performed and the rites to be done everyday starting with the *sandhyavandana*, and so on. Though in life, I have never been a typical religious 'madhava', but I have strong faith in the Almighty which I prefer to refer in this book.

My mother always backed me. Later on in my career, when I became the Chairman, Telecom Commission and met at that time a so-called laughable prediction that we will create a situation in India, where a telephone connection was a very difficult thing and people had to wait for more than six years to get a phone connection. In this background, when I took over as Secretary, DoT, I had predicted that we will have telephone on demand. In other words, instead of two years which was the waiting period, the Department of Planning in the Eighth Five Year Plan, which lasted till 2000, I had said that we will create a situation where a telephone connection can be had in two days, instead of two years from the date of registering one's demand. Everybody laughed at me and Gita, my wife, herself pulled me up for opening my mouth and putting my foot into it. But my mother stood by me and told me quietly, I know that you will do it, if you say that you will create a situation of telephone on demand, you will do it. In fact, right through my career, whenever I undertook any effort, she was fully confident that I would succeed. I have already mentioned how when I appeared for the IAS, she was confident that I will make it and as an additional incentive, perhaps an insurance, said that if you succeed in the IAS and if her brother offers his daughter Gita to me, as my daughter-in-law, I will immediately grab it. But, I will not take any initiative, unless you first pass the IAS, and as I mentioned earlier, this fortunately was a great blessing in my life. It really so happened. One of the happiest things in my life for which I am eternally grateful to the Almighty, Lord Venkateswara, is my marrying Gita. In my boyhood, there have been occasions where I had created a lot of tension in the family by suddenly deciding to walk all the way from school to the Trichy Airport at Chempet, which was seven kilometre away and that too on a day when there was a local festival, thus, there was every danger that I would have been lost and I don't know, what horrible life I would have led. Fortunately, I was traced and when I came home, my mother probably and others were all greatly relieved and neither my father nor my mother said a word or shouted at me. My mother offered me thick milky coffee which I used to like in those days.

I have described many such incidents in my life in the course of this book. But, this personal influence she had on me is something for which I am eternally grateful. Apart from literally teaching me the Tamil alphabet at the age of 5, when I started learning to write, she also induced values of faith in Lord Venkateswara as well as our holy saint, Guru Raghavendra. My father and mother both were religious and had intense faith, and they were not very visual minded. They maintained highest values and transmitted those values which we all observed. All these were done by their actions and not by their lecturing us. One of the happiest thing that happened in my life was that later in my life, after I settled down in the IAS, many a time, my mother would come and be with us for long periods of time. But she always wanted to go back to Chennai because, she did not know Hindi and as she could hardly enjoy her stay in the North where I spent the bulk of my career. She used to say that it felt like being dumb, even though one knows the language. She was comfortable reading English, though I have not heard her speak much in English. Otherwise, she was a self-confident person with intense faith in God and believed in absolute integrity of character, morally, intellectually and financially.

I have mentioned about my wife in another chapter and how she transformed herself from my dream girl to become my *dharmapatni* but there is one point on which my mother, perhaps like all mothers are, shows that she ultimately has a divine element of infinite mercy.

GRANDFATHERS

(i) Paternal Grandfather

It is not only our parents who shape our lives, our grandparents and their forefathers also do in their own ways. When joint families were the norm, their influence might have been more but in our time of nuclear families, their impact is much less.

In the seventies, I read the book *Roots: The Saga of an American Family* by Alex Haley, a black American, which had become a bestseller and which was made into a 13 part TV series. It portrayed in moving graphic details, the wrenching story of a whole generation of blacks from Africa and their harsh replantation in the cotton fields of the American south. The legacy of slavery had cast a dark stain in the social history of the West, especially the WASP (White Anglo-Saxon Protestant) dominated United States.

The author of the book was a cook in the US Navy and had traced the tortured story of his forefather, Kunta Kinte, from Gabon in West Africa. Later on, it turned out that the author has in fact passed off as history, and that was a work of fiction.

Nevertheless, the book made a deep impact on me. I realised that we were speaking Marathi in a land of Tamils. As Madhwa Deshastha Brahmins, we were a minority within a minority. The Brahmins formed only 3% of the population.

When I went to school, the rationalist self-respect movement of the Dravidar Kazhagam was on the ascent. EVR, the social reformer called father Periyar by his followers lived next door to our Bishop Heber High School, Puthur. I could sense the element of hostility towards all the Brahmins around.

All this made me feel that one day, I must trace our family history and identify how we came to live in Tamil Nadu. After my retirement, I gave a talk on "Maharastrians in Tamil Nadu" on 29th June 2003 at the TAG Centre on TT Krishnamachari Road. The next year, it was published as a booklet. That traces the broad history of my community.

One of the distinguishing features of Maharashtrians is the surname. I read somewhere that Maharashtrians have perhaps the greatest variety in surnames. Names like *'Poldukle'* (suffering from stomach ache) and *'Elclote'* (one fingered) are really amusing. What is our surname?

On my father's side they were using the surname 'Rao' which is not very distinguished. It is fairly common to come across Telugu and Kannada Brahmins with the surname Rao. In fact, like *'Bhai'* which is the term of affection and respect added to every Gujarati gentleman's name, in Maharashtra, 'Rao' is added to every man's name.

My father dropped even 'Rao'. He became plain Mr N Nagarajan, a typical Tamil name. Even the style of writing our name followed the Tamil system. First came the initials of the village name or the father's name and then one's own name (or 'Christian' name).

My name also follows the Tamil tradition. In Maharashtra and Gujarat, the name of the person is followed by the father's name and then the family surname. Thanks to my being in Gujarat, my children's name followed the local tradition. Sharad Vittal and Smita Vittal carry on my family tradition. As I write this, the third generation is already on the scene. Ashwin Sharad and Anjali Sharad are US citizens. My son Sharad carried on the diaspora tendency of my forefathers of the 17th century and has migrated to the US. My daughter's daughters Niharika Praveen and Aditi Praveen are happily in India.

Hindu tradition thus built in systems to ensure that the family tree is not forgotten. Especially during the *shraddha* ceremonies, we have to offer the *'pinda'* to at least three generations of our forefathers. Thanks to this, I know that my father's father was Narayana Rao, his father was Subba Rao and his father was Keshava Rao. Sanjiva Rao was Keshava Rao's father.

What were they? What did they achieve in life? I know nothing.

All that I have heard from my father is that we were landlords in Salem. The Deshiha Brahmins of Desh area (near Pune and Bijapur) were considered good for administration. When in 1676, Shivaji's step brother Ekoji (also known as Venkiji) established Maratha rule at Thanjavur, he encouraged a lot of the Deshastha families to migrate to the South. Temptations by way of *jagirs* and land grants were offered. I can therefore, guess that one of my forefathers decided, 327 years ago, to migrate to the South. We are living in Tamil Nadu thanks to that unknown forefather's decision to migrate.

When the British established their rule in Tamil Nadu, my forefathers were among the first to go for the modern English school system. One of father's paints of pride was that we were graduates from my great grandfather's time.

My great grandfather, Subba Rao, was a minor official in the Taluka office of the revenue department. He died fairly young at the age of 40 years or so. Nothing more is known about him.

Subba Rao had two sons and at least one daughter. Jivan Rao was the eldest and Narayana Rao, my paternal grandfather was the second. Janaki was the sister. Janaki married her cousin K Raghavendra Rao who retired as a deputy collector. He opted for the title of Rai Bahadur from the British. He was known as an honest and bold officer. In my aunt's house, there was also the title signed by the then Viceroy.

Jivan Rao became a clerk in the AG's office after graduation. He was known to be an irascible hot tempered person. I recall him as an angry old man who used to care and stay with us once in a while. He was demanding and it was always a pain for my mother to ensure that he did not get upset or angry.

I still recall one incident. Like all old men in those days, Jivan Rao also had a small tuft (hardly 10 hairs) and a clean shaven head. Once the barber Velu, who used to come to our office for our hair cuts, shaved off his tuft by mistake. I remember, Jeevan Rao showing and railing the whole day "What he should have done, he did not do! What he should not have done, he has done!" Jeevan Rao, did not rise higher in his life. He had only one daughter, Sonabai.

My grandfather Narayana Rao was a total sturdy in contrast. He was fair, 5'6" and had the kindest face, as far as I remember. As all grandparents are, he was very fond of us. We had an old cradle in the house at 67, Pattabiraman Pillai Street, Thennur, Tiruchirapalli. Four or five of us, my sister, brothers and cousins would sit in that cradle and grandfather would rock it gently. He would tell us stories from our Puranas. I still remember the story of Shashirekha Parinayam and Ghatotkach.

He hardly had any hair except for a small tuft. When you are young, all old people look alike. He had a remarkable appearance and reminded me of Gandhiji. I remember one occasion when the cradle came down with a thud when grandfather was rocking us. Fortunately, no one was hurt.

Father used to tell us about how our grandfather used to function. He was a District Munsiff (District Judge trying civil cases) and Krishnagiri was where he served. We hailed from Namakkal (Salem) but we had never been there. It appears we had a large house which was acquired by the government for a Post Office.

In his younger days, my grandfather must have been quite handsome. It seems his nickname was 'Son-in-law Munsiff' (*Maappillai Munsiff*). He was always for settling cases through compromises. He was, therefore, also called *'Raji Munsiff'*.

Apparently, one serious illness he had was perhaps in 1934 when he came down with dropsy. I have already described how my father had to give him blood transfusion.

One story I heard was that on the day when my grandfather was to be married, he disappeared and went to a Lord Vinayaka temple. Anyway, he married and had a long married life. Tulasi Nagarajan (my father) and Saraswati were his three children.

Grandfather called my grandmother by the pet name 'Ammani'. No one remembered her real name. Years later, when I got married on 28th June 1964, my wife Gita had to be given a new name, as is the custom in our community. I remember everyone asking what my paternal grandmother's name was. My aunt, Tulasi Bai then recalled that her mother's name was actually 'Krishna Bai'. So, Gita got christened as 'Krishna' but we still call her by her original (maiden) name till today.

I recall, during 1946 and 1947 my grandfather became seriously ill. He was apparently worried about his death. So much so, if any funeral procession passed along the street, he would shut the door and avoid the sight.

In spite of his illness, he had a sense of humour. Our uncle Rama Rao (husband of Tulasi Bai) was also with us during this period. When my grandfather was sick, my father or my uncle used to shave him. Grandfather used to joke: "How lucky I am? I have got graduate barbers to shave me!"

The most vivid memory, I have of my grandfather was the moment of his death on 17th April 1947 at 13.35 hrs.

It is said that the way a man meets his death is an index of his character. There is a Telugu proverb, *"Manchi Vaduluku Margname Sakshi!"* (the proof of good people is the manner of their death). If this test is applied, my grandfather surely was one of the best human beings to live on this earth.

Grandfather was fully conscious right up to his last moment. Right from the morning of 17th April 1947 he was reciting all the prayers and the Ramanama. Around 1 PM, he asked for all of us, my parents, aunts, uncles and us grandchildren to gather around his bed. He formally took leave of each one of us with "I am going away." Finally, he called Kannappan, our peon and folding his hands said, 'Kannappa, Nan Po...' (Kannappa, I am going). Well, those were the last words. He closed his eyes and he was gone forever.

What was remarkable, my father said was that grandfather, who was so afraid of dying, never felt the fear and met death with supreme calm. He must have been a really great noble soul.

The last thing I remember about him was walking along with his dead body, holding a torch in my hand along with my cousin Parthu, son of my younger aunt Saraswati Bai. We walked up to the end of the road and the procession proceeded further to the cremation ground.

My grandfather was fond of English. Typical of his generation, he could recite long passages from Shakespeare. I wish god had spared him for a longer period. At this distance, all I remember is his kindly presence and love for all of us.

Fortunately, my maternal grandfather C Balakrishna Rao lived for a longer period.

(ii) Maternal Grandfather

My maternal grandfather was Shri C Balakrishna Rao (C stands for Canchi, the old spelling of the city). In fact, among my grandparents, he was the person with whom I spent most time while I was growing up. I was fortunate that he lived long enough to see my getting into the IAS at the age of 22 on 16th May 1960. He has always been a great source cf inspiration for me.

As I look back at my life, it appears that his life and mine have uncannily great parallels. Among my relatives, he was the one who occupied a distinguished position in public life. He was the Chief Engineer of the State of Travancore in the 1930s when HH Chithira Thirunal was the ruler of the State of Travancore with Thiruvananthapuram as the capital. Having graduated with a BE degree in Civil Engineering from the Guindy Engineering College, one of the oldest engineering colleges in India in the 1920s, he got employed in the Government of Travancore and became the Chief Engineer after a brilliant career noted for sheer professional excellence. He was excellent at his work and one standing monument of his achievements is the Trivandrum Water Works, which provides drinking water even to this day to Trivandrum.

This was commissioned in 1930s and it is held up as an example of excellent planning and effective implementation of a public works project. The fact that the Vellayambalam Water Works, which is a tourist site for all visitors to Trivandrum is his creation. Even to this day, he is remembered by an Annual Seminar in honour of his memory among the Engineers in the Department of Water Works in the Zoo where the water supply works headquarters is also located. As one goes up the stairs upon the first landing, a full sized portrait of his is displayed as a mark of respect of his association with the works.

The implementation of the water works was a project which not only has an engineering dimension but also a lot of social impact. The project appeared unbelievable! The opposition to the water works was from the trustees of the temple on the ground that providing a common water supply went against the Varnashrama Dharma codes like untouchability. We may recall, in those days, early part of the 20th century, the practice of untouchability was very prevalent. A common water supply, was a challenge to the orthodox Brahmins particularly, and they wondered whether it was a good measure at all. In such a situation, my grandfather planned the whole water supply for the city and implemented it without any time overruns or cost overruns. I have heard from my mother that Lord Willingdon who was then the Viceroy and who came to inaugurate the water supply system was surprised that an Indian engineer has implemented such an excellent project.

While implementing the project, naturally, many streets in the city of Thiruvananthapuram had to be dug up and my grandfather acquired a nickname 'Peruchali Rayar'. Peruchali in Tamil and

Malayalam means the bandicoot. Just as the bandicoots dig holes all over the place, my grandfather had to dig up the roads!

The project also demonstrated his great sense of commitment to duty and integrity. Apparently, he was sought to be bribed by one of the contractors. My grandfather promptly rejected the offer and credited the amount into the Treasury. His work was so much appreciated by the ruler of Travancore, HH Chithira Thirunal, that he was given the title 'Vastu Vidya Kushala'. This was one of the high points in his career.

He did not stop with this. He went on to work along with Sir CP Ramaswamy Iyer, who was the Diwan, to set up the Government Engineering College which has built an excellent reputation over the years. When I became the Managing Director of Gujarat Narmada Fertilizers, I came across a couple of students who fondly recalled my grandfather's lectures and the effectiveness of his lectures.

I also got another confirmation about his engineering vision from my own boss, Mr R Thirumalai (IAS, 1948 Tamil Nadu cadre), who was the Additional Secretary, Commerce when I was the Development Commissioner, Kandla Free Trade Zone in the Ministry of Commerce (1974 to 1977). When he visited Kandla in 1976 and during the course of our conversation, he came to know that my grandfather was the Chief Engineer who built the water supply works in Trivandrum, Mr Thirumalai, who was also Secretary, PWD, in the state recalled how he had come across many neat plans and meticulous records maintained by my grandfather C Balakrishna Rao when he was the Collector of Kanyakumari district. He had personally seen the records and greatly appreciated the vision of my grandfather.

There are many aspects of my grandfather which I still continue to admire. The first was his sense of discipline. He was a diabetic and was conscious about his food habits and controlled his taste buds very effectively even though he was as fond of sweets as I am. I am also a diabetic like him and perhaps, I had inherited his genes, so far as this aspect is concerned. Years later, in 2012, when I got the Padma Bhushan, I also recalled that in my family, after my grandfather, I was the person to be so honoured by the state. In my career, I also had an opportunity to start a college like my grandfather. With the help of Bharatiya Vidya Bhavan, in 1986, I was able to launch the Narmada College of Science, Arts and Commerce in Zadeshwar in Bharuch district when I was the Managing Director of Gujarat National Fertilizer Corporation.

The sterling character of my grandfather, so far as integrity is concerned; have been a source of inspiration for all of us in our family and all we grandchildren fondly recall his dignified appearance, majesty and immense love for children. He was the one person with whom I could argue on issues like soul, birth and death and all other aspects of life, big and small. In fact, he played a great role in supporting the idea of Gita becoming my wife. Moreover, he had become an expert in astrology, especially in the later years of his life and following the death of my grandmother and the meticulous person that he was, every subject he took up, he became thorough and very systematic. I still think that my marriage with Gita is the best blessing, he conferred on me as his gift.

When I joined the IAS, he was particularly interested in giving tips to me to help me in my riding. He was an excellent rider and horse riding was a professional necessity for him. I have described my problem with riding in the chapter 'The Year of the Horse' learning how to control the horse. He himself had a horse called 'Mary' which was very devoted to him and we used to hear stories about how the horse had saved his life many a times in the jungle where, during the course of his work; he had to travel and wild animals and elephants were a constant threat to those crossing the jungle.

I still retain the letters, he wrote to me almost till the week before his death, which was at the age of 79 in 1961. In them, he advised about how to control horses.

GREATEST BLESSING IN LIFE – MY WIFE GITA

There is a well-known saying that behind every successful man, there is a woman. I have realised this on the eve of my celebrating the Golden Jubilee of my marriage with Gita on 28th of June 1964. There are cynics who say that behind every successful man, is a woman telling him that what he is doing is wrong. Well, my wife also passes this test because most of the decisions, I have taken in my life are those to which she took serious objections and was literally against them.

Many a times, this must have hurt her feelings, because she is a very intelligent person and has a pragmatic mind. I have a tremendous ego and I cannot see anything beyond my own nose. Gita provides an effective corrective for me. I may claim to be a very clever person, intelligent, and so on. But she is the one who looks at every issue from the other person's point of view. In fact, she is very good in disaster scenario planning. People have different attitudes to life. Most of us in the professional services are brainwashed by management literature. Motivation speakers preach that we should look at everything from a positive point of view. After all, for a pessimist, everything looks negative. In fact, worry is one of the common weaknesses of human kind. I remember, Dale Carnegie made a pile of money in the 1930s with his two popular classical books, *How to Make Friends and Influence People* and *How to Stop Worrying and Start Living*. I have also read Dale Carnegie books and a whole lot of books sold on literature on those lines. Even today, in every airport and many railway stations, the most popular books sold are self-improvement books. Many of the authors of such books are those who were themselves failures. Those who advise the readers how to stop worrying have been themselves worry warts. Those who advise how to become a millionaire have never become real millionaires in life. George Bernard Shaw was bang on target when he said that "he who can does and he who cannot teaches."

I don't know whether it was Oscar Wilde who spent his life minting aphorising by making the truth stand on its head and throw light on a lay neglected reality performed functions which in the old days of monarchy, the court Jesters of emperors did. Court jesters like Tenali Rama to Krishnadeva Raya, Birbal to Akbar. All had an important role to play. They were the only persons in the *darbar* or the court of the king, who could tell the king the truth without being afraid. They had the shield of humour to protect themselves. If the king or the emperor did not like what the court jester said, it could always be laughed off as the jester performing his tricks to amuse the audience and keep the king happy. Many a times, however, they performed very vital functions in an atmosphere where only 'yes men' were encouraged. In the court of absolute power like the kings and emperors, there was no safety valve against the danger. Lord Acton said, "power corrupts and absolute power tends to corrupt absolutely." Many a time emperors and kings have been prevented from launching a foolish course by the timely caution and advice provided by the court jesters. What they did was simple. They made their kings see the reality when everybody else was brainwashed in the group or persuaded by the momentary whim and fancies of the king or emperor. A classic example of how in such an atmosphere, a totally ignorant person or an innocent person can bring everybody back to reality is the well-known story of the emperor's new clothes. When the emperor was brainwashed and the whole court was also hypnotised into thinking that the confidence tickers have come claiming that they have got perhaps the thinnest of the dresses. They went to the extent of making the emperor naked with their hypnotic words and elaborate gestures to create a halo that the emperor was indeed wearing a very thin and costly dress. It was a child in the street, when the king went about in a procession displaying his 'new dress', who said, "Look, the emperor has no clothes." It was then with a rude shock that everybody was brought to reality and could see with their own eyes, how they have all been taken for a ride and hypnotised for the moment.

All of us, go through such moments in life, where we are fascinated about an idea about a particular course of action is the best, we never see the negative side of it. It is in such situations, the corrective was provided by the child in the case of the fairy tale and by the court jesters in history whose records are available.

But in modern times, when we lead a settled life with our spouses, the role of providing correction and caution by raising doubts about the wisdom of the course of action chosen is provided by the spouse. Wives are particularly experts in this because, in every home, the husband is basically accustomed to think in a male dominated world. Till recently women were not present in large numbers in offices to commit the error of group thinking. In such a situation, it is the wife who points out the alternatives and how the entire course of action could be wrong and questions the assumptions under which a particular course of action was being contemplated. My wife, Gita, particularly, I find is a great expert in taking a pessimistic view and visualise a disastrous scenario so that before I take any action, at least I am alerted to the wisdom of the course of action I chose. It is not as if I have always gone by advice but many a times, after the act is performed, I have come to regret and realise how mistaken I was. This is particularly true when it comes to interacting with other people. Women basically have better instincts and can read the body language of those with whom they are interacting and their minds are wired to look into details. This probably arises from the basic function assigned to men and women over generations in the evolution of human kind. Men have been hunters and trying to go outside and bring food to eat and it is the women who took care of the children, who delivered children and took care of their nourishment. By nature when men can afford to be single minded and focused on one subject at a time, women by nature of their functions, which nature seems to have assigned for them, their brains are wired for multi-tasking. Rightly therefore, there are very popular books which claim that men are from Mars and women are from Venus. They come from different planets with different backgrounds. While this may be the common human experience of many, looking at my own life it will be obvious in this book, my wife has been performing a signal service and I consider marrying Gita as one of the greatest blessings I have had from Lord Venkateswara.

Apart from this general aspect, there is one signal service my wife has been performing for me in my life and of all the saints and great men I have read about, the best manner in which it has been summed up is by the Saint poet Kabir of the 16th century. Kabir says, "if you want to lead a clean life and you if don't want to avoid becoming too haughty and if you want to conquer your ego and have peace of mind which will help you to evolve spiritually and come nearer to God, then you should always keep around you people who will not praise you but who will constantly find fault with you and put you down." Kabir says, *"Nindak niyare raakhiye, aangan kuti chhavaay"* (keep those who abuse you or curse you near you as much as possible). Because, if you keep such people they will point out your defects and your failings and you will be able to correct yourself.

I am not a perfect man and many a times, in our married life I have been annoyed and in the heat of the moment, uttered words which have hurt my wife very deeply. Some of these words, which I have used in the moment of anger and stress have indeed caused her lifelong sadness. I deeply regret the words I uttered years ago, but looking at the long lasting hurt they have caused to Gita, I realise the sad fact that words are like arrows. Once they are shot, they cannot be retrieved. I realise the bitter truth of the valuable words of Tiruvalluvar, the Tamil Saint who wrote *Tirukkural*. He says, a wound caused by fire will heal, but never the scar caused by abusive words:

Theeyinal sutta punn ullaarum aaraathe naavinaal sutta vadu.

(Kural 129)

He advises very rightly, whatever else you do not careful, it does not matter but do control your tongue.

Yakavar aiyinum nakakka kavakkaal Sokappar chollikzikkup pattu.

In the later part of our life, in old age, virtually every day I have a list of all the wrong things I have done in our long married life. We Hindus believe that Chitragupta (the divine accountant), a major assistant to God of Death, Yamaraja, keeps an account of all the sins we have committed and all the good things we have done, and once we die and go off to the heavens, we will be confronted with the recorded career of our lives with the list of the sins and good things done. Most of us, as human beings, would probably have more sins on our side than merits. I do not know whether there really is a Chitragupta, keeping an account of the wrong things done in life. But definitely, Gita is perhaps his authorised representative on earth, reminding me every day with the complete and detailed list of all the wrong things I have done in my life, particularly harsh words I have spoken from time to time in my life.

Perhaps, this is the duty of the *dharmapatni* and I realised that she is doing the essential function of recording all the worst things I have done. Even when my lapses were reported to her in our married life, she will mildly suggest that I could have behaved better, words to that effect and that too in a very gentle way. These days, when I am at the end of my innings in this physical world, I wonder that the only being who can show infinite mercy on me and forgive all my sins which Chitragupta is taking note of is Lord Venkateswara. My mother was his representative, a walking image on this earth and I could feel how God would treat me as amongst the very humblest of souls on this earth created by him. No wonder that all religions, particularly our Hindu religion, reminds us of Gods on earth – *matru devo bhava, pithru devo bhava, acharya devo bhava, atithi devo bhava*, and so on. The mother takes the most primary position so far as our Gods on earth are concerned.

CHAPTER 5

NIMITTA MATRAM: MY JOURNEY THROUGH THE SPECTRUM OF GOVERNANCE

(i) MOTIVATION: THE ROOT FOR EFFECTIVENESS AND GOOD GOVERNANCE

There is this story about a girl who, before getting married, had four different theories on bringing up children. Many years after her marriage, one of her friends asked her: "Before marriage you had four theories on how to bring up children. Now that you are married and have children, tell me which theory works in practice?" The lady replied, "Well, before marriage I had four theories and no children. Now I have four children and no theory!"

One of the interesting aspects of life is that as we live from day-to-day, we come across different situations and act upon them. Very rarely do we try to analyse which of our actions bring out results and which do not. There is an old joke about advertising. Fifty per cent of the money spent on advertising works. We do not know which 50%. This chapter of the book is an attempt to pin down that 50% which works.

When we come to think about it, we realise that most of us react to situations depending upon our temperament.

In the third chapter of the *Bhagavad Gita*, Lord Krishna says:

Nahi kashchit Kshanamapi, jatu
tistatya karmakrit kritu

Karyato yah vasha karma sarrashya
Prakritirjaigunai

which means, nobody can remain still for a moment and all of us act at all times according to our nature.

This is the essence of the concept of work ethics or work culture. We can apply this to an individual, an organisation or a nation. "Character is destiny", is an old saying of the Greeks. Character determines our performance. After all, character represents one's values. Values determine actions. The link is therefore obvious. Culture is nothing but, the aggregate of the culture of the individuals. This may explain the mystery of success or failure.

If all of us act according to our nature, then how do we get results in any group or organisation? This is the perennial problem of management. Sir John Harvey-Jones titled his book of management as *Making It Happen*. The essence of management after all is to make things happen. There is also a view that the successful manager is the one who makes others do what the organisation wants. It is said that the inscription on Andrew Carnegie's grave reads, "Here lies a man who knew how to make people better than him work for him."

When we look at the whole issue about how to make things happen or how to get things done, we must recognise that there is a certain amount of determination or pre-ordination because of the individual characters of the people. At the same time, the specific individual nature of people itself can be utilised to get things done. After all, the perennial problem in management is the problem of choosing the right people for the right task. Peter Drucker in his 60 books and seven decades of experience ultimately focuses on people's decisions as the most important decisions.

There is a story in ancient Greece about how Socrates came to realise his own identity as a philosopher. It is said that Socrates was taken aback and he came to know through some of his friends from Athens that the Oracle of Delphi declared him as the wisest man. He asked his friends why the Oracle considered him the wisest man. When his friends had no answer, he said in one of his throw away lines, "It is because I am the only person in Greece who knows that he knows nothing". In fact, it is this awareness of ignorance that is the starting point of the Socratic method of inquiry and objective analysis. Socrates apparently also realised that the Oracle of Delphi can never be wrong and if the Oracle has said that he was the wisest man, there must be a reason why he was rated as the wisest man. Probably this line of thought triggered his questioning methods.

Comparisons are odious. When made by a person which reflect positively on himself it may be considered worse than odious and positively disastrous. Even at the risk of being considered as a disastrous exercise, I can claim that I had a Socrates-like experience. In August 1997, *Business Today* magazine came up with a cartoon of 50 men and women who contributed to the economy of India and (surprise, surprise) I figured in that. The cartoon portrayed me with a computer and a phone because of the role I played in the area of telecommunications and information technology as Secretary of the Department of Electronics from 1990 to 1996 and as Chairman of Telecommunications from 1993 to 1994. It boosted my morale and I treasure this distinction as more precious than the other awards.

As already mentioned, our culture has two negative characteristics. Our society is feudal and hierarchy-minded. Our organisations are work-shy. India can be compared to a snake, with its head in the 21st century and the tail in the 17th century. When it comes to our mindset and approach to life, I am afraid that a majority of us are in the 17th century feudalistic era. The distinction conferred on me by *Business Today* will be a useful input, if I could analyse the techniques, the approach and the philosophy I adopted to get things done in spite of our organisations being work-shy and our society ridden with the feudalistic mindset. This book, therefore, in a way is an autobiographical exercise with the focus not on blowing my own trumpet but objectively analysing the work environment in which I performed for more than four decades and how results were achieved. There is always a difference between one's own perception about oneself and meta-perception, which describes how others see us. This is an exercise in meta-perception that is trying to guess how others think I achieved my results. In the ultimate analysis, it is the perception that matters. And perception that leads to action may be worth examining.

If I am perceived to have been an effective bureaucrat and if I articulate the techniques and the philosophy, which I adopted, this may influence the readers to adopt similar techniques in their work environment. Who knows? This may be a small step in India getting rid of its work-shy nature and come out of the feudalistic mindset and join, psychologically, the 21st century. This may sound positively grandiose.

Dr Abdul Kalam, our idealistic President always used to say: "Low aim is a crime". At least, I would not commit a crime in the eyes of our beloved President in writing this book. Where do I begin? I will begin by analysing what is it that shapes my behaviour and approach to life and how it influences my functioning in the work environment. To begin with, I do not make a distinction between personal life and my functioning as an officer. There is an interesting story about a strict Imperial Police Officer, Mr Ram Iyyar who was the Inspector General of Police, Gujarat in the 60s. Ram Iyyar was the Police Commissioner of Ahmedabad. Once when a visitor met him at his residence, Ram Iyyar asked him: "Have you come here to see the Police Commissioner or Ram Iyyar". This visitor was puzzled. He said, "I have come to see Ram Iyyar, the Police Commissioner". Ram Iyyar's reply was: "If you want to see the Police Commissioner, you come to my office tomorrow at 10 o'clock. If you want to see Ram Iyyar, you can meet him right now". I have not been able to make this sort of a distinction between my role as a bureaucrat and my role as an individual. Professional management experts may consider that not maintaining such a distinction is bad. In fact, one of the criticisms I always face from my wife is: "You are a Secretary to the Government of India and you are not behaving like a Secretary". Perhaps in the mind of the people, there is a certain behaviour pattern expected of a Secretary.

I remember when I was a junior officer, one of my seniors said that a senior officer is one who is talkative without being communicative. I can never be talkative without being communicative. In fact as Chairman, Telecom Commission or as Central Vigilance Commissioner (CVC), I have been very easily accessible to the media and what is more, I have been openly communicative my views. There is, however, a Lakshman Rekha, I draw. If something is considered as an official secret, even under great provocation, I will not give up the secret. I was put to a severe test once when I submitted as CVC in March 2001, a study on the defence deals and the allegations of corruption relating to them. There was a debate in the Rajya Sabha in the Winter Session of 1999 when Jayant Malhoutra, the Member of Parliament made an allegation that even though the Government of India had a policy that there would be no middlemen in defence deals, in every deal after 1989 when the 'no middlemen' policy was in-force, there have been middlemen and kickbacks paid in the deals for procurement of weapons. Mr Fernandes, the Defence Minister gave an assurance in Parliament that he would ask the CVC to inquire into the matter and true to his word, he entrusted the task to me on 14th February 2000. There was no time limit and the terms of reference were:

(i) Have there been middlemen in defence deals even though the government policy visualised that there will be no middlemen from 17th April 1989?

(ii) Twenty allegations of corruption made by Mr Jayant Malhoutra in Parliament. Seven allegations of corruption

> made by Rear Admiral Purohit in a court case filed by him. All cases of more than ₹75 crore after 1989 must be explained to see whether there has been any corruption or violation of laws.

There is no time limit. Prof Northcote Parkinson of the *Parkinson's Law* fame says: "If you do not want to commit yourself, committee yourself". I could have looked upon this inquiry as an opportunity for a long, never-ending quest and taken my own time. The Central Vigilance Commission would have been fully justified because this was a wide-ranging inquiry and spread over a long time. After all, we have seen the Warren Commission in the US taking ten years and the Jain Commission on Rajiv Gandhi's assassination also trying to beat that Commission's record, though unsuccessfully. It was wound up in six years. For producing our report, we had to go through more than 500 secret files. Every file in the Ministry of Defence is 'secret' or 'top secret'. When our inquiry was based on the documents, which were secret, we had no alternate but to classify our report also as 'secret'. We submitted a preliminary report on 7th August 2000 and the final report on 31st March 2001 to the government and left it to the government to decide whether the report should be made public or not.

There was a continuous pressure on the government to make the whole report public. The tehelka.com expose of 13th March 2001, which also dealt with the issue of corruption in politics and defence added some urgency to the demand. When I was asked about what I had to say on the issue of the tehelka.com expose because the CVC was also studying the issue of corruption in defence deals, my reply was: "The tehelka.com has only confirmed what the CVC said in its Preliminary Report of 7th August 2000." Within 18 days of the Tehelka expose, by 31st March 2001, we had submitted our final report. There were persistent efforts being made by correspondents of *The Indian Express*, especially by Ritu Sareen, who is an investigative journalist. I did not reveal the contents of the report except to say that we had pointed out the need for transparency in our report, the Government of India on 2nd November 2001 modified the policy and indicated the guidelines under which agents could be appointed.

The issue of making public the CVC report on defence deals became once again a matter of public concern when in 2001, the Chairman of the Public Accounts Committee wanted a copy of the report. The government claimed privilege and the media once again asked me for my comments. I said that as it was a confidential report, it was for the government to decide. They can claim privilege and they were fully justified. I quoted a case when I was Secretary (Electronics) and Atal Bihari Vajpayee was the Chairman of the Public Accounts Committee. He wanted the report of the silicon project, but we did not oblige and claimed privilege. Atalji with his persuasive skills called me twice and used all his charm but I could not unfortunately agree with him and we continued to claim privilege. I gave this example to show that the government was within their rights. Ritu Sareen was persistent. She said: "I want to interview you about the CVC report on defence deals". I told her that apart from the policy change in procurement, we had pointed out lapses in various deals and we had asked the Ministry of Defence to fix the responsibility and initiate action. I had also taken up the matter with the Defence Minister George Fernandes who replied to me within 24 hours to the effect that he would be looking into the matter. Ritu Sareen, further probing the issue, wanted to know whether I would publish the names of those who are involved in the deals who have been found guilty. I said that once the Ministry of Defence fixed the responsibility and as per the procedure, departmental inquiries were conducted and somebody was found guilty at that stage, as we were doing in other cases on the CVC website, their names would be published. She wanted to know whether I could give a time frame within which this could be done. I told her that it was difficult to give a time frame but in view of the facts, the Defence Minister himself had agreed to pursue the matter, perhaps we could expect within six months the whole issue to be wound up and the names to be published. On the same day I attended the wedding reception of the son of the Defence Secretary, Mr Yogendra Narain. Mr Fernandes was also present, and I told him about the interview I had given to Ritu Sareen. I also mentioned to Mr Fernandes that for a specific question I had replied that so far as defence deals were concerned, my judgement was that Mr Fernandes was sincere. Being a very shrewd and pragmatic politician, Mr Fernandes's reply was quick. He said: "I am sure, she is not going to publish it in her story." Mr Fernandes was proved more than correct. Not only was that reference about Mr Fernandes' sincerity not mentioned, the next day *The Indian Express* published a story under the headline 'Six Months or I Go Public, says CVC'. It showed how the CVC wanted to publish the names within six months of those found guilty in the defence deals. That day in a programme on 'Aaj Tak', Mr Fernandes was interviewed and the headline was 'CVC se Raksha Mantri Naaraz' (Defence Minister is angry with CVC). I saw Mr Fernandes with a very sorrowful face addressing the camera: *"Hum kitne logon ka bojha uthayenge?"* (For how many people should I carry the load?) "CVC himself said that the report was secret and how he wants to publish it." Immediately I tried to contact Mr Fernandes on the RAX, he was not available. I therefore wrote a letter to him the very next day explaining the full sequence of the case. I ended my letter saying: "In journalism, bad news makes good copy but truth makes a better copy in life". Mr Fernandes rang me back at once and said that he received my letter and he wanted to know whether he could publish the letter in the media. I happily and readily agreed but, true to the theorem of journalism, though this letter must have been given to senior journalists, it was never published. I could guess this only because when Mr Prabhu Chawla interviewed me for a programme on 'Seedhi Baat' some months later, he gave a hint that he had seen this letter. I give this instance to show that as a bureaucrat, I have tried to maintain my limitations so far as secrecy is concerned. Apart from this 'Lakshman Rekha' – limitation of secrecy, I have been very communicative and had not behaved like a typical senior officer.

The significance of my nature that I am not different in office from what I am at home was brought to my notice sharply by one of my architect friends who had met me when I was the Managing Director of the Gujarat Narmada Valley Fertiliser Company (GNFC) (1982-87). Rajnibhai Patel, who was just starting his career, met me later on in the office as MD, GNFC and remarked that there was no difference between what he saw in me in my house and in the office. This perhaps shows the perceptions people have about the role of body language and behavioural characteristics of a person when one is in a position of authority.

There is an old Tamil proverb, which says that if you have to play the role of a dog in a play, you will have to bark. Perhaps it is necessary that one should be donning the expected characteristics of a particular role while performing one's functions. Here is a possible explanation as to why I might have been successful and effective when others who probably go by the conventional norms of behaviour and etiquette might not succeed. Ultimately, what motivates people is credibility which comes from being sincere and straightforward. In my case, what you see is what you get. Many a times when people assume roles and modulate their behavioural characteristics for that role, perhaps what they communicate fails to bring out their real personality and commitment. Since I have been probably the same in whatever role I played, what came through ultimately was me as an individual which got translated into credibility so far as communication with the people with whom I was concerned. In fact, for getting anything done, communication is very vital. If we put artificial barriers in communication, which perhaps is the professional hazard for a bureaucrat, to that extent we are designing for sub-optimal performance. Many have commented upon my outspoken nature. I have also been accused of being a loud mouthed person.

However, nobody had pulled me up for being talkative or being communicative. There might have been an element of jealousy as well.

In our system of governance, ministers being politicians have to be in the public eye and try to hog all the credit for any achievement. Perhaps a classic instance of this truism was the launching of the trial run of the Delhi Metro. This is a remarkable engineering success, thanks to the dedicated professional leadership of Mr E Sreedharan. He had earlier earned a name in setting up the Konkan Railways. The whole lot of technocrats and engineers under his leadership built the Delhi Metro, without disturbing the chaotic traffic. However, when the formal programme was organised, there were so many people in politics who were trying to hog the publicity that one newspaper commented that it was made to appear as if it was the ministers who have built the metro system but not the silent dedicated engineers. There is, therefore, an unwritten rule in our civil service where the civil servant is supposed to maintain a low profile and calm. Statesman once called bureaucrats, as faceless non-entities of the South Block. In government programmes, the entire credit is taken by the political leadership.

We also see repeatedly in our democracy the truth of John Kennedy's lament that "success has many fathers, failure is an orphan". The statement was made after the Bay of Pigs fiasco. Since the media had easy access to me, there was a lot of coverage about me. The Minister apparently was annoyed. Here was a situation where he could not directly give a directive that I should not communicate because I happened to be the Secretary of the Department. Even under the rigid confines of the Conduct Rules, the Secretary is authorised to talk on behalf of the department and that was what I was doing. The minister was very unhappy with me. My driver brought this to my notice and commented in Hindi: *"Mantriji chahte hain ki kaam aap karein aur namm unkaa ho"*. This was not happening and hence the problem. Perhaps, the need for communication and sincerity transmitted by one's behaviour, might in turn, bring credibility. This is perhaps the starting point for getting anything done. If one retains one's natural self, one behaves without putting on airs or without adopting the expected body language appropriate to the office and status. Thus, among the status-conscious colleagues also there is a positive impact. If the boss is not status-conscious, to that extent it encourages the juniors to overcome their shyness. Perhaps the feudal culture is also overcome partially, if the boss does not put on airs. If he is transparent, as in the computer language, "What You See Is What You Get" (WYSIWYG), there is an automatic credibility in communication. Communication is vital for successful leadership, which is measured in terms of achievement.

Successful communication is the basis of charisma. Charisma was once defined as the capacity to simplify and exaggerate. Mahatma Gandhi's 'Salt Satyagraha' is a classic instance of charismatic leadership. By focusing on the salt tax, Gandhiji was able to communicate to the entire nation of 300 million that because of the foreigners' rule, even the poorest of the poor who cannot do without salt in their food had to pay a tax. The 'Salt Satyagraha' became a turning point in our struggle for independence.

I have described elsewhere the experience I had of this type of communication when I became Managing Director of the Gujarat Narmada Valley Fertiliser Company in 1982. I began by pointing out that our objective was to produce 100% ammonia and 100% urea every day. The non-adoption of the standard behavioural pattern and body language one is expected to have at a particular office has not only the advantage of credibility, putting the subordinates at ease and helping them to come out of the feudal mindset of clamming up before their bosses but also brings in an element of sincerity. When a leader in an organisation communicates in this manner, the goals are very clear and the fact that action must be taken becomes an unwritten message, which evolves from the environment of the transactions taking place.

When I became CVC, we introduced a system of marking attendance through a smart card every day. I insisted that I would also do the punching. This had a much unintended positive impact. Right down to the peon the message went that the CVC himself was punching the card. As a result, overtime was totally controlled because nobody could fudge the time about his or her attendance in the office.

Walking the talk is very essential if anything has to be got done. When we talk about getting things done, we are all the time talking about making the organisation perform to achieve its goals. The first step in the whole effort is motivation of the people in the organisation.

I am for transparency in everything. In fact, as CVC, one element of my strategy in fighting corruption was to bring in greater transparency in governmental systems. Greater transparency means greater communication. The question is, where do we draw the line so far as transparency is concerned? I would say that what we must aim for is transparency and not striptease. In striptease, there is also greater exposure with the added dimension of titillation. Many a time, the media is trying to titillate the readers by coming up with exposes, which are likely to cause embarrassment. In fact, the embarrassment that will be caused can itself be a check. If there is truth, there is no need to be embarrassed. I have also passed through situations where I thought I was acting within my limits but still the way the media publicised the issue, led to possible misunderstandings. This was in January 2000, when one day a person came to me with the information that the Income Tax Department had completed their inquiry into the Hawala case and had identified some bureaucrats and political leaders who had undisclosed incomes. The Hawala case was a very prominent case, which ultimately led to the judgement of the Supreme Court in the Vineet Narain case and which, in turn, led to a series of accidents ending up in my becoming the first CVC with enhanced powers. As this was an important case, I referred this to the Central Bureau of

Investigation (CBI) indicating that this was source information and they may like to inquire into it. The allegation was that the Income Tax Report was being diluted and was suppressed. On the same day, a correspondent from *Jansatta* met me and wanted to know whether somebody have given me information about the persons involved in the Hawala case. I said that I got some information and have passed it on to the CBI. Next day, *Jansatta* published the information saying that the CVC had asked the CBI to inquire into the Hawala case, especially relating to the concealment of income by certain political leaders and bureaucrats. The *Jansatta* then added by saying that "according to the information available with the *Jansatta*, the names of the politicians/bureaucrats as well as the amount involved were as given in the report." It may be noted that I had never mentioned any details about what I had communicated to the Director, CBI, except the mere fact that I have received information and I have passed it on to the CBI.

This took a totally dramatic turn. I became the target of attack by various political leaders and I was told that the government was very upset. The stand I took was that the CVC did not have any jurisdiction to inquire into cases against political leaders who were also public servants. But the CBI was the agency capable of conducting such inquiries. When I got information from a source which I considered was reliable, I was duty-bound to bring this to the notice of the Director, CBI and it was for the Director, CBI to take further action. This was interpreted as my being a publicity hound or crossing the Lakshman Rekha of the job of the CVC. As this campaign went on for some time, I came out with a statement that the CVC has been formed to check corruption. The question before the country was whether the CVC should be checked or corruption should be checked. That put an end to the controversy.

I still believe that it is worthwhile to bring in maximum transparency in the system. When Mr Ram Jethmalani was the Minister for Urban Development, he proposed to make all files available on payment of a fixed fee to any person who was interested in that file. This would put a check on not only corruption but also bring in greater firmness and objectivity on the part of the civil servants who advice the government. Thereafter the Government of India passed the Right to Information Act, which came into force from August 2005. These measures should be carefully designed. It must be ensured that public servants who give their objective opinions are not harassed or made subject to litigation for what they have said on the file. Even though the file may be made public one day, when the notes are being recorded, the civil servant does not know whether the file will be made public or not. There should be sufficient provision under the law to ensure that the civil servant is not faced with litigation related to defamation, etc. These days we keep hearing about the need for better governance and greater transparency in the system. Better governance means less corruption. Less corruption will follow if there is greater transparency in the system. Action on the lines, as I have mentioned, I am sure, will go a long way in cleaning up our system.

People get motivated if the message is clear and if they know that the boss means what he says. In fact, I would go to the extent of even endorsing the bad master's strategy as a means of getting 'things done'. V Iswaran (ICS), who was the first Chief Secretary of Gujarat was also my Secretary. According to him a bad master keeps the dog and does the barking himself. If the boss himself is capable of doing the work in case the subordinates do not work it will certainly embarrass them and make them work. The fact that the boss is capable of doing the task shows that when the boss gives a task, he knows that it is feasible to achieve it. Explanation for non-performance will only be reflecting on the incompetence of the subordinate. This, I think, acts as an unarticulated motivation, which makes people act and perform.

Many leaders have been successful by practising, what is called, "management by walking about." What happens in management by walking about is, the boss is accessible, the boss is able to look at the cutting edge of operations and is able to get a realistic feedback about the field conditions and because he is in touch with the reality, the solutions he suggests are also pragmatic and implementable. We can therefore see how this process of management by walking about, breaks the ice generated by feudalistic mindset and the work-shy culture. In the normal management process of getting things done, the work is supposed to be delegated by the boss and supervised effectively. Supervision could be by management by exception. These are ideal textbook perceptions but under Indian conditions, perhaps a little dose of the bad master's syndrome and effective communication are absolutely necessary to get things done.

As I started this analysis on what has been behind my success in getting things done in my career, I found that there is a problem faced by the Information Technology (IT) experts in developing artificial intelligence systems for knowledge management. The IT experts have realised while there is a standard method of doing a thing and the process can be written down in terms of instructions in the form of manuals, ultimately what distinguishes a real effective expert from others is the extra factor which can be called as the 'x-factor'. This is like the distinction between a chef who is a master cook and the short order cook who is just learning to cook. The recipe may be the same, the ingredients may be the same but the manner in which cooking is done brings in the element of experience of the master chef who knows just when to switch off the heat and how much salt to add so that the flavour of the dish is fully maintained. What I am trying to do in this book is to analyse myself and see whether there are such 'x-factors', which generally are not articulated, which if made explicit can help for a better management of the organisation, and consequently lead to better results and increasing expertise.

Time-consciousness and effective time management are vital for getting anything done. I have an uncanny feeling that my perception about extreme value of time can be traced to the fact that I became a diabetic at the age of 25. This was a traumatic experience which may have had a negative impact on my life. I could have become a hypochondriac. Somehow, it did not have the negative impact on me. Instead, I became aware of the extreme value of time. I have been extensively preaching the principle that between perfection and speed, vote for speed. It is this focus on speed, which perhaps is another reason for my personal success in getting things done in my work environment. Speed can be brought in by certain technical improvements also. Everybody is aware of IT as a means of speeding up any process. IT can also lead to re-orientation of work and business process re-engineering becomes a fashion for some time.

In 1981, I discovered the tremendous potential of the Dictaphone. Dictaphone, I find, can enhance one's effectiveness, at least, tenfold. In a way, Dictaphone is an instrument for testing your readiness to be transparent. Whenever journalists were interviewing me and they thrust the Dictaphone in front of me, I was quite comfortable because I have always been of the view that there is nothing secret in our life, particularly, for a civil servant, who is like a goldfish in a glass bowl, constantly under watch. In the civil services, when you reach higher levels, particularly in a democracy like India, there is a greater scrutiny of one's behaviour. That is where, I think, the great advantage of not trying to put on different roles and being consistent and transparent has a tremendous effect. It has been said that if you do not lie, you do not have to remember what you said because whatever you say is basically the truth. The Dictaphone is an instrument, which will in a way, psychologically, make you speak the truth because it is on record.

Sometimes, people who are over guarded become non-communicative or less communicative or devious when facing the situation of being on record. If you are basically sure of yourself and if you are honest then, when the question arises of being on record, there is a great advantage. From the 80s, whenever

I held meetings, I recorded the decisions in the meeting itself. In this case, I was behaving like a bad master because normally in our governmental systems, the junior-most officer is supposed to maintain the minutes and the issue of the minutes after due approval by proper process takes a lot of time. One can cut-short all this sort of waste of time and manage in a better way by using extensively the Dictaphone. When I was the CVC, I realised that the use of Dictaphone has another great advantage. People from all over the country telephoned me at all times of the day, to my residence to lodge their complaints. When a person takes the trouble of making a long distance call and talk to the CVC late at night, say at 11 o'clock, he does so because he is under tremendous pressure and he thinks that talking to the CVC is the last resort. I got innumerable calls on a day-to-day basis, apart from 110 complaints per day and 50 files per day in my four-year tenure as CVC. I adopted the practice of recording immediately, after any such telephonic conversation, the contents of the conversation and send the note to the Secretary of the Commission. In this way a record was built-up of all the complaints that were received and even after months when people rang up, even though I may not remember the specific details, I could always assure them that the matter would be looked into and in most cases, it was. In this way, as CVC, I was perhaps able to build the credibility into our system. The credibility will be obvious from the fact that while I became CVC, the number of complaints received were about 2,200 in the year 1998; it went up to more than 17,000 in the year 2001.

Credibility is the starting point for anything getting done in our country. My term as CVC from 3rd September 1998 to 2nd September 2002 brought me a certain degree of nationwide recognition. In fact, the organisation of CVC was known and it also became credible and effective. Perhaps, one can explore the roots of how this visibility, credibility and effectiveness were brought into the CVC during my tenure. The very first step I took was to continue to be myself. One of my colleagues advised, since I was the CVC, that I should stop contributing to *The Economic Times*. The logic given was, because the CVC was a statutory authority, the government was responsible for whatever he says or writes. This according to me was a restricted view and indirectly contributed to the tradition of invisibility and ineffectiveness being of the highly dignified officers in our country. Dignified impotence is what is expected in our country from people holding high offices. Perhaps we as Indians are so much ritual-minded that some of the high officers themselves become more ritualistic. This focus on rituals arises because of the basic mistake of emphasising on doing the thing right than on doing the right things. If the dignity of an office is maintained by silence, to that extent it contributes to the lack of communication. Lack of communication leads to lack of effectiveness. In fact, lack of communication also leads to lack of transparency and further complicates the process of getting results. The breakthrough I was able to achieve was because I allowed myself to be the same even though I was occupying a job where perhaps one is expected to be silent and non-communicative. One cannot make an omelette without breaking the egg.

In a country like India, thanks to the feudalistic and the ritual-ridden traditions, high-level posts are seen more as decorative or impotence clothed with a lot of dignity. Perhaps with dignity being inversely proportionate to effectiveness, we create a situation by which governance is compromised. The steps I took for better communication were responsible for making the CVC into, at least a visible organisation. This visibility also led to credibility as mentioned earlier. Effectiveness comes if one can use techniques that overcome the problems of implementation. The CVC is an organisation to advise departmental authorities about the action to be taken and the punishment to be meted after departmental inquiries. I went in for computerisation of this information and also published it on the CVC website. This right away brought out the fact that in many cases, even after the advice was given after due inquiry, no action was taken by the disciplinary authorities for more than five years.

This, in turn, helped me to write to the disciplinary authorities, pointing out that such a situation would mean either their organisations were inefficient and therefore they did not take action or worse they were trying to protect the corrupt. This had some good impact and the follow-up action was expedited. Here we can say how in the Indian work culture, the corrupt at the higher-levels can easily escape because there is no chasing or monitoring of the cases and worse – lack transparency. Perhaps, during my tenure as CVC, the one most widely noticed and commented upon step I took was to publish on the CVC website, the names of the charged officers, who have been found guilty in corruption cases in departmental inquiries. This led to an uproar but the public welcomed it. Ninety-three per cent of the people who were polled by the *Hindustan Times* said that it was a welcome measure because it showed for the first time that action was being taken, even against senior officials. The fact that action will not be taken against senior officials is the result of our feudalistic approach. Eighty-three per cent of the people polled by *The Economic Times* felt that it was a good deterrent measure because exposing the names on the CVC website showed that some of the charged officers were in responsible and sensitive positions. This transparency highlighted the weaknesses of the system and, as mentioned earlier, also added to follow-up action where the disciplinary authorities were lackadaisical in implementing the advice of the CVC.

The CVC's website experience in exposing corruption perhaps shows how in the Indian environment, one can get things done and also overcome the action-shyness and the feudal approach. We can use technology like the IT to reach a wide section of the public to publicise the facts. In fact, IT is better than the normal print media. In the print media a subject may grab a headline for some time and then disappear, whereas once information is made available on a website, it is available not only worldwide but it is available for a long time. IT can be an instrument by which one can overcome the twin dangers of the work culture in India namely, feudal mindset and action shyness. The second step is transparency, so that public opinion and monitoring is done more effectively as in the case of follow-up action. The third one was the building up of a public opinion, which also creates an environment in which action could be taken against the corrupt.

One of the techniques we can adopt in getting things done in India is to follow what I would call the Michelangelo approach ? Michelangelo was asked how he made beautiful statues out of marble, which had no shape. He said that his focus was on the statue and he went on removing from the marble whatever was not part of the statue. Lo and behold! The statue emerged soon. If we want to get results, we have to find out what comes in the way of our goal and take steps to see that they are removed. I noticed as CVC that in certain departments whenever there were reports by the CVO (Chief Vigilance Officers) against corruption at higher levels, the disciplinary authorities not only diluted the charges but played safe by delaying actions. Question arises as to how to overcome this problem because CVOs are mostly at junior levels? On a visit to Mumbai in the airport when the flight was delayed, I had discussions with a couple of my officers and they came up with the interesting suggestion that an advanced copy of the CVO's report may be asked to be sent by the CVOs to the CVC. This did not dilute the authority of the disciplinary authority and if the CVC gives the direction that the advanced copy can be sent, the CVOs cannot be held guilty of not following the official channels for communication. Once such information comes to the CVC, it can monitor whether the department was trying to go slow and trying to protect the corrupt. Accordingly, in November 2000, I issued the order and this had a good impact. Here was a case where the weakness of the system of protecting the corrupt and preventing vigilance from going after the corrupt was overcome by a procedural change.

Another procedural change which had a wide impact was the order I issued, that in government procurement systems, once the financial bids are opened, there will be no negotiations except with the lowest bidder. I realised the importance of this step during my experience as the Chairman, Telecom Commission. The Department of Telecom, being in a position of monopoly buyer, was able to pitch one bidder against another. This led to endless possibilities of corruption because in the subsequent discussions with all players, even after financial bids have been opened, the lowest bidder may not get the contract and the contract may be awarded to someone else who is favoured by the powers that be. In order to put an end to this, I consulted all the heads of large departments and issued a simple order that once financial bids are opened, there should be no post-tender negotiations except with the lowest bidder. This had a healthy impact. This type of focus on the specific factors that come in the way of performance comes from experience and a detailed understanding from an insider's point of view of how the governmental system functions. Michelangelo was right.

Are Indians essentially work-shy? When I look at different sections of our country, I find that at the lowest level, most of the poor in India are very hard-working. The Indian agriculturist probably toils the hardest. I have seen how hard is the life of the daily workers who have to earn their bread on a day-to-day basis. Indians, because of the nature of the environment in which they function, have to work hard. Indians by nature cannot be said to be avoiding work. Avoiding work probably becomes a part of the educated class. This avoidance of work is also encouraged by our system where those who work are loaded with more work and those who do not work get pay, promotions and perquisites. This is, what I call, the 'Vittal's Law' and the logic is understandable. Any boss who finds that he has an urgent task to be done is likely to give it to a person who is known to work and deliver. In a way, therefore, the entire playing field gets tilted against the sincere working person and he gets more work all the time. More work means that there is also a possibility of some mistakes happening. These become, in a way, obstacles to the hardworking man's progress in career. The man who avoids work automatically gets less work and is also less likely to commit any mistakes. Further, we have got, as a fact, working environment, the trade union movement and the labour laws. These are such that a person who does not work is further favoured by the law and is protected. Even if we have a system of fair judgement by way of confidential rolls, if adverse remarks are given, the employee concerned can raise all types of objections and bring extraneous considerations. In our society where affirmative action is the policy for asserting the rights of the weaker sections, if the employee against whom adverse remarks are made happens to be from the weaker section, the employee can invoke the myth of his or her caste being a factor, which led to the adverse remarks. In other words, we have created, through our legal system and our system of governance and rules, a very cosy atmosphere for those who do not want to work.

Having created such an environment, how can we expect that in India there will be a work culture for getting things done? The fact is that Indians basically are not work-shy but our problem of work culture is, thanks to the structures and organisations we have developed. This will be obvious from the fact that the same Indians when they go abroad work very hard and are successful. The NRIs today are the classic example of the willingness of the Indians to work very hard. Indians are not shy of working and the poor people work hard anyway. But when it comes to the educated class in the organised sector, we have by policy created an environment in which there is positive discouragement to those who want to work. There is even legal protection given to those who do not want to work. In such an environment if you want results, you will have to think in terms of changing the rules and procedures, which discourage people from working. The emergency is a classic example of why at that time the trains ran on time. Consciously, the whole cushion of safety and the security blanket which has evolved was withdrawn temporarily. Thanks to a series of court judgments and policy measures starting with the protection given under Article 311 of the Constitution of India. The bureaucrats realised that they will have to perform and hence the sloth and the culture of not working was temporarily given up. The other factor that comes in the way of getting things done in India, namely the feudal culture is more difficult. The feudal culture leads to extreme status-consciousness. The entire French Revolution and subsequent development of modern European nations have brought out the central fact that modernisation comes when the social relationship moves from status to contract. In India, we have not been able to move in this direction of status to contract. It is true that we have a democracy where everybody has equal rights and everybody has the vote, but the policies of reservation and the caste arithmetic which has become the basic theorem of politics in our country have created vested interests in which if a person does not work, he can still go ahead in life because of the argument of social justice. This is a fact that has to be realised, if we want to move India towards a modern, efficiently-running state.

Social change in India, in the process of moving from the status to contract, has witnessed increasing assertiveness of the weaker sections encouraged by conscious government policies to not only protect them but also ensure constitutional support. The policy of reservation and preference in various programmes of the government for uplifting the backward and the depressed classes has created a situation, which goes against the development of a work culture. As discussed earlier, those who work sincerely get more work and those who evade work enjoy all the benefits. This disastrous vicious cycle which I call the 'Vicious Cycle of Vittal's Law' is one of the factors why the work culture in India is not conducive for greater productivity or efficiency or getting things done. If, by policy, we encourage not working and asserting individual rights, how can we expect a better culture? In fact, the Kerala experience shows what can be the impact of education in the Indian context. Though education has been the common factor for the economic development of the miracle of the South-East Asian countries, in India, Kerala, which became the first 100% literate state, found that the people have become more assertive of their rights neglecting their responsibilities. The issue of the work culture can be resolved not only by moving from the status to contract but also by building a culture of responsibility. This means that every person will have to own that he has the responsibility for results. The increasing application of the labour laws which protect labour also lead to ridiculous situations where people can probably also resist the opportunity for becoming multi-skilled. It is very common that in a government office the sweeper is supposed to sweep the floor and a farash is supposed to wipe the tables and keep them dust-free. The farash will never do the work of the sweeper and vice versa. Perhaps, this goes back to our Indian culture of casteism and the Indian penchant for extreme analysis and division and also the tendency for each one to stick to his knitting. The reason why in many of our organisations, the performance level is low is because our human resource potential is not fully explored. An organisation in which people are multi-skilled and are willing to switch jobs and take additional responsibilities is likely to be more effective than an organisation where each person's work is so strictly defined and there is a sort of a Lakshman Rekha that they cannot cross and take on additional responsibilities. In times of economic trouble when organisations try to downsize, there will be need for multi-skilled workers but this probably is also resisted and the movement towards multi-skilling is also made difficult by the labour laws which guard every person's right to stick to his own defined sphere of work. The lack of work culture in terms of people's commitment and getting results can thus be traced not only to caste consciousness but also to the legal protection given by the administrative policies.

In the ultimate analysis, for getting anything done, there has to be an overwhelming desire on the part of someone to achieve results. The reason why in many large organisations like government, things are enormously delayed or do not get done within reasonable timeframes is because there is no individual who owns the particular objective or has an intense desire for getting the results. This lack of commitment may be also due to lack of adequate information and an awareness of the overall picture. This is where the importance of communication comes in. One of the characteristics of any leader has been described as a capacity to communicate and sell his vision to the people in the organisation.

Let us go back to the basic issue of desire. If any person desires to achieve results, that intense desire becomes a commitment. I had this experience when I was posted as the Chairman, Telecom Commission. The entire Department of Telecommunications had become a mini empire ruled by the technocrats of the Indian Telecommunication Service. The winds of change were blowing from 1991 when the Athreya Committee was appointed. After all, telecommunication in our country has a long history and for 100 years the Department of Telecommunications had the monopoly of this sector. As a result, it had become an inward looking organisation and the approach was of distribution of patronage. When I was appointed the Chairman of the Telecom Commission, there was an organisation-wide resistance to my appointment. The first objection was that I was not a technocrat and belonged to the universally-hated generalist service of IAS. Secondly, I was also perceived to be a person very much in favour of liberalisation and was dubbed as the 'dot buster', the sobriquet used for me in the editorial of *The Economic Times*. I got this reputation because from June 1990 I was the member of the Telecom Commission being the Secretary, Department of Electronics and I have been all the time arguing for liberalisation and increasing the options available to the customer of telecom services by injecting more competition in the century old monopoly of telecommunication services.

The 1991 Athreya Committee was appointed to examine the issue of corporatisation of the Department of Telecom. This was necessary because Sam Pitroda, the Telecom Czar of India, took the first step to separate telecommunications from the postal department and telecom became, on the model of the Atomic Energy Commission, the Telecom Commission. Out of the telecom services provided all over the country by the Department of Telecom, the external services were corporatized in the form of Videsh Sanchar Nigam Limited (VSNL), which was earlier known as Overseas Communication Service. The services in Delhi and Mumbai were corporatized under the aegis of Mahanagar Telephone Nigam Limited (MTNL). When I came on the scene as Chairman, Telecom Commission in October 1993, there was an organisational diarchy with Delhi and Mumbai, which accounted for 22% of the telephones in the country under a corporate structure and the rest of the country under a departmental structure. I was arguing for corporatisation and the Athreya Committee was appointed under the chairmanship of the well-known consultant Dr MB Athreya in 1991. A majority of the Committee recommended corporatisation of the Department of Telecom into six different corporations, four zonal ones and one for long distance communications. But there was no unanimity in the Committee and it was a fractured report. The report remained largely a dead letter. Subsequently, when I was appointed as the Chairman of Telecom Commission, it was seen by the 4.5 lakh employees, who were strong and organised into 41 unions and three federations, as an attempt at corporatisation and virtually arranging for the hara-kiri of the department. The Indian Telecom Service (ITS) realised that if corporatisation and liberalisation came, their well-known service, which had given them a monopoly over an important infrastructure sector, will be lost. The idea of further liberalisation, therefore, was resisted strongly, by practically the entire organisation. The Minister was also not very enthusiastic and openly opposed corporatisation. The pressure for reforms came from outside the department, i e from the PMO and the Ministry of Finance under Dr Manmohan Singh with Montek Singh Ahluwalia as the Secretary. The 1991 liberalisation process itself was a result of external factors like the foreign exchange crisis and the whole attempt was at dismantling the licence permit regime and pegging the Indian economy more closely to the global economy. For achieving this, it was necessary to ensure that the telecom, an important sector, was also liberalised. When I became Chairman, Telecom Commission, I found that I had to carry out the mandate for liberalisation. Nobody, specifically in government told me that I should go in for liberalisation. The Zeitgeist was there. How does one push for reforms in an organisation when there is total hostility to the idea? The first requirement, I think, is intense commitment towards bringing change. I had developed this intense commitment because of the fact that I had spent the bulk of my career in Gujarat, which has been known as an industry-friendly State, where the culture of administration was different. In Gujarat, being Managing Director of a public sector enterprise carries greater status than being Secretary to the Government. On the other hand, in the Government of India, it is totally the other way. Senior officials probably take pleasure in making top executives of the public sector enterprises wait for appointments and hence the general perception is, it is better to be in the driving seat of the government which makes the policy rather than in the public sector enterprises which is perceived as subservient to the dictates of the administrative ministry.

All through the fifty years and more of our experiences in the public sector, one constant theme of the public sector executives has been greater autonomy and accountability. The autonomy perhaps will never be provided because the public sector enterprises provide a convenient source for improving the perquisites of service for those who are in the administrative ministry. In fact, when I was the Chairman of Public Enterprises Selection Board, I was appointed the Chairman of a committee to go into all the 821 guidelines issued by the Government of India from time to time to regulate the various aspects of public sector enterprises and I came up with the proposal that bulk of the instructions should be scrapped. It is to the eternal credit of the Government of India under the Industry Ministry headed by Mr Murasoli Maran that 696 guidelines issued by the Department of Public Enterprises were scrapped in 1997. This provided a great sense of relief to the public sector enterprises and sent a positive signal that the government was serious about giving greater autonomy to the public sector. Along with this, in our committee, I also recommended adopting a model code of conduct, which would regulate the relationship between the public sector enterprises and the administrative ministry.

Unfortunately, this has not taken off. The hostility of the ITS officers for the corporatisation idea therefore can be easily understood. If reforms have to happen and bring a change, how are we to achieve it? I therefore behaved like the 'bad master'. Knowing that if I ask for any policy paper on liberalisation or corporatisation, I will not get a comprehensive paper or a paper on the lines which I visualised, I myself prepared the three papers on – (i) Policy for Liberalisation of Telecom Services, (ii) Corporatisation of the Department of Telecom, and (iii) Finding Resources for Telecom Reform, in November 1993.

I also took the initiative to have four times in the second half of December 1993 the meeting of the full Telecom Commission which, apart from the permanent members like the Chairman, Telecom Commission, Member (Services), Member (Finance), Member (Production) – also had Secretary (Electronics), Secretary (Industry), Secretary (Planning) and Secretary (Finance) as members and hammered out a policy for liberalisation as well as corporatisation. I submitted the papers to the then Minister of Communication, Mr Sukh Ram on 5th January 1994. Thereafter, the matter rested there. There was no action. Then on 11th April 1994, the Prime Minister's Office reminded the department and wanted a presentation to be made to the Prime Minister when the Minister for Communication was also present. I made the presentation and the Minister disagreed with my view, especially on corporatisation. The Prime Minister was annoyed and said that he was under the impression that there was a consensus about reforms and corporatisation of the DoT and was annoyed at our difference of opinion. He gave us a time limit of one week within which we were expected to resolve our differences and come up with an alternative proposal. The work could not be done within a week and finally on 22nd April 1994, we met the Prime Minister at his residence. The Minister had prepared a five page note arguing why corporatisation would cost about ₹9,000 crore and should not be done. I had seen the note in the file and re-submitted with the file a note to the Minister running up to eleven pages arguing why the corporatisation should be adopted. I explained that it would not cost ₹9,000 crore but much less, and this measure can be sustained. When the issue came up before the Prime Minister on 22nd April, I conveyed my views and gave the note to the Prime Minister. It was unusual that a Secretary should disagree with the Minister and give his views in writing to the Prime Minister on a policy matter. I did this because I hold that the highest authority in the land – the Prime Minister, should have all the facts before him before he takes a policy decision. I submitted what I considered to be correct facts for a policy decision. The price I had to pay for this act was to be transferred and shifted unceremoniously on 7th September 1994 back to the Department of Electronics. The government added insult to injury by suggesting my name as India's candidate for the post of Director of Telecom Development Bureau of the International Telecom Union and shifted me from the post of Chairman, Telecom Commission on the eve of the election to the post to be held at Kyoto in Japan. But the success I tasted was when the Telecom Policy for liberalisation was announced on 13th May 1994.

I am mentioning this to show that in getting things done in India, especially when there is hostility to any change, what is needed is the sense of commitment and motivation on the part of the individual who is trying to bring about the change. This also includes a capacity to find arguments for every counter argument and solutions for every problem that is posed by those who are opposed to change. In spite of my experience, I still hold that being frank and open is always desirable. Though I might have a setback in the form of being shifted from the Department of Telecom back to Department of Electronics, I had my reward later on. The Prime Minister apparently appreciated the fact that I was independent in thinking. I was made the Chairman of Public Enterprises Selection Board on the eve of my retirement on January 31, 1996. My subsequent selection as the Central Vigilance Commissioner also, I suspect, may be due to the general perception of my being independent. This only shows that perhaps the basic requirement for making things happen is intense commitment.

We see in successful cases in other fields also, the change agents have been those who are intensely committed and are quite open about their views and vision. Without such an articulation of a vision and being open about it, communication will be difficult. Without communication, an idea cannot catch on and the public opinion or opinion in any organisation cannot be influenced. There is thus a close linkage between the need for developing a vision, intense commitment to the vision, communication and winning public opinion for bringing about any change. People who are hostile to any change will come up with a lot of operational objections at the implementation stage. Generally, what I call as the RAMA process takes over. In every situation which is evolving, once the critical point is crossed, the entire situation changes. In nuclear physics once critical mass is achieved, there is a chain reaction. It will be interesting to identify in each major change that has taken place in our country when such a critical mass was achieved where when the resistance to change was given up and the inevitability of the change accepted. This is the period where we would have moved from rejection(R) to annoyance(A) to mellowing(M), where the environment is created for achievement(A). Incidentally, my friend Dr Thyagarajan of the Department of Science and Technology first conceived the RAMA concept.

I have always found that trusting people and giving them a pat on the back when they do well, pays rich dividends. One of the earliest problems I faced was a strike organised by the State Bank of India in Gujarat that coincided with the financial year ending on 31st March 1969. I was then Director of Accounts and Treasuries and one of my basic responsibilities was to see that the salaries were properly disbursed to all government servants in spite of the strike by the State Bank of India. I had a batch of dedicated Treasury Officers and we coordinated with the Reserve Bank of India and the State Bank of Saurashtra to move ₹6 crore in cash. This was an unimaginably large sum in those days and the entire operation of disbursement of salaries went on without difficulty. It was such a success that I wrote to Mr VB Eswaran (who later on became Finance Secretary in Government of India), suggesting that a letter of appreciation must be given to Mr CH Shah who was the Treasury Officer of Bhavnagar and who had moved nearly four crores from the State Bank of Saurashtra. I was pleasantly surprised when one afternoon Mr VB Eswaran rang up and said: "Not only we are issuing letter of appreciation to Mr Shah but also to you for what you have done." Throughout my career I had continued this practice of giving letters of appreciation. Whenever any task was completed, it normally was taken for granted and where some initiative was shown by any officer, I promptly wrote DO letter to him ensuring that a copy was filed in the Annual Confidential Report. I found this measure immensely motivating and I have watched with satisfaction many people, who worked with me, rise high in their careers.

Mao Tse-tung in his *Little Red Book* had laid down the principles for guerrilla warfare. One of his principles was never attack unless you are fully prepared. I find that this principle is very effective in getting things done. A thorough preparation is necessary if one has to succeed. One must be able to anticipate all possible objections to any proposal and be ready with the answers. Basically one strategy I always adopted was to remove all alibis for non-performance. I had many times in my career tried to apply this logic. One was when I was Industries Commissioner and in 1978 the District Industry Centres (DICs) were introduced. Gujarat became the first state, which covered all the districts with DICs. I had to personally visit all the 17 districts of Gujarat and select the sites for construction of buildings for the DICs. The Government of India was giving an amount of ₹5 lakh as well as a vehicle for the office. This was a great luxury in those days. We could hire buildings but the hitch was the rent was to be certified by the PWD engineer. I found that their estimates were conservative. The Gujarat Industrial Development Corporation (GIDC) also had Executive Engineers. I adopted the strategy of utilising the services of the engineers of the GIDC for certification of the rent, so that we would not have any complexity. Till the permanent building of DICs came up, we had very smooth operations. In fact, Gujarat became the first state in the whole country to have all the 17 districts come up with DICs and I got a personal letter of appreciation from Mr George Fernandes who was at that time the Industry Minister. This was something unique because Gujarat was the only state, which got the distinction. The point I want to emphasise is that in implementing a programme of this type, one has to anticipate the likely pitfalls and dangers and make thorough preparations so that the system does not fail. I had mentioned that between perfection and speed, I always suggested that we should vote for speed because Gujarat became the first state, it got the full benefit of the ₹5 lakh per district funds available for the DICs and subsequently the scheme itself was diluted and the grants were reduced. As we were quick to take advantage of the schemes, Gujarat got the full benefit.

Talking about thorough preparation, another technique I always adopted was the application of the PERT (Programme Evaluation Review Technique) or the Network method, the critical path method. When I was Secretary, Civil Supplies, the Cabinet took a decision in August 1980 that the Civil Supplies Corporation should be set up on 2nd October 1980. Between the decision of the Government on 14th August and 2nd October, there was two months' time. We planned the operation working backwards from various steps to be taken and here again we had to go through the whole process of registering the corporation, drawing the policies, mobilising funds, so on and so forth. All this was done because of the thorough preparation and planning in time. The need for thorough preparations, identified by Mao Tse-tung in his book on guerrilla tactics, is required to be applied in administration also. Choosing the right people for the right job and entrusting them the full responsibility is one of the basic requirements for success. For example, in the Narmada Auto case I was having an excellent support from Mr Kanak Trivedi who was a great leader and organiser of men and when it came to setting up of the building, I entrusted the job to Mr Dhimant Ojha who was a young enthusiastic engineer, thoroughly honest. Choosing the right people and entrusting them fully by the task is the simplest method of ensuring that the task gets done.

Commitment is only another name for intense expression of motivation. How does one get motivated? Looking at myself, I am trying to analyse what motivates me. I have already mentioned in the chapter, about my reaction when I was diagnosed to be a diabetic at the age of 25 and which, by some curious coincidence did not make me a hypochondriac or a valetudinarian but as a person intensely aware of the need and the preciousness of time. This awareness probably pushes me to see that the things are done as fast as possible. Hence I value the slogan, "Between perfection and speed, vote for speed". Perfection probably gives a convenient psychological cushion for those who want to procrastinate. While procrastination is the thief of time, an indulgent attitude is taken towards the thief because the person who is procrastinating can take a view that he is only trying to achieve perfection. Nothing done by human beings can ever be perfect. One can only try for perfection. As the old concept of fullness *'poornotva'* says:

Om purnamda purnamidam
Purnat purnamudachyate
Purnasya purnamadaya
Purnameva avasishyate

Out of perfection comes perfection. I therefore see, even quality as a quest for perfection. If we are trying to get things done in India and if we try for perfection, we are not going to succeed. We must be able to see what is pragmatic and what is feasible (I have, explored elsewhere) – the chemistry for achieving things considered possible with the help of the five principles. These are the principles articulated by Bertrand Russell, Victor Hugo, Alexis de Tocqueville, Bernard Shaw and Michelangelo. Against this broad framework of the change dynamics, one can try to draw strength and get results.

A point for consideration at this stage is, whether reading books on management or techniques of management helps one to improve one's performance. As I look back at my career, I find two specific cases where I have been influenced by what I read or was taught. The first is the concept of productivity. In 1964, I attended a National Productivity Council programme on 'organisation and methods' and I was exposed to the elementary principles of 'work study' and 'method study'. Somehow, this has had a great impact on me and developed in me a capacity to analyse and provide ready tools for exploring alternative methods of doing things. The elements of method study namely, elimination, combination, re-sequencing, modification, and substitution have become part of my thinking process. Perhaps, this is at the root of many innovations I have done throughout my career in administration.

The second important influence I had is from my exposure to the books by Edward de Bono. In 1982, I started getting exposed to Edward de Bono and his style of innovative thinking. His basic concept that ideas are the spectacles with which one looks at facts has been internalised by me.

Each one of us also is the product of the experience we are exposed to. It so happened that I was fortunate to start my career in Gujarat, which had just been formed on 1st May 1960 out of the bifurcation of bilingual Bombay. Gujaratis are known to be pragmatic, enterprising people and my exposure to them, I think, was also responsible in a great way in my adopting a pragmatic outlook to work. Unlike in other parts of the country, the IAS moniker in Gujarat does not carry a heavy brand equity and automatic social respect. In Gujarat you are judged by your performance. Perhaps, that also made me realise that whatever one has to achieve, one has to achieve on one's own effort and the fact that one belongs to a particular service would not give an automatic advantage.

How does one learn? The entire life is a learning process, if one knows how to reflect on one's experience and internalise the lessons. One of my favourite stories is the story of the donkey of Jesus Christ. Jesus used to travel on a donkey. He delivered those excellent memorable sermons on the mount. People like Peter and Paul, who heard them became apostles. The donkey also heard all those sermons remained a donkey! The question is, whether in our life, we are like the donkey of Jesus Christ or like the apostles? This book is an exercise on reflecting how I was able to learn from my experiences and learn to get things done in India in spite of the twin cultural factors of hierarchy and work-shy nature of the people. The hierarchy part we can understand, we have a long tradition and the hierarchy was perpetuated by social structure like Varnashrama Dharma. Thereafter, we were ruled by foreigners for a long time and hence the concept of respect for authority and behaving like courtiers (the *darbari* culture) came naturally to us and which has perhaps still remained within, even though special changes are being made by affirmative action. Even the process of affirmative action seems to be an exercise in Sanskritisation, to use the words of the eminent Indian sociologist, MN Srinivas.

What about the work-shy nature? The work-shy nature perhaps comes from our tolerance for alternative points of view.

Hinduism has survived because of its sense of tolerance and the basic concept that there could be alternative methods of looking at the world. It is this sense of tolerance perhaps which further gets extended to tolerance of sub-optimal performances. The *'chalta hai'* (satisfied with whatever is there) attitude is well-known. This is perhaps at the root of our lack of killer instinct, which many have commented upon. Many a time, we do not seem to have the energy left for the last mile effort and we are satisfied with the sub-optimal performance. This may be one more reason why we do not seem to have succeeded like South Korea and Japan. These countries strengthened themselves by external discipline imposed by military rule or at least the military culture.

All generalisations run the risk of exceptions. It is exception that proves the rule. It has been well said that whatever is true of India is true and the contrary is also true. India is a large country of a billion plus people with a tradition going back to more than five thousand years. Therefore, one can extract the twin concepts of hierarchy and an easy-going work-shy culture as a factor that comes in the way of getting things done. However, it is not as if that there are no achievements to celebrate in the 70 years of India's independence, where perhaps for the first time India as a united country is governing itself.

(ii) YEAR OF THE HOUSE

Distance in time and space lends perspective. As I look back at my year at Charleville from June 1960 as a Probationer in the IAS at the National Academy of Administration, the most striking thought is how ignorant, naive and wet behind the years was I. When I left the Academy, I was a different person.

To be honest, I was the first IAS officer I had met. Competing for the IAS was never my idea of a career. As a student of BSc Honours Chemistry (equivalent to a post-graduate), at Loyola College, Madras (now Chennai), my dream was that I must go for a career in research in Chemistry. I visualised future generation of students studying about the Vittal Reaction just as we studied Grignard Reaction.

My father, the most gentle, ever smiling and the politest person I have ever seen in my life and the person who never got angry or raised his voice, told me that I must take my chance at the IAS. "If you fail, you may go for research," he had said. He was the only son of his parents and when he wanted to appear for the ICS, his parents had not agreed. I could not even think of refusing his advice. In fact, it turned out to be the best advice I ever had. By the grace of God, I got through in my first attempt and found my name in the list of successful candidates for the IAS in February 1960.

I was just 20 when I finished my BSc (Honours) course and I had to wait for a year to complete 21, the minimum age for appearing in the IAS. I took up the job of a Lecturer at Jamal Mohammad College, Tiruchirapalli in 1958 and wrote the examination in 1959.

I had a senior colleague in the college faculty whose nearest relation Mr Venkatanarayanan (1957 Uttar Pradesh cadre) was the member of the IAS and was visiting him in Trichy. Before leaving for Mussoorie, I met Mr Venkatanarayanan, to get his advice as a new member of the service. He made an insightful comment, "Vittal, when you go to the Academy, you will naturally find many brilliant people, who have joined the IAS, but you will also find chaps, who will make you wonder, how they ever got in."

I was really a boy from boondocks. I had never travelled north of Tirupati and my first visit to Delhi was when I had to appear in the UPSC interview for the IAS on 18th January 1960. I was allotted Room 65 in the Happy Valley block of the Academy overlooking the riding grounds and commanding an excellent view of the mountains.

Two people played a key role in our life at the Academy. The first of course, was the Director Late Mr Aditya Nath Jha (ICS), the roly-poly jolly officer who never took a class. The other was

Senior Deputy Director Shri Ramakrishna Trivedi (IAS), an ever serious intense, dedicated officer. They made an excellent pair complimenting each other.

Mr AN Jha used to take, once in a while, tutorial classes for batches of Probationers. When the foundation course was on, one of the IRS probationers asked him, "Sir, as Director, what exactly are your functions? We hardly see you." The unflappable Mr Jha explained with a smile, "Have you ever been on a ship? You will never see the Captain rushing about. If you ever see the Captain of the ship rushing about, it means that the ship is having a trouble. I am like that Captain."

Years later, I have heard him explain the concept of what a senior officer must be. According to him, a senior officer must be like the master of the native oil press, quietly smoking his hookah while the bullocks go around pressing the oil seeds in the oil press. He certainly believed in delegation of work and would have agreed with the first Chief Secretary of Gujarat, Shri V Iswaran (ICS), who used to say, "He is a bad master who keeps a dog and does the barking himself."

The remarkable aspect of Mr Jha was his bubbling sense of humour. Throughout the entire year of our training, he gave in all, three lectures. One of them was on humour, another was on his trip to Australia to attend a conference which was also full of cracks. One comment I recall was about how the popular Erle Stanley Gardner would have come out with the novel *The Case of the Dozing Delegate* if he had attended the conference. Another was about an Australian minister who was called a bastard by his political opponent. His old mother commented in the next day's paper, "I don't mind my son being abused. But why should my name be drawn in the controversy?"

In the course of his lectures, he shared his experiences as an ICS probationer. Horse riding was one of the key aspects of the ICS training as it was for us in the IAS also. When Mr Jha who must have been roly-poly in his youth also turned up at the riding ground, the riding master had one look at him and said, "Boy! I am afraid you will have problems in riding." Jha shot back, "Why should I have a problem? The horse might."

Unfortunately, I did have a problem in horse riding. I had a number of falls from the horse and twisted my ankle a couple of times. Riding was not only a part of the training but one had to pass the test for completing one's probation. This test was of course, supervised by the Director himself. When at the end of the course, I took my test, the horse did not cooperate and I failed. I was to appear again after three days for a second attempt.

As luck would have it, that night was a Friday. Fridays were nights for formal dinners which were called 'Penguin Nights' because all of us probationers had to wear the black and white *bandhgala* outfit making us look like Penguins. Formal nights also involved cultural programmes presented by the probationers.

That night in the programme, my friend T Padmanabhan (Andhra Pradesh cadre), and I made a brave attempt to present the classical Ragamalika Malaipozudhainile sung by MS Subbulakshmi, the great singer. It was a total disaster, thanks to my off key rendering but was highly entertaining to the audience which included the Director. Anyway, my effort was worth it. It helped me to pass my riding test. Soon after our presentation, Mr Jha said generously, "Vittal! For that efforts of yours I am going to pass you in the riding test!" Sure enough he kept his words and I completed my probation successfully.

At the end of the year, we probationers left our parting remarks in a register kept in the Academy Administration Office. My colleague, V Venkatesan (Maharashtra cadre) had commented – riding was great fun.

I added in my comment – riding was great fun for the horses.

But life in the academy was not all horses. The training programme was in effect a process of continuously discovering new horizons and experiences. The range of lectures covered art, literature, history, linguistics, economics, law and the Constitution. We were exposed to experts from various fields who stretched our mental horizons. Verrier Elwin came to speak on tribal people. Sivaramamurthy spoke on epigraphy, sculpture and numismatics. Ramachandran spoke about the archaeological work in Nagarjuna Sagar (Andhra Pradesh). SS Khera (ICS), impressed us with his systematic analysis of district administration as well as the public sector. Mr Mathur (ICS), Director-General of All India Radio gave us a tool d'horizone of Indian dances and music.

Senior Deputy Director Mr RK Trivedi (IAS) was really a serious master and teacher. He taught us to adopt a systematic approach to work. He emphasised the importance of integrity as well as the roles of an ideal civil servant and the political leaders. As an honest officer, he had also faced problems and recalled the words of Mr Govind Ballabh Pant, the then Chief Minister of UP, "a milch cow also has to suffer kicks from time to time."

Mr Naval Singh was the riding master. He was a colourful character. He was a tough disciplinarian in the riding field but gentle outside. He had a philosophic streak about him. If any of us were afraid of falling from the horse, he would say, "Sahib, god who has made you an IAS officer after such a tough competition, will not let you down."

Among the professors each one had his own special features. The most memorable was Professor Pathak, who taught law. He was a close observer of the probationers and in his farewell address in the mess, when he left, he gave detailed thumbnail sketches of each of the 70 probationers. I recall that he described me as a great jurist as I perhaps did well in law. My grandfather and father were in the legal profession, I suppose I had some genetic advantage, so far as the subject of law was concerned.

Prof Bhattacharya who taught economics was opposed to using jargon and insisted on using simple English. He used to say that a steel mill can help to build a hospital but not the other way round.

It was at the Academy that the idea first dawned on me that I had become a Sahib. When I was addressed as such, by the boy allotted to attend to our personal needs, like Jeeves to Bertie Wooster. My Jeeves was a young fair *pahadi* boy named Ranjit Singh. He was allotted to do all the odd jobs including ironing of clothes, polishing shoes, etc.

It so happened that after leaving the Academy in 1961, I did not have any opportunity to re-visit it till 1983. After a gap of 23 years, I visited the Academy with my wife, son and daughter when I was working as Managing Director of the Gujarat Narmada Valley Fertiliser Company, a joint sector enterprise of the Gujarat government. A lot of changes had taken place in the meanwhile. The Director and the faculty had long changed. One constant factor was Ranjit Singh still playing Jeeves to all the successive generations of trainee officers.

I located Ranjit Singh. The years had taken their toll. The fair young man I had known as a probationer had now become old and haggard.

I felt a twinge of sadness for him. I tipped him ₹100 and took leave.

I am afraid I was what my smarter colleagues described as a KTP (Keen Type Probationer). Nevertheless, I feel I was all the better for being one.

(iii) MY PHILOSOPHY, MY ACTION

It is more than twenty-one years since I joined the Indian Administrative Service. I would have never got into this service but for the insistence of my father. In the tradition bound Madras state, as it was known then, IAS was a magic passport to status and prosperity. Even today, the service enjoys a status in Tamil Nadu which is unimaginable in the pragmatic, commercial and industrial culture of Gujarat.

My first reaction to the idea, when my father mentioned this to me sometime in April-May 1958, was very cool. I had just cleared the BSc (Honours) from Loyola College Madras. I was viewing the world from the Olympian heights of a scientist and my ambition was to become a renowned scientist. First, I must get my Doctorate and then the world of science.

It was not to be. My father made the very practical proposition that I make an attempt at the IAS and if I fail, I can go to science always. The family dictated decisions. I took a chance and in the 1959 examination I got through.

I joined the service on 16th May 1960 and was allotted to Gujarat, the new state carved out of Bombay on 1st of May 1960, just sixteen days before.

Twenty-one years is a long time and I sometimes wonder whether I have evolved any administrative philosophy in all these years. Do I have any values? Are any values left at all? How far all the theories and principles of administration relevant in practice on the field?

Before undertaking this exercise, one may as well ask whether it is worth having any value at all. One can come across any amount of sterile cynics in administration. Perhaps, they have had bitter experiences which have rendered them so. Perhaps, one can even make out a convincing case that a mere bureaucrat in the leviathan of organisation is powerless. Even if he holds power for a moment the results are transitory.

I believe in the positive approach to administration. Perhaps one can decide the basic orientation of an administrator as positive, negative or neutral. Perhaps the basic cause of this is in the genes or constitution or background. I will not be able to precisely identify the factors, but as one floats along in the stream of bureaucratic life, one comes across the different types and also gets, I suppose, typecast.

For me, a positive approach to work is a basic condition for survival. Out of 24 hours in a day, eight are lost in sleep and at least eight hours are for office work. If one third of one's life is going to be engaged in similar activity, then, it is better that is enjoyable rather than being a burden. If you adopt the neutralist stance, you are living life in a state of detachment. For the learned followers of the *Gita*, this attitude of water on the lotus leaf may be an ideal. Not for me. The leaf shrugs off the water drops and nothing is left. A neutralist is reduced to the level of mere spectator, in his work. He just watches one third of his life slip away. One of the banes of bureaucracy is that it is heartless and impersonal. Neutralist administrators contribute a lot for developing this characteristic of the bureaucracy. I have seen the same neutralists, once out of power or removed from position, petitioning to the power that they be more helpful or sympathetic in their own case. Perhaps, a neutralist derives the special delight of a sadist voyeur in adopting an objective, a cold and a correct stance in handling problems, perhaps, he is protecting his own stain. For the neutralist, the cockroach for survivability and the tortoise for instant withdrawal from any involvement, should be ideals.

The negativist administrator is hostile to work and the work environment. He is perhaps an active sadist and delights in being the abominable 'No man' of the department. Alternatively, he lets off his bottled-up frustrations in wrecking proposals which try to be constructive. The negativist is generally intelligent and perhaps corrupt. It pays to be negative because you can put a price on every 'yes' of yours.

The great delight of the negativist is forever acting Cassandra and sometimes things will go wrong and prove him right. If things do not go wrong, he has the satisfaction of continuing support of powers that be, to be cautious and perhaps the success of the idea because the perils anticipated by him, have been taken care of.

Somehow, temperamentally, I never liked the "nattering nabobs of negativism" to quote the phrase of Spiro Agnew. As one of the successful senior IAS officers, KT Satarawala, once told a batch of young officers, what this country needs "are people who are maniacally optimistic." I think that one is positive and optimistic, the approach to problems in administration look totally different from the traditional conservative approach. It makes a world of difference. Administration, instead of being a mere 'maintenance' function, becomes a creative, active and lively 'design' function with tremendous potential.

What exactly is the positive approach? Administration can be visualised as a daily encounter with a series of problems and decisions to be made to solve the problems. Books have been written and a few have evolved about the art of decision making. Essentially it is one of analysing all the available facts in a given situation, evolving sets of options to resolve situations and choosing one to go ahead with.

In reality, there is no neat classification of the three stages of decision-making. They tend to overlap. Most of our decision making is intuitive. According to my colleague BS Raghavan, what LP Singh was trying to achieve while working as Home Secretary was to make the decision making process less intuitive and more rational, tangible and articulate. In a way, the entire system of bureaucratic device of files and noting can be visualised as one collective effort at decision making which is done in a patient and explicit manner in view of the administration's accountability to the public.

Well, in the anatomy of decision making, what is the relevance of mental orientation? The orientation is like a compass which sets the direction in which movement takes place. Given a set of options in a situation, the neutralist may opt for the path of least resistance. For the negativist, the course which results in greater short term financial saving to the government and thereby claim the satisfaction of having been the moral guardian and financial watchdog of the public and the society. The positivist will try to select a course that runs some risk but is likely to bring benefits to the public on a large-scale and also provide some immediate satisfaction.

Is the person with the positive approach trying to play to the gallery? Is he trying all the time to win some cheap popularity? Being a human being, like most of us, I like being praised. I caution people that I am perhaps susceptible to flattery. Nevertheless, in the course of my career, I have taken decisions which have not been immediately popular. In fact, they have invited hostility but subsequent events have shown the very people who opposed the idea that it was a desirable step and the decision implemented. An example of this will not be out of place.

I was Director of Geology and Mining in the State of Gujarat from December 1970 to May 1974. One of the organisational weakness of this department, leading to low morale was, that there was no difference in responsibilities between the senior experienced geologists and the junior most ones. There were three categories of geologists – Senior Geologists, Geologists and Assistant Geologists. All were doing more or less the same type of surveys.

Another added problem was that while for eight months in a year they were all in the field, for four months they all came together and there was more office politics than technical work done. With increase in price of petrol and diesel, especially after the OPEC price hike of 1973, the centralised system was proving to be costly also.

I therefore proposed and got the approval of the government for decentralisation of the system. Four regions were to be created at Ahmedabad, Baroda, Bhuj and Rajkot, each under a Senior Geologist with a compliment staff of Geologists and Assistant Geologists. This could resolve the problem of morale and bring a system of better technical supervision with increased responsibilities on the senior geologists.

There was tremendous opposition to the idea from the staff. I have anticipated all the likely problems like accommodation, both for the office and residences of the officers and staff, and made arrangements in consultation with the Collectors and the Gujarat Housing Board.

In early 1974, the proposal was approved. By sheer coincidence, the Nav Nirman agitation, which resulted in the dismissal of the

Chimanbhai Patel ministry, started in January/February 1974. Our decentralised scheme was to be effected from 1st April 1974. The staff of the Directorate, with the assistance of the State Karmachari Mahamandal General Secretary, Om Vacharajani, went on a strike. The government, elided and dropped the idea of decentralisation. It was a decision that virtually eroded the base of my effectiveness as a Director. Fortunately, I was transferred by 30th April 1974.

Time and history vindicated my decision. Two years later, the same proposal of decentralisation was implemented and I was told that for accommodation the staffs were asked to fend for themselves.

I am giving this illustration to show that a positive approach to administration need not necessarily result in one becoming an artist gunning for cheap popularity. At the same time, one should be aware of this as an occupational hazard.

Coming to the main line of arguments, the correlation between the mental set and decision making can be further explored a little more. Perception of facts in any situation, is coloured by the mental stance of a person. In scanning the environment, a positive minded person looks for the strengths and opportunities more than at the weaknesses and threats. Any student of management is familiar with the concept of SWOT analysis – a scanning of the strengths, weaknesses, opportunities and threats before evolving a suitable business strategy. A negative administrator will concentrate on weaknesses and threats. A neutral administrator, may list some of all the factors but his lack of commitment and interest may result in his perception limited to the obvious and the tangible factors only.

At the stage of evolving options the mental makeup plays an important role. A positive administrator who is committed is likely to evolve more options based on the perceived strengths and opportunities. This provides the basis for new approaches in decisions.

If we consider the questions which one is likely to ask as a part of evolving the options, the negativist will always ask why? The positive person, why not? The neutralist may merely say, why bother at all? I think these are the questions, at the subconscious level, that must be arising in every case of decision making.

While I shall rate a positive approach as one of the values, I have held dear to my heart in administration all these years, another related value is that of the ethical element in administration. What is administratively ethical? In a changing society when one finds every organisation in a state of flux, is there any principle worth holding out for?

There could be a view that administrative ethics is a contradiction in terms or at best an avoidable luxury. If administration involves delivering of the goods, so long as that objective is achieved what does it matter whether an individual is honest or corrupt? Years ago, in 1962, when I was an Assistant Collector, there was a seminar organised in the old secretariat at Ahmedabad. The first Chief Secretary of Gujarat V Iswaran observed, in a project costing a crore of rupees, he would much rather have a corrupt official who can complete it and deliver on time rather than a person who may be honest but incompetent or delay decisions on moral considerations with the result that the project cost ultimately far exceeds the original limit. In short, corruption is sometimes cheaper and efficient. Honest is costly and inefficient.

At the national level, it was Nanda who started a campaign against corruption while he was the Union Home Minister. The Sadachar Committees became objects of ridicule. Honesty got a bad name. The Boeing pay off scandals in the mid-seventies exposed the fact that even kings and Prime Ministers are not above temptations. Corruption, it was clear, was a worldwide phenomenon.

I think that the ultimate rationale behind any ethical principle is that it helps an individual to have a sense of self-respect and the society to prosper. Corruption and dishonesty mitigate against both in the long run and that is the reason why I hold that honesty should be a value worth driving for and cherishing.

I am acutely aware that ethics should be viewed in the context of a prevailing situation. Honesty may be a value which goes against the very possibility of survival in certain circumstances. I am not entering into a general discussion on this which could be endless. I am concerned only with limited issues so far as administration is concerned.

Perhaps factors like poor pay, working conditions, low morale and a number of similar factors may have contributed to the growth corruption in administration. Generally, the corrupt officials are more intelligent than the honest ones. He has to know the rules thoroughly to know how to beat them. When he is caught he must know how to get out. Our elaborate inquiry procedures designed with a view to protect the honest official only succeed in providing easy loopholes for many corrupt officials to escape.

Another feature I have observed is that among the honest officials, there is many a time a fear of the rules and the system. The corrupt officer is generally bold in decision making than the honest one. I have a suspicion that many of the officials who are honest are so because they are afraid to be dishonest. The giveaway line is the adoption, vigorously, of Caesar's wife principle. Many a time such officials are convinced that a given course of action is desirable but will hesitate to take action because it will be viewed as an act of partiality or favouritism.

The anonymous letter is a great terror to such officials. Such letters when received by a timid but honest official result in starting of inquiries. The endless government circulars always contain some clauses which can be twisted to order an inquiry rather than file the papers or better still destroy them as recommended by the ICS officer, who wrote the *Assistant Collector's Manual* in old Bombay.

I would classify this category of honest officials as those who are honest in a negative sense. They are honest because they are afraid to be dishonest. I would recommend adopting a positive approach to honesty. If I am honest, I must be so because I feel it is a value worth having rather than one based on hypocrisy and fear.

I also realise the limitation of the honesty principle. One cannot change the world or even an organisation by starting a campaign like Nanda or the prohibitionists. One can however be quietly effective in creating a temporary atmosphere where honesty and efficiency can flourish.

A positive approach to honesty is what I rate as a desirable value. Such an approach gives a person a greater degree of freedom of action and is essentially a healthy attitude. The virtue of this lies in the sense of undivided worth and dignity it gives to a person.

What about compromises? After all, administration is not an ivory tower activity of spinning airy and golden phrases. It is concerned with delivering the goods. How does one apply the principle of positive integrity in this context?

I had to deliver a talk in London in 1972 on 'Ethics in Administration' to a group of officers from Commonwealth countries. What could be common between an administrator from Nigeria, India, Greece and Australia? I found after some thinking that there is a golden thread common to all. There could be a test common to all when it comes to public administrators, irrespective of the countries or the style of the government.

I argued that the basic test is, if any action of a public servant is, in the public interest and for the public good, then it is ethical. I have found this to be a useful operational principle when it comes to deciding on courses of action in every administrative problem.

A positive approach to administration leads not only to the concept of positive integrity but also to the principle of speed over perfection. In the bureaucracy, there are always the forces for defence and perfection competing with speed and initiative. Between speed and perfection, I have always voted for speed. It is also because in a service like the IAS, one never knows how long one is going to last in a job. It is better to score as much as possible when one is at the crease.

The fourth value, I hold dear is perhaps a luxury. This is the principle of elegance in work and the work place. We spend at least one third of our prime of life in the office, but what type of office? Somehow, cleanliness, sprightliness and a general atmosphere of cheer is considered alien to most of the government officers. Everywhere I have gone, I have tried to adopt at least the following techniques:

(a) Physically shift useless muck of old records which as a rule clutter every office – at least to a place where it is not seen.
(b) Get a few painting to brighten the drab atmosphere.
(c) Have bright and cheerful curtains.
(d) Insist on wastepaper baskets for every table.

Essentially based on the principle of elegance in administration is my partiality for what can be called administrative or management cosmetics. These normally care in the fashionable packages of techniques on which Institutes of Management and Consultants thrive. Most of the times, the techniques are nothing but organised common sense dressed up in some uncommon fancy name. Still, some of the techniques have a basic medium of use and can be adapted. I have particularly found work study techniques, PERT Operations Research to be useful.

Well, at the end of twenty-one years, if I had to distil the values in administration which I have adhered and found to be relevant, they came down to these four – (i) a positive approach to integrity and administration, (ii) a preference for speed over perfection, (iii) a weakness for elegance in offices and (iv) management cosmetics. Can there be the best or the most desirable? Well, in the ultimate analysis each one has to make his own choice. I have made mine.

(iv) INTRODUCING CHANGE: THE McNAMARA TECHNIQUE

I had mentioned earlier that one of the strong points of the IAS is ignorance. How can ignorance be a strong point? It is the innocent and ignorant child in the Emperor's New Clothes story, who asked the question why the emperor is not wearing any clothes. All other courtiers and elders had been conditioned to look at the emperor as if he was wearing some advanced type of clothes.

But then ignorance cannot be a source of strength unless you know how to use it. The inspiration for using ignorance came to me indirectly when I read the book *A Thousand Days: John F Kennedy in the White House* by Arthur Meier Schlesinger. Jr Kennedy has always been a hero to me, despite all the revelations about his private life long after he was assassinated. Kennedy for me is a role model of vigour and a capacity to explore new options. I was in Mussoorie in the National Academy of Administration, undergoing training as an IAS officer, when Kennedy got elected in 1960. In early 1961, I remember a Senator coming to the academy. He said that in the history of United States, it was the Kennedy administration that had the maximum number of intellectuals in key positions.

Schlesinger describes in his book, the way McNamara was drafted to be the Secretary for Defence. After the November elections when Kennedy was building up his team, he asked McNamara to become the Secretary for Defence. McNamara said that he had no experience of defence. All that he knew was about Ford and Harvard. Kennedy silenced him by saying him that he also had never been the President of the United States. The obvious option was to learn on the job.

When McNamara became the Defence Secretary, Schlesinger says that he sent questionnaires to various Generals asking for specific information within a specified time. According to Schlesinger, some of the questions were so sharply worded that if a Japanese General had received them he would have committed hara-kiri. I read this in April 1969 when I was Director of Accounts and Treasuries in Gujarat. When I read this, it occurred to me that an IAS officer like me was also like McNamara in so far as that he is all the time asked to handle organisations about which he may not have full knowledge and expertise. So, I also thought of sending a questionnaire to all my officers. In the Department of Accounts and Treasuries there were 120 officers. I sent questionnaires to them asking for information within a month. The questions were simple. "What is the object of our organisation?" "Are we achieving the objectives?" "If no, why not?" "Is your talent being used?" "Is there scope for corruption?" "If so, how can corruption be tackled?" At the end of one month, I received about 15% response. I went through the replies. Going through these replies gave me an idea of areas where action was possible.

What I was doing was basically this. I was ignorant myself about the department and I was picking the brains of the people for specific suggestions. In 1982 when Peters and Waterman came up with their book *In Search of Excellence: Lessons from America's Best-Run Companies*, 'Productivity through people' was listed as one of the qualities of excellent companies. What my questionnaire did was to achieve productivity through people. In any effort at getting things done in India, from my practical experience I can say that the questionnaire method or the McNamara method is very effective.

The positive impact of this measure has to be seen to be realised. The first advantage is that in any new organisation which you take charge, you come to know within one month who are the people in the organisation who, when you give them a task to be completed within a time limit, are capable of doing the task.

Secondly, you also get an idea about who are the people who are thinking about the job. Thirdly, you also get enormous information and feedback about the issues that are bothering people at the cutting edge level. One of the problems in any organisation particularly for those who are near the top is that they do not know what is happening at the grass roots.

One of the problems of Indian Administration is the power paradox. So long as a person is in power for day-to-day things like getting a cheque cashed, paying electricity or telephone bills, etc, there are junior officers and assistants to do the task. But when a person retires and becomes an ordinary citizen, he realises that when he goes to the bank, telephone or electricity office, how difficult it is to get even small things done. Then he realises how bad our administration is. In fact, in India you will find that the most vigorous, vocal, voluble critics of government administration are the retired public servants – what I call the power paradox. When these officials were in positions of power when they could have brought about changes for the better, from the citizens point of view, they were totally ignorant of the ground realities. When they come to know the ground realities they are out of power. This is the power paradox.

The same concept of knowing the ground realities in management jargon is known as 'Management by Walking About' which has been very much praised by management writers like Peters and Waterman. A recent vigorous version of Management by Walking About is what Jack Welch did in his Workout. It is worth looking at what Jack Welch says about the human potential and how the workouts were effective:

> "Workout was nothing more complicated than bringing people of all ranks and functions – managers, secretaries, engineers, line workers, and sometimes customers and suppliers – together into a room to focus on a problem or an opportunity, and then acting rapidly and decisively on the best ideas developed, regardless of their source.

> At these workout sessions, all the things that people used to mutter about around the water cooler on the weekends were finally brought up openly, and in many cases, resolved on the spot. These meetings are predicated on a belief that the people closest to the work know it best and are best qualified to make it better." (*Jack Welch Speaks: Wisdom from the World's Greatest Business Leader*, p 131)
>
> "Workout evolved its own language. Low hanging fruit are problems that are easily solved. Rattlers are problems that are easy to recognise because they make a lot of noise. Pythons represent problems that are hidden and entwined in bureaucracy. Pythons can put up a good fight." (*Jack Welch Speaks: Wisdom from the World's Greatest Business Leader*, p 133)

Another important advantage of the questionnaire method is that it is a great morale booster. Definitely in the government we do not ask people for their opinions. We always only call for explanations. If the boss is willing to practice the idea of a questionnaire and asks the opinions of the people, this has tremendous impact on the morale of the people in the organisation. It probably creates the right psychological atmosphere for development.

In every office, which I have held after 1969, on the very first day or definitely within the first week, I sent such questionnaires to all the officers, irrespective of their levels. Incidentally, it also provides an opportunity to reach all the officers instead of being confined to the number two or number three levels. This is particularly necessary because, especially as one goes higher and higher in the civil service and in management, one is always surrounded by only a small number of senior people who report to the boss. When I took charge as Additional Chief Secretary (Home) in 1987 in Gujarat, I issued a questionnaire, which can be seen at the end of this chapter. Actually, this got some publicity in the media. People found that it was an unusual experience and it was reported that this was the first time that the ACS (Home) was asking the officers to give their comments.

I sent my questionnaire to about 700 officers, up to the level of Deputy Superintendent of Police. I got the usual 15% response. When I was going through the replies, the Police Commissioner, Ahmedabad looked into what I was doing and asked me, "Sir, are you reading the replies?" Probably, what he had thought till then was that all this issuing of a questionnaire by me was only a publicity stunt, which would be quietly forgotten. What shocked him was that I went through the replies also. Incidentally, he had not replied to my questionnaire. After all, it was not compulsory and I had also mentioned in my covering letter to the questionnaire that the information I received would be kept confidential.

If this McNamara method has to be successful, then what is needed is that you should be able to walk your talk. The reading of the replies is the most taxing part. I had to put in special efforts to complete the reading. Unless I do this fast in every organisation, there is no impact, generally one of the occupational hazards of the IAS is that there is no certainty of tenure. You can be in a job for three months or three years or even more. This uncertainty of tenure is generally given an excuse about why IAS officers cannot be effective. The first argument is that in this age of highly advanced, technology and specialisation, IAS officers who claim to be generalists are an anachronism. The second argument is that they are ignorant of the subject and therefore cannot be effective. The third argument is that they are like birds of passage and therefore cannot be effective. Perhaps, this may be an appropriate place to examine all these issues, which generally are flung against the IAS and also examine whether they can be really effective in getting things done in India.

This generalist vs specialist issue and the relevance of the IAS in the 21st century need to be sorted our first. In fact, the great management guru Peter Drucker, wrote a book in 1989 about the shape of things to come. Looking at the management models for the 21st century he picked upon three as the most likely models. The first is the model of the President of an American University who has to preside over an institution, which had a lot of specialists and he had definite roles to play in coordination, raising resources and running the organisation of the university. The second is the Superintendent or Health Administrator in a hospital. This also was an organisation, which had specialists, and the superintendent or administrator had a coordination role to play. The third model he selected was the Collector coming from the ICS in British India. The IAS incidentally is the service, which succeeded the ICS. For an objective management guru like Peter Drucker, the ICS model, the generalist administrator model whose role is coordination, has relevance even in the 21st century management.

There are more serious arguments also about the role which a generalist service can play in the age of technology. Have you ever wondered why even though when a human child and a chimpanzee are born, both have the same brain size but the chimpanzee remains a chimpanzee and the human child becomes an intelligent person? This is because in a period of two to three years, the baby chimpanzee becomes an adult whereas for the human childhood goes on till the age of 16 or 18. It is this prolonged childhood called neoteny that distinguishes human being from others. The characteristic of a child is curiosity and capacity to learn continuously. The IAS can be looked upon as an exercise in administrative neoteny, at least which is what I have tried to practice.

It is quite possible that many IAS officers may also have an alternative view. Having entered the IAS, they may think that they have achieved what they wanted to achieve in life and thereafter the chair will teach them. The very fact that they are appointed as Secretary of a department or the head of an organisation like electronics or agriculture, they presume that the knowledge comes to them from the chair like the shepherd who became very skilful as a ruler when he sat on the throne of Vikramaditya according to one of the fairy tales. You will generally find that the less confident a person is, the more anxious he is to cover up his lack of knowledge and invoking the powers of his authority pull rank or become a nitpicker to assert his authority. One should never commit this mistake if one has to be effective and take advantage of what I call the unique strength of the IAS, namely ignorance.

The McNamara method is one method of overcoming the problem of ignorance or the technique practised by management icon Jack Welch, mentioned above, like work out is another method at continuously learning and motivating people.

There is another serious reason why IAS has an advantage. Because an IAS officer is never posted in a particular job for a long time,, there is a constant effort at learning. This administrative neoteny is an occupational advantage. Added to that is the fact that the IAS also gives enormous opportunities to practice what Edward de Bono calls 'lateral thinking'. This unique and powerful concept promoted by Edward de Bono was that when you want to find innovative solutions, you will have to think not only vertically but laterally. You will have to explore paths, which normally people would not explore and that may be where the solutions are lying. The advantage of the IAS is that it provides a person to bring his experiences from different fields, practice lateral thinking and find innovative solutions.

For example, when I was managing director of GNFC, one of the problems we had, was the number of snakes in the GNFC township of Narmada Nagar. We engaged a snake charmer to catch the snakes and paid him ₹25 per snake. But the snake population did not go down. Ultimately I located Tiruvengadam who was a Security Officer in the State Bank of India and also an excellent table tennis player. Tiruvengadam was a great snake lover and also a real sport. So, he started collecting the snakes and we set up in the township of Narmada Nagar a mini zoo. Bharuch was a backward place in Gujarat and the addition of a mini zoo to the township was a source of attraction. From this experience of snakes, I wanted to go further, drawing on my experience as the Secretary, Health, the post I held before becoming MD, GNFC, to see whether we could set up a snake venom project. Unfortunately, I was transferred. Therein lies the chance of innovation and lateral thinking which IAS provides. I was however successful because of my experience as Health Secretary to make the hospital set up in the GNFC not only serve the employees of the GNFC but also the local population on payment of reasonable fees. Beyond this we also set up a mobile dispensary so that about 100 Adivasi villages could benefit. Another person who is appointed as MD of GNFC may not think of making the hospital a focal point for making some small contribution to public health administration in place.

Years later I became Central Vigilance Commissioner after having had nearly a decade of experience in Department of Electronics and Telecommunication. Because of this exposure, one of the first things I did as the CVC was to put up a website of the CVC. I could use the advantage of the website to publish the names of the charged officers, i e officials who were found guilty after departmental inquiries and against whom major penalty was recommended like dismissal, reduction in rank, etc. This itself became an exercise in serendipity.

Because of my exposure in Department of Electronics I could also focus on the banking sector. I found that out of the 65,000 branches of the banks only 10,000 were computerised. The Harshad Mehta scam took place in 1992 because the public debt office of the Reserve Bank of India among other things was not computerised and there was a fifteen-day float available. This was exploited to perpetrate the scam. Like locking the stable doors after the horses have fled, the RBI computerised the public debt office after the scam. The state of computerisation in 1998

September, when I took over as CVC, was such that hundreds of crores of rupees was lying to be reconciled and this was a major area where corruption could take place.

I therefore invoked my powers as CVC and set a target to the banks that they should computerise at least 70% of their business by 1st January 2001. I must say, to the credit of the Indian public sector banks, they took this seriously and 24 out of the 27 banks computerised their operations by January 2001 and by the end of 2001 all the banks had computerised and the average level of computerisation was 74%. In fact the CVC directive was able to overcome the problems, if any, between the Unions of the bank employees and the management and gave a push to the process of computerisation. This is another example of how the generalist services of the IAS, which exposes the officers to different departments, can also help to bring in the advantage of lateral thinking and overall contribute to the enhancement of effectiveness of administration. I have already explored in another chapter the larger issue of administration, which is action shy, and what can be done.

I had mentioned about my experiences in the home department in Gujarat. The replies to the questionnaire made me realise that how pathetic was the condition of the constables who did not have enough housing facilities and the constables in Surat were living in the slums owned by bootleggers. That was one of the strong motivations for me to push for setting up the Gujarat Police Housing Corporation in which I succeeded.

When I became Secretary, Department of Electronics, now Department of Information Technology, I also issued the questionnaire and this helped me to locate a talented officer who said that for seven years he had been in Japan and he was fluent in Japanese. I had seen that MITI of Japan had projected that by the year 2000, there will be a shortage of 1 million software engineers in Japan. This helped me to launch a programme for teaching Japanese to the software engineers which I initiated.

Perhaps equally effective was the questionnaire I issued when I became Chairman, Telecom Commission (see at the end of this chapter). This was really a challenging assignment.

The first challenge was the high degree of hostility to my becoming the Chairman, Telecom Commission. It was felt that IAS was grabbing the posts meant for technocrats. There were four and a half lakh employees in DoT. There were forty Unions and three Federations. In my first meeting in July 1993 with the Unions, I was very clearly told by one of the union leaders, Chaudhury, that I was not welcome in the DoT. There were 5,000 officers to whom I sent the questionnaires and 490 replies were received. Many of the replies were very sarcastic and hostile. For example, I had suggested that in the area of television even though only 24% of the country was covered by television in 24 years from 1960 to 1984, thanks to the technology of the low power transmitters in six months the coverage went up from 24% to 76%. If this was possible in the electronic media, why not in telecom. One of the replies I received was – your question shows that you are a bureaucrat and do not understand technology.

After all, television is one-way broadcasting whereas telecommunication is two-way and they are totally different.

My basic question was that there should be a possibility of finding technological solutions to this problem, which of course I later on projected. For example, we can use networks available in other government organisations like the railways, PSUs like SAIL, ONGC, BHEL to supplement the government network. When it comes to transmission equipment, by changing the terminal equipment, it was possible through fibre optics to enhance capacity by 400%. But the very idea that it is possible to make a radical change was probably not the thinking of the traditional technocrats.

I received another cynical reply to my question on why we do not have telephone on demand. The reply was, "Sir, do not worry, our officers are so good at cooking up figures that on file they will show that even this possible." So, if one wants to use the McNamara method of questionnaire in India to get results, we cannot expect the potential hara-kiri by the sensitive people who receive the questions as pointed out by Schlesinger that you may expect brickbats, sarcastic comments and negative responses also. But this is a small price to pay because of the positive advantages of this technique, which I have consistently used from 1969 till 1998 and beyond.

I have been propagating this technique but except one officer, Shri Pujari of Karnataka cadre, not many seem to be following these footsteps. I do not know why such a successful technique cannot be replicated widely.

That brings us back to the issue which I have explored elsewhere namely, if you want anything to be got done first you yourself must be committed to the idea and must be prepared to not give-up easily and also be prepared to use techniques like the questionnaire to pick up other people's brain so that you can leverage on your ignorance and get results in the work.

As we look back on my continuous use of the McNamara technique in the form of questionnaires, it is worth examining how this tool has been successful. After all, the questionnaire gives only a feedback. How does it provide for an action plan or help in clarifying the objectives? The simplest benefit of the questionnaire is that it helps you identify what people in the organisation knew about the tasks that deliver the results in a given time limit. Correct people-decisions are the root of getting things done in any situation. One of the questions I always asks in the questionnaire is the objective of the organisation. The feedback tells me the different perceptions about the objectives of the organisation and the extent to which we have been successful.

Questionnaire of the Department of Telecommunications

1. According to you, what are the objectives of DoT?
2. Are we reaching these objectives? If not, why?

3. Is it possible for the Department of Telecommunications (DoT) to accept that the customer should be the most important person and our entire policies and procedures should be designed to satisfy the customer?
4. We are accustomed to thinking of satisfying demand in terms of years. But, in the light of the new industrial policy that has been adopted, it is necessary that telecommunication in the country emerges as one of the strong factors supporting India's competitiveness. Today global competition is based on velocity of business and we in DoT are in a position to make a real contribution in this area.

   We have a situation where we have 7 million lines and 3 million people on the waiting list. If we accept that the customer is the king, we can focus our effort on removing the waiting list and ensuring that as in the developed countries, the customer gets the telephone connection he needs preferably the same day if not within 48 hours.
5. If resources, financial and human, are a constraint, have you any ideas of how we can raise new resources?
6. If with the resources of the DoT and its organisations we are not able to meet the ideal of ensuring that there will be practically no waiting list for telephones, what objections can there be for allowing non DoT organisations as well as industry in the public sector/private sector both Indian and foreign to supplement DoT's efforts? The only precondition should be that the technologies must be acceptable and compatible.
7. In 1984, after nearly 24 years of television, hardly 24% of the country was covered by the telephone network. In that year a decision by the government was taken to put one low power transmitter every day and in six months, the coverage went up from 24% to 78%. Is it possible to

repeat a similar strategy and success in the area of telecommunications?

8. As you are aware, as a result of the new policy, we are trying to attract foreign direct investment. India is not alone in the race. There are 60 other countries, which are also privatising and as I indicated, velocity of business is the critical factor. How can we improve the velocity of business? How can we compete in attracting forcing direct investment through better telecom services? Have you any idea?
9. Should we allow, if we allow non-DoT organisations to compete, to have total freedom in tariffs? After all if the market is going to decide the winner, automatically tariffs will be kept in check. Alternatively, when special services are provided as in the case of courier services in posts people will be willing to pay a higher rate for a better service. Why not adopt a similar strategy in telecom?
10. At present our system of field-testing and type approval takes a long time. India in size is comparable to Europe. If the dozen countries of Europe can have different systems and still have inter-connectivity, why not adopt a similar model for India? After all the systems that are being offered have worked in some country and thanks to the CCITT (Consultative Committee for International Telephony and Telegraphy) and other international norms, are compatible with other systems. Why should we be so restrictive about selection of technologies and approving them for implementation?
11. Delay due to red tape in procedures is the bane of our system. Have you any idea about how we can reduce delays? What are the systems and procedures, which you would like to see, abolished or modified?
12. The Indian Telecom Service (ITS) has grown along with the DoT. If we are going to allow competition from the

private sector, what is going to be the future of ITS? What ideas do you have to see that the career prospects of the ITS are also taken care of while serving the national interest of better and state-of-the-art facilities in the country?

13. What is the future of the 4.7 lakh people who are employed in telecom services, if there is going to be abolition of the monopoly of the DoT not only in the value added services but even in plain old telephone service?
14. Under the present system the Telecom Commission and the DoT span all the three years, namely, regulation, service providing and manufacturing. Why do we not follow the practice in other developed countries where the Telecom Commission becomes a regulatory body, takes care of the interests of the consumers and ensures fair competition and so far as service and manufacturing is concerned, there is free competition?
15. We have had problems of court battles in the cellular phones. Perhaps a similar development may take place in the case of the paging system. Can you think of any innovative or alternative method by which there is transparency in decision making, decisions are taken fast and therefore such court battles are avoided and India can join the race in technology in providing state-of-the-art telecommunication facilities to the telecom user in India?
16. One of the problems we are having is the dichotomy in service conditions arising as a result of MTNL, for the cities of Bombay and Delhi and DoT serving the rest of the country. Have you any idea about resolving the issue?
17. What are your reactions to the recommendations of the Athreya Committee?
18. What are your ideas about amending the Indian Telegraph Act?

19. What are your ideas about making rural telecommunication profitable?
20. What are your ideas about popularising value added services? Today it is a small fraction of the overall telecom network. Can we not think of an incentive scheme by which the initial tariff costs are low so that the services become popular?
21. What are your ideas on making the best use of the physical assets we have and improve our productivity?
22. What are your ideas to make the best use of the human resources we have to improve our productivity?
23. As an individual, do you think your talents are fully utilised? What ideas you have to see that your talents are fully utilised?
24. What are your personal problems as an officer? Do you have any suggestions as to how they can be resolved?
25. What is the scope of corruption in the DoT? What are your ideas for checking corruption?
26. Have you any idea to resolve this issue of cellular phones?
27. Have you any other comments and ideas about how we can achieve the following goals:
    (a) Making the Indian customer of telephone services happier with a better telecom service which will be comparable to the best in the world;
    (b) Improving and protecting the career prospects of the officers and employees of the DoT; have you any creative ideas about how we can achieve these goals?

(v) FROM IDEAS TO ACHIEVEMENT: FIVE INSPIRATIONS

The focus of this chapter is on understanding the Indian work culture, so that we can get an insight into getting things done in India. Getting anything done also requires a sense of commitment and effort on the part of oneself. It is the poor general who blames others. It is the weak person who finds an easy way out by pointing his fingers at others and it is the poor workman who blames his tools. A capacity to own responsibility is one of the important features of leadership. It is only the leaders who get things done. It is increasingly being realised that management is ultimately to be replaced by leadership, especially in these days of globalization when competition is the way of life.

There is a story about a fat man who went to a doctor to get advice about how to reduce his weight. The doctor said that he should walk for one hour every day in the morning on an empty stomach. The fat man asked, "on whose?" The doctor had to emphasize "on your own".

If we want to get anything done, we should realise that we ourselves have to make the effort. I find that this is what many a time is lacking in people who cannot get things done. One of my former Chief Secretary, V Iswaran (ICS), used to say, if you want to get things done, you have to be the 'bad master' who keeps a dog and barks himself. It is alright for management experts to claim that you should delegate work. Mr Aditya Nath Jha was the Director of the National Academy of Administration when I joined service. Jha opined that a senior officer should be like an owner of an oil press – quietly smoking his *beedi*, while the actual pressing of the oil was being done by the patient, hard-working bullocks. I am afraid, only if you yourself are working in an organisation, those who report to you also will work like the patient hard-working bullocks. I have found, by and large, that what makes people work is the awareness of the capability of the boss.

That brings us to the whole dynamics of how work gets done. What I say is based on my experience in India and I do not know whether these observations are universal. I find that ultimately what motivates people to work is your credibility. Credibility comes from integrity. When I became Managing Director of GNFC, Harish Jani, one of my managers told my wife, "Your husband's predecessor also used to ask us to work. He also used to speak well, but, after listening to him we used to go and do whatever we were doing. When your husband speaks we feel like going and doing something." What is the difference? I think it is a good practice to say what you mean and mean what you say. Diplomacy may be left to those who have chosen diplomacy as a career. Of course, the only diplomacy I have used is in the sense Walter Lippmann had defined. He said diplomacy is the capacity to put in the other fellow's words what you want. As Managing Director, GNFC, I applied this diplomatic technique in converting Dahej (a minor port, 32 km from Bharuch) into a port to import fertilizers.

I think every successful manager knows that ultimately what works is the strategy of enlightened self-interest. If you want others to follow or approve what you are doing, you must be able to point out to them what is of interest to them. So, when I approached the Gujarat Government to get their support for the Dahej project, I pointed out that in spite of spending ₹78 lakhs on the Port hardly any ship ever came there. Only boats and dhows seemed to utilise but not the ships. The government was behind me in the effort to make Dahej a port fit for importing fertilizers. I then presented to Ministry of Agriculture the fact that if Dahej port was approved for import of fertilizers, the Government of India will save ₹100 per tonne in transportation charges. That sort of economy normally appeals to any financial adviser in any Ministry and thus the Ministry of Agriculture was with me. I then approached the Central Board of Excise and Customs. Mr Dutt was the Member (Customs). I told him that the Customs and Excise Board was very reluctant to sanction new ports because Custom officials see occupational hazards in new ports.

Just as for the person affected by jaundice, the whole world appears yellow, for Customs officials the whole world is full of smugglers. I had a first-hand experience when I became Development Commissioner of Kandla Free Trade Zone (KAFTZ).

I realised that all my predecessors who were Customs Collectors looked upon KAFTZ, declared as Customs Free Zone under Section 25 of the Customs Act, as vulnerable to smuggling. Instead of focusing on export promotion, their focus was on prevention of smuggling. That is the reason why even in the zone after 9 years (from 1965-1974) there were hardly 9 industries, mostly small-scale. I was the first IAS officer to succeed the Customs officials as the Development Commissioner of KAFTZ. Incidentally, I was the only IAS officer to be delegated with the power of Collector of Customs. After I was transferred, power was taken away from my successors. I could use whatever power I had as Collector of Customs to see how exports can be promoted. As a result, when I left at the end of three years, the number of industries in the zone had gone up from 9 to 32 and exports had gone up from ₹1 crore to nearly ₹4 crore and the number of people working had gone up from 500 to 1,500.

So, I met the Member (Customs), CBEC, with regard to the Dahej port and told him about the saving which the Government of India would make in transport charges. The Bombay Port was congested and the government was paying a demurrage of US $30,000 per day in those days. This probably went home and Customs agreed to make Dahej a port for import of fertilizers.

The next question was making the port operational. It is here I would draw attention to the fundamental principle for getting anything done, namely commitment. If anything has to be achieved in life one must have a desire to do it. When you have to achieve with not only your own effort, but with the effort of others, the related principle is the principle of enlightened self-interest. I would suggest that if there is a simple principle for getting things done, you may look at any issue and first see whether you would like to reach the objective which you set for yourself. Then you should intensely desire that objective. This intense desire becomes a commitment. Once it becomes a commitment, you can use techniques like what I did in the case of Dahej port to sell the idea all-round. In the ultimate analysis, the whole essence of getting things done is to mobilise a set of people who may have their own different agendas to see that they work together towards attaining the goal. In the Dahej port, within a period of three months with the enthusiastic support of fine team of officers I had, set up all the facilities needed for importing fertilisers. As Harish Jani pointed out, the central issue in the entire exercise was whether the Managing Director of GNFC was sincere and whether he was willing to 'walk his talk'.

All of us, in this context of getting things done, must learn a lesson from Mahatma Gandhi. How was this frail old man able to mobilise a whole nation of 300 million people at that time to fight against the British? His greatest strength was his transparency, sincerity and integrity. In the language of computers, Mahatma Gandhi was WYSIWYG – What You See Is What You Get. There was no shadow between what he preached and what he practised. So, in understanding the dynamics of getting things done, we come to the fundamental issue of integrity. It is not surprising therefore, successful managers like Jack Welch, Narayana Murthy or Azim Premji also highlight the importance of integrity. If any collective exercise is to be done, there has to be a leader with a vision. That vision has to be communicated. It should be communicated in such a way that other people can buy into it, and they also put their efforts to achieve that vision. Credibility is vital in the whole process so that trust and a sense of team spirit is generated. Credibility comes only if people perceive that you are sincere about what you are doing and there is absolute transparency in your dealings.

This process can be seen in everything Mahatma Gandhi did. He was also a great communicator. The idea behind the Salt Satyagraha is really stunning. In a land of 300 million people he had to convey that because of foreign rule, even an essential commodity like salt that is necessary for the poorest of the poor, was being taxed. The Salt Satyagraha perhaps communicated more dramatically the evils of foreign rule than any amount of theories, speeches or logical analysis would have done.

Gandhiji was charismatic. What is charisma? It is nothing but the capacity to simplify and exaggerate. Gandhiji's concept of Salt Satyagraha was an exercise in charisma. In my own life, when I became Managing Director of GNFC in April 1982, the plant was ready for commissioning but had not gone into commercial production. We were operating the world's single largest Ammonia-Urea plant. The feedstock was fuel oil which has its own problems. So, we coined a slogan "100% urea and 100% Ammonia every day". This slogan was written everywhere. Right from the Managing Director down to the office boy, everybody knew this was our goal. I was fortunate to have a team of executives and workers whose average-age was 30. Therefore, automatically the youthful energy could be focused on the effort to achieve 100% Ammonia and 100% Urea every day.

Slogans are easy to coin. But the test is whether you are able to walk your talk. For example, political leaders talk about zero tolerance of corruption. But, in practice, they are not keen to act against the corrupt, and people can at once realise the hypocrisy. The whole credibility of the leader's slogan is lost. We can, therefore, see how in getting anything done there is a close relationship between commitment and intense desire on the part of whoever is in-charge of any project to get a thing done, communication of that concept by appealing to the principle of enlightened self-interest, and, the capacity of the leader to put himself on the line so that if things go wrong he could follow Iswaran's 'Bad Master' strategy.

Ultimately, it all came down to the values you cherish utmost. Each one of us have different values. A former Chairman of the Union Public Service Commission in a seminar, had some years back raised an issue which was intriguing him. He said that when it comes to selection of officers for the All India Services like IAS, IPS, the candidates who appear before the UPSC are idealistic, bright, committed and sincere. However, once they join the service, within a period of five years or so, they seem to become cynical, negative and possibly even corrupt. He was wondering how this change takes place.

This set me thinking about the whole process of how we imbibe, adopt and apply values in our life. I have come across many offices where a junior official would be honest whereas his senior is corrupt. There is the eternal debate about the need vs the greed basis for corruption. Definitely if need was the basis of corruption, then such a phenomenon cannot be explained. Values, therefore, are important.

The first time I had to look into myself to analyse the reasons for my success in the various assignments I have held, was when Dr Khandwala, who was the then Director of MM, Ahmedabad, invited me to talk on 'My Philosophy, My Action'.

We do not generally stop to analyse the cause of our successes and failures. I had to talk to students of management about the reasons of my success, I had to do an honest analysis of what the characteristics were in me which might have helped in achieving whatever success I achieved. I came up with an analysis of three factors which subsequently I have replaced endlessly whenever I had to deliver a convocation address because these three, I realised, were the root of my success and perhaps could carry credibility when I talked to the youngsters about how they could succeed in life. The first of the three factors is – having a positive attitude.

My positive attitude is perhaps the result of a number of circumstances. This was earlier discussed in the previous chapter. This positive attitude helped me to look at the opportunities to be provided by every post and not look at the negative side. For example, when I was the Managing Director of the GNFC, our colony Narmada Nagar was in a backward area in Bharuch in Gujarat. That was built on a ravine land acquired for the project. As it was on a ravine land, there were snakes. This should be a nuisance. Initially we paid ₹25 per snake to the people who helped to get rid of the snakes. But then somehow there was no effective reduction in the number of snakes. Then I accidentally came to know that, Thiruvengadam, the Security Officer in the

State Bank of India was a lover of snakes. I brought him to GNFC on deputation and he started collecting snakes. We developed a snake farm and very soon a mini zoo was created in Narmada Nagar, the township of GNFC. This was a bonus to the place, which was a backward area with no zoo. The mini zoo of GNFC became a point for entertainment to the people around. Thus, a problem was converted into an opportunity.

I adopted the same principle while looking at the whole issue of pollution. If one man's meat is another man's poison, one industry's pollutant is the raw material for another industry. I believe that the best solution for sustainable development is to see how we can make useful products out of waste. The GNFC in those days was producing large quantities of solid, liquid and gaseous pollutants. We were burning thousand tonnes of coal per day resulting in 400 tonnes of ash. Normally, ash is disposed in ash ponds. This means using valuable land and I had learnt that in Britain and New Zealand the ravine lands are levelled by using fly ash. I also adopted the same strategy and pursued the Government of Gujarat to allow the ravine land to be levelled and then entered into a deal with the government to sell the ravine land and share the profits. I remember, in my time 30,000 sq metres were recovered at a cost of ₹30 lakhs. We sold 25,000 sq metres and recovered ₹25 lakh. The city improved because the ravine land, which was a breeding ground for mosquitoes, was levelled and valuable commercial land was created in the heart of Bharuch city.

The liquid pollutant was the effluent water – 6.5 million gallons of which was being used by the plant every day. We improved this water by treating it through an effluent treatment plant to ISI irrigation standards. Very soon the farmers in the downstream villages accepted this water very gratefully. Cotton and wheat, which were difficult to grow in that area, were grown, thanks to the effluent water of GNFC. The gaseous pollutant was sulphur oxide, the sulphur content in the fuel oil, which was the feedstock of the plant. We put up a Claus unit for the recovery of

Sulphur. This elemental sulphur recovered was sold like hot cakes to the sugar factories and sulphuric acid plants in the adjoining areas. We thus made productive and positive use of every pollutant. Generally, we adopt a policeman's approach to the problem of pollution. Pollution is a crime and the polluter must be punished and the factory closed. Or we adopt the problem-solving-approach – we do not want pollution in our backyard, the NIMBY (Not In My Backyard) Syndrome. We treat the pollutant and dump it far away, out in the sea or a river. The third approach, which I strongly advocate is a productivity-oriented one. If one man's meat is another's poison, one industry's pollutant is the raw material for another. We must explore how each pollutant can be used for some value-added purposes. It is quite possible that sometimes it may be uneconomical to do so. In such cases, either by policy or subsidy, such production can be made economical or alternatively may resort to incineration, so that there is no pollution.

> A positive attitude is the starting point for another mental attitude, namely a creative attitude.

When we look at a problem as a potential opportunity, we automatically get creative solutions and begin to explore options. For instance, when the Claus unit in GNFC was under construction, it was July 1982. I was told that the unit could not be commissioned till the monsoon was over because underground tanks had to be built. I asked, "If we cannot go underground because of the monsoon, can we not have some tanks over ground?" This led to the location of some pickling tanks, which were lying in the scrapyard of GNFC after the project was over. These were used for trapping elemental sulphur. Thus, even though we started commissioning the project of the Claus unit in the monsoon, we were able to make profits of ₹10 lakh per month.

Positive attitude leads to a creative attitude but this must be based on a third attitude namely, sound common sense. Idealism can provide the spark but for getting things done on the ground, what you need is sound common sense. I think that the characteristics, which have helped me to achieve success, are:

(i) positive attitude,
(ii) creative attitude, and
(iii) sound common sense.

I have repeated this three-point formula endlessly as the *mantra* by which we can succeed in getting things done in India.

Positive approach also gets translated into an exercise in pushing up the envelope in every job I held, so that instead of merely looking at the post as given, I have tried to push, to the extent possible, the scope of the job. For example, when I became CVC, I tried to see whether the CVC can be a focal point for fighting corruption in India. I have explained in this context the well-known story of the three brick masons and the attitude of the third brick mason. I tried to find out how the CVC can be considered to be an organisation engaged in fighting corruption and improving the nation. Similarly, when I became the Chairman of the Telecom Commission, I was not looking at the department as one dealing with telecommunication, but as dealing with an important infrastructure, which was crucial to development, in the context of India plugging into the global economy. I think all these exercises, which I undertook, my being an outsider, gave me a perspective which the insiders may miss. This probably came out dramatically in the case of the Department of Telecom where the ITS officers, accustomed only to their departmental thinking, could only think in terms of gradual improvement and not the dramatic radical change like telephone on demand. When it comes to the work culture and the results, I must also acknowledge the advantage I enjoyed as the Secretary of the Department of Electronics.

I grew in Gujarat as an officer and Gujarat has a different work culture. Thanks to the dominance of the entrepreneurial culture in Gujarat, the IAS moniker does not carry, the same clout or automatic respect, which it commands probably in certain States like Tamil Nadu, Andhra Pradesh or Uttar Pradesh. The Gujaratis as a community are more oriented towards business and do not look to the government for job opportunities. If India were ever to become a developed country like the United States, perhaps it would be Gujarat writ large where the people would have the entrepreneurial spirit and the government does the basic regulatory function. Gujarat, in those days, also had an interesting and healthy tradition so far as funning the public sector enterprises was concerned. The chairmen of the public sector enterprises were always industrialists and the chief executives were IAS officers. This, in a way, brought the best of both the worlds for developing a different and effective, result-oriented culture in the public sector. While the IAS officers learned from the chairmen, who are businessmen, about the entrepreneurial way of looking at every issue, the IAS background of the MD ensured that proper rules and procedures were followed. Incidentally, when it comes to prestige being a chief executive of a public sector enterprise carries more weight than that of a senior government officer. In the Government of India, the Secretary of the department commands more respect than the chief executive of even a large enterprise like BHEL or SAIL. This association of running enterprises with the industrialists as chairmen also brought a different approach to the officers in industrial development in Gujarat. We did not look upon the industrialists as somebody waiting with an application for getting a concession from the government. There was an easy attitude of collaboration with industry.

I was able to build on this advantage when I became Secretary (Electronics). One of the first things I did, as Secretary (Electronics) was to call all the industry associations and tell them that they could approach me freely. In the next 5½ years when I was Secretary (Electronics), I acted as the champion of the industry and the spokesman for the industry within the government. This was something unusual in the Government of

India. Those officers, who come from states which have an authoritarian culture and where the civil servants are supreme, tended to look upon the industrialists who were approaching the ministry as favour-seekers and their attitude was not one of a partner. This change in perspective, which I got because of my Gujarat background, helped me a great deal in developing a strategic alliance between the industry and the government during my tenure as Secretary, Department of Electronics. This is where we see the impact of the work culture including the regional culture, like that of Gujarat in administration and in getting things done.

To understand how to get things done in India, it is better to begin by looking at those instances where something had been got done in India. For example, our administration does not generally move very fast. However, in times of crisis like the situation on the eve of the Bangladesh War in 1971, when one crore people migrated to India or the partition of the country which led to massive migration of population, the Indian administration was able to rise to the occasion. In conducting the games like Asiad 1982 also, the Indian administration showed that they could rise to the occasion and meet the challenges. Practically, every year some place or the other suffers due to natural calamities like flood, earthquake or cyclone and we find that the Indian administration rises to the occasion. However, there have been incidents like in the Orissa super cyclone of 2001, the administration could not rise to the occasion. By and large, wherever we find administration rising to the occasion, the reason is may be that the objectives are clear and there is tremendous pressure for performance and the civil servants have to perform. If we have to get things done in the normal course, what we must do is to recreate artificially some of those conditions, which arise in the time of external stress as in a natural calamity or similar situation. The classic example of effective performance of our bureaucracy is at the time of general elections.

The Election Commission has been entrusted with the task of conducting elections. It has an excellent track record of conducting elections peacefully, regularly and as per rules, for over more than fifty years. This is made possible because there is a time limit laid down and within a schedule the election process has to be completed. The stakes in an election are high and the Election Commission has emerged as an independent body. At the level of an individual officer, it is possible to create and assimilate these conditions. I adopted a method of creating this condition by fixing up timelines. I have mentioned about it elsewhere about how fixing a timeline automatically creates a pressure on the organisation. When V Krishnamurthy was CMD, he was probably able to create such artificial conditions to improve the performance of Bharat Heavy Electricals Limited (BHEL). Even though the company enjoyed protection, he said that BHEL would undertake the responsibility of delivering their goods and services on time and were willing to accept liquidated damages for failure to do so. One method of creating a condition for success may be, to artificially create a pressure on the entire organisation through a timeline. This alone will not do. What is needed is the motivation of the people to perform. The motivation of the people in an organisation comes, if the officer in-charge himself is motivated. People watch and evaluate your behaviour constantly. What you do, speaks much louder than what you say. I have therefore referred the need for not only management by walking about to get a feedback about the reality of the field conditions but also adopting the 'bad master' strategy of V Eswaran, that the boss must be able to carry out the work which he wants his subordinates to perform. This probably creates the atmosphere for performance.

An equally important issue is the recognition of the good work done. I had excellent experience of this when I was Managing Director of Gujarat Narmada Valley Fertiliser Company. We started a suggestion scheme. People initially were sceptical. They said: "After the first two weeks what we are going to get are suggestions about transfers and postings and complaints." In fact, I did not realise at that time, according to Toyota, even a complaint is looked upon as a suggestion for improvement. In the five years (1982-87) I was in GNFC, I carried out the suggestion scheme. What we did was to supplement the normal financial incentive by other non-financial incentives also. We published on the notice board the names of those who gave valuable suggestions in the various plants of the GNFC like ammonia, urea as well as sulphur recovery, etc. Whenever any VIP visited the plant, I introduced good suggestion makers whose names were in the roll of honour to the VIP. This was a great morale booster. We ran the scheme for five years. Every Saturday we used to open the boxes and within eight weeks, decisions were taken to accept or reject the suggestions and every month, on the last day, the awards were being given in the presence of the senior management and the union representatives. All these went on to create an atmosphere such that in five years I was there, there were 5,000 suggestions received, 450 were accepted and the company saved ₹65 lakh per annum. The total cash award given against the total saving of ₹3.3 crore was just ₹1 lakh! The suggestion scheme is one method by which one can tap into the brainpower of the people and get results.

Values are formed by a series of processes of interaction of the individual with his environment. As we are born, we are subject to the values and concepts of our parents, teachers and colleagues. Peer pressure probably these days is more important especially since the joint family has become a thing of past. In my case, I think I was fortunate to have parents who were very God-fearing and also scrupulously honest. In fact, this perhaps runs in the family. My maternal grandfather, Mr C Balakrishna Rao who was the Chief Engineer in the State of Travancore, at Thiruvananthapuram, Kerala, is remembered even today for his integrity. It is said that when he was implementing the water supply scheme, (which has stood the test of time) in order to meet the demands of water supply of the city, the contractor probably offered him a bribe of ₹3 lakh, which in the 1930s must have been many times more worthier than it is today. My grandfather ensured that the entire amount was credited to the government. He was also able to complete the project in less than the project cost, which drew the attention and admiration of the then Viceroy Lord Willingdon.

The commitment to integrity has, I think, a direct bearing on religion. Religion, if we come to think of it, ultimately has its influence upon the society because it ensures smooth and all round growth. It ensures that the members follow the religious precepts. In Hindu religion we talk about the need for speaking the truth and observing Dharma – *satyam vada*, *dharmam chara* (tell the truth, take the righteous path). In the case of the Christian religion, there are the Ten Commandments. Religion I think is a very important fact to nurture cultural values. Perhaps, it is the decline of religion in our socicty, which has also led to erosion of values. In the advanced countries today, we find six year old school boys shooting and killing their friends. This can be explained only in terms of erosion of values and the lack of parental guidance supplemented by the gun culture which perhaps gets an indirect boost from the television, video games, etc, all of which have significant elements of violence.

I am not praising myself but making an honest attempt to find out the roots of my approach to work – this apart from the fundamental values imbibed from my family and also shaped by my senior colleagues with whom I had worked. This also is perhaps an example of the process of value osmosis by which individuals absorb values from others. Rajaji pointed out aptly that the charcoal in the kitchen, the graphite in the pencil and the diamond in the jewellery are all forms of carbon. If a lifeless substance like carbon can be a low value charcoal, middle value graphite or high value diamond depending upon temperature, pressure and the circumstances, how much greater is the potential of human beings who are alive and who are much more evolved?

In the ultimate analysis, values adopted and practised by an individual depends upon the following:

(a) **Enlightened Self-Interest:** After all everyone wants to survive and thrive. Values, which are perceived to be helpful in this effort, will be accepted.

(b) **Desire for Improvement:** There is an inherent desire for improvement in everyone's heart. This is the root of jealousy, ambition or keeping up with the Jones. Role models help to ingrain values because of this craving for moving towards an ideal.

(c) A variation of (b) is the hierarchy of needs of the psychology of Abraham Maslow. We adopt values depending upon where we are in the hierarchy of needs, be it basic physical needs, safety/security needs, self-actualisation or ego needs or social needs.

When we analyse the dynamics of values, we should also not forget that there is always a potential for change in the human behaviour. Probably this explains why suddenly people change their behaviour. It is well-known that every sinner has a future and every saint has a past. This shows that when it comes to values there could be dramatic changes depending upon the circumstances. Therefore, we come across officers, who, towards the end of their careers, when under severe financial strains due to social requirements like dowry for their daughters, etc, become corrupt. It is in such circumstances that a person's mettle is tested.

This is where the second aspect of sustaining values comes. While the individual imbibes the values, they can be sustained only if the atmosphere is also conducive for certain values. Unfortunately today we find a dissonance between the social values as accepted by the society and the ideals, which everybody pays lip service at the individual level. For instance we have a society, which honours only money power. Knowledge and individual achievements are not honoured. I was once speaking to Professor Chao of South Korea who built the Pohang Steel Plant. He said that in South Korean society a Professor is more honoured than many others and as a result Koreans had no difficulty in getting non-resident Koreans to come back and help in building the Pohang Steel Plant or other major projects in Korea. The incentive offered to the non-resident Koreans was that they could get the treatment and honour of a professor in Korea. Perhaps, there is something in the Confucian ethos, which gives respect to the learned person. We have also in our society and our Hindu ethos the concept that

Swadeshe pujyate raja, vidwan sarvatra pujyate

(A king is honoured only in a country, while a scholar is honoured everywhere.)

Nevertheless, in practice, it is money power and clout that matters. Criminalisation of our politics and society is the direct consequence of this erosion of values.

Cricketers are great heroes for many, particularly the youth, in our country. The match-fixing scam has shown that these heroes had also feet of clay. The societal values are the result of the general consensus. Even where a general consensus in terms of traditions and laws lay down certain values, depending upon the implementation of the laws and traditions, ultimately the values prevail. In this conflict between the positions on values, it is the social values which ultimately prevails.

We can now go back to the question raised by the Chairman of UPSC about how the transformation or metamorphosis of idealistic young officers into hard-headed, money-grabbing, corrupt bureaucrats takes place. This is the result of the combined impact of the system, the seniors and the social values. Globalization and the impact of satellite television have promoted a culture of high consumerism. Everybody wants to keep up with the Joneses, even if they know that financially they cannot afford to do so. An understanding of the dynamics of the values and how perhaps those dynamics can be operated for achieving social good may be helpful in any effort at social reformation for better governance.

While an individual can resist the society and be on his own, majority fall into the pattern of conformance. After all, common behaviour is common because the majority subscribe to that behaviour. When it comes to corruption, for example, in our country, if we take the population, 10% may be honest, whatever we do, 10% would be congenitally dishonest. 80% depend on the system. In our country we have created a system which tolerates corruption. In fact, our democratic system itself is based on corruption starting with political fundraising through black money operations, and so on. We have to focus on the 80% of the majority and see how the system can be modified so that the overall values for good governance are encouraged. If delay comes in the way of good governance, we can have systems and application of IT, etc, to improve the system. If corruption is perceived to be a low-risk, high-profit activity and hence encouraged, we can ensure that corruption becomes a high risk activity by appropriate change and its implementation. If we find that good governance has eroded because of lack of transparency and right to information among citizens, by providing greater transparency and the right to information, this problem can be overcome. In other words, a continuous focus on the system to encourage the values which ultimately encourage good governance may be the only option for realising a better and a less corrupt India.

In the process of developing an effective work culture in India for achieving desired changes, I believe in the five principles enunciated by five eminent men. If anyone internalises these, there is a possibility of success. Unfortunately, none of them is an Indian. These are the principles, which have motivated me when I took up, for example, an issue like tackling corruption when I was the CVC. The first principle is that of Bertrand Russell. He says that every opinion becomes respectable if you hold it for a sufficiently long time. When I was the Chairman of Telecom

Commission, the technocrats of the Telecom Department in the 8th Plan had worked out a strategy that by the year 2000 the waiting period for getting a telephone in the cities of India will not exceed 2 years. I raised the question in my questionnaire (the McNamara Technique). Why cannot we provide a telephone to a subscriber in 2 days instead of two years? The replied I got were cynical. One of the officers said that our officers were so good at cooking up figures that they would show on paper that even this had been achieved. When I became Chairman, Telecom Commission, I took upon myself and practised the 'Bad Master' strategy. I prepared the basic paper for telecom reforms, restructuring of the department and financing myself. I held a record of four complete Telecom Commission meetings in the second fortnight of December 1993 and submitted the reform proposals to the government. The matter went up to the Prime Minister and the new National Telecom Policy was announced on 13th May 1994. On the 9th of May, I had submitted in the draft Telecom Policy in which I had recalled that the waiting period for getting a telephone in cities of India according to the 8th Plan would not exceed two years, but the policy now visualised was that we must have within three years, telephone on demand, i e a new connection within two days. PV Narasimha Rao, who was the then Prime Minister cut out with his own hand the reference I had made to the 2 year waiting period visualised at the end of 2000 in the 8th Plan document. Telephone on Demand, a concept ridiculed in October 1993 had become the official policy in 1994!

I have tried the Russell principle elsewhere also. As Secretary (Electronics) one of my objectives was to ensure that every department focused on IT. As the perennial problem in the government department is shortage of funds, one method by which this problem could be overcome was to earmark 3% of the budget of the department for applying IT in the department. This way, no additional funds will be required and at the same time Application of IT would focus in departments. I made the proposal in 1990-91. When I was the member of the Task Force on Information Technology in 1998, I could also persuade my colleagues in the Task Force to make it as a recommendation. This recommendation was also promptly approved by the government.

In fact, what is needed for getting things done is persistence. No wonder that one of the shlokas of Bhartruhari points out the distinction between three types of people – *uttama*, *madhyama* and *adhama*. The *adhamas* or the lowest type of people are those who do not want to take any initiative at all. They wonder how they could bring in change at all. Such people can never change easily. The *madhyamas* or the middle class are the people who are prepared to have initial enthusiasm – *arambhasuratva* – and once they come across a problem, give up. The *uttamas* are the people who persist and get results. In fact, persistence is essential for success. It is said that Churchill visited his school once. He was in a hurry and could not give a long speech. He could say only three sentences. "Never give up. Never Never give up. Never Never Never give up."

Some people may say consistency is the virtue of a donkey. Some people may call you pig-headed. I have also found that to get anything in India you should have the characteristics of a donkey. Two characteristics of this much maligned animal are required – patience and optimism. There is a story about a circus donkey which was being treated very badly by its master but was still very cheerful. When the people asked the donkey why it was cheerful despite bad treatment by the circus master, it said, "Do you know, one day I heard the circus master tell the girl who does the trapeze, if you fail on any day, I am going to marry you off to this donkey." So, the donkey was patient and optimistic. In India I feel the qualities of patience and optimism are required because as Russell says that if you hold an opinion sufficiently for a long time it becomes a respectable, one.

I give another example from my personal life. When I was Additional Chief Secretary (Home) in Gujarat, I took up the issue of having a Police Housing Corporation. I had seen the pathetic conditions in which Gujarat police constables lived. Some of them, for example, in Surat were living in slums owned by bootleggers. In Gandhiji's Gujarat, prohibition is a sacred principle. However, if the constables who were supposed to enforce the law of prohibition themselves were living as tenants of bootleggers, how can they implement the law? There was a proposal for setting up a Police Housing Corporation and the proposal was going on for the last 14 years. I took up the issue and pointed out all the advantages that would flow in having decent quarters for the police. My argument was that the police must be treated more or less on the lines of the armed forces as they are expected to be a disciplined uniformed force. The police are the instruments with which the state has to maintain law and order. The then Chief Minister Amarsinh Chaudhary, who incidentally was also the Home Minister, supported my argument. I told the Chief Minister that even Rama's *vanavas* was only for 14 years and ... this file on police housing was older than 14 years. There was no reason why we should not go ahead and set up the housing corporation. In fact, the Cabinet overruled both the Finance Secretary and the Chief Secretary who opposed the proposal and approved the Gujarat Police Housing Corporation. The policemen greatly welcomed this action.

I am only giving it as one more example to show that, if you have the persistence, you will automatically be able to win over the resistance. The process underlying the Russell principle can be described as the RAMA process discussed earlier. Whenever you try to sell any new idea, initially what you get is the R – ridicule, resistance, rejection and refusal. But if you persist, soon people are annoyed with you. That is the A of the RAMA process. If you further continue to pursue then it comes to the stage of M, which is mellowing. And finally comes A – achievement and acceptance.

The RAMA process is the one, which enables anything to be accepted and implemented. How does this process take place?

For this, we have to understand the principles articulated by three other eminent persons. One is Victor Hugo, the French writer who says that there is nothing more powerful than an idea, whose time has come. India was a colony of the British. It was said that the Sun never sets on the British Empire. But after the Second World War, came a period when the idea of anti-colonisation became dominant. Today, we have to look very hard to locate a place where the Sun rises on the British Empire. This is because decolonisation was an idea whose time had come after the Second World War.

How does an idea, whose time has come become powerful? It is because of a phenomenon noted by Alexis de Tocqueville, the French thinker. He says that the inevitable becomes intolerable the moment it is perceived to be no more inevitable. I have seen on October 5th, 2000 on the BBC how the people of Belgrade poured into the streets of Belgrade, rushed into the Parliament, and Slobodan Milosevic who was ruling as a strong dictator for 12 years had to go into hiding. The same thing happened when the people's power removed Ferdinand Marcos and again replaced Joseph Estrada both of whom were the Presidents of the Philippines. In our own country, we have seen during the emergency how Indira Gandhi became a virtual dictator. It was said India is Indira, Indira is India. But in 1977 when she announced elections, the inevitable Indira became intolerable and she was defeated. So, the process by which an idea gets accepted can easily be traced to these psychological changes represented by the RAMA process.

The fourth idea is that articulated by Bernard Shaw. He said that the reasonable man accepts the limitations of life and leads a peaceful life. The unreasonable man wants to change his environment and in the process makes progress. Change has always come from such 'unreasonable' men. Mohandas Karamchand Gandhi was the unreasonable coloured lawyer who did not swallow his humiliation of being thrown out of the 1st Class railway compartment in the middle of the night in South

Africa. Satyagraha was the dramatic result which played such a great role in India's independence.

We then come to the basic question of how to bring about the changes in practice. This book is about understanding the Indian work culture and how to get things done in India. My favourite story is one which I heard from Mr TA Pai who was a banker and also a minister in the Government of India. A rat was being harassed by a cat. It went to the owl to get an idea of how to tackle the cat-problem. The owl being a wise bird, thought about it and said, "As a rat you are very weak compared to a cat. You should also become another cat. Then cat vs cat will be no problem!" The rat went to its hole, thought through it and went the next day to the owl and said "I agree in principle that from being a rat if I become a cat there will be no problem. But how do I become a cat from a rat?" The owl wisely intoned, "I am here to give you policy directions, and implementation is your problem!" This book is of course not written from that owl's stand point. This is written more from the point of view of the rat which to some extent has been able to take on the challenges posed by the cat.

The best advice for the rat to cat transformation is the observation made by Michelangelo Buonarroti, the great sculptor who made beautiful statues out of marble which had no shape. So, that is the secret of getting things done. Once you have a vision you must be able to sell this to others. The whole enthusiasm for selling the vision comes if there is commitment. Commitment comes if you have intense desire, a sense of responsibility and ownership of that vision. No idea ever gets translated unless it is transformed into action. Mere vision is only day-dreaming. When vision and action are combined then everything is possible. In fact, the last shloka of the *Bhagavad Gita* distils the essence of this need for synthesising vision with action:

Yatra yogeswara Krishno yatro
partho dhanurdharaha

tatra shreer vijayo bhutir
dhruvo nithir matir mamaha

Meaning: Yogeshwara Krishna represents divine vision. Partha or Arjuna the archer is a man of action. Even he alone cannot succeed. But when they come together, when vision and action are combined together, then three things happen – there is accumulation of wealth (*shree*), there is success (*vijay*) and there is justice (*nithi*). So, the formula for getting anything in India at one level is the same as getting anything done anywhere in the world. Ultimately, it is the people who get things done. The leaders are distinguished from the followers by the fact that they have a vision, a commitment to that vision, and they are able to communicate that vision. Charisma comes if the vision can be simplified and exaggerated, so that everybody can buy into the vision like what Mahatma Gandhi did in the Salt Satyagraha. These ideas have to be pursued with the persistence advocated by Russell so that the ideas become acceptable. This acceptability of ideas come because of the RAMA process. Once the ideas are accepted, they have to be translated into action. For translating ideas into action what is needed is the application of the Michelangelo principle namely, go on removing systematically whatever comes in the way of realising that vision.

Working out a strategy comes from the old chestnut analysis of Strengths, Weaknesses, Opportunities and Threats (SWOT). In the Kandla Free Trade Zone or KAFTZ, as mentioned earlier, from the time the Zone was started in 1965 to 1974 when I went there, hardly 9 industries had come. My Chief Secretary, Mr IR Dala, questioned me why I was going there which was just one industrial estate. I told him about the 9 year failure of the Kandla Free Trade Zone. If I succeed then there would be something worthwhile to write about. If I fail, I would be one more failure. As it happened, I succeeded.

One of the first things I did on joining as DC, KAFTZ in 1974 was to make a SWOT analysis. The strength of KAFTZ was that it already existed and it had 770 acres of land. The weakness was that Kandla was a backward area. Psychologically people felt that Kutch was more distant than what the real distance was. Even basic facilities like telex was not available. The opportunity was that in 1973, the petrol price hike had brought prosperity to the Middle-East and Kandla was less than two hours flight from the Middle-East. The threat was that government was thinking of other free trade zones like in Kolkata and Cochin (Kochi). SEEPZ (Santacruz Electronics Export Processing Zone) in Mumbai had already started under the dynamic stewardship of Mr S Rajgopal (IAS), who later on became Cabinet Secretary in the Government of India. I therefore worked out a SWOT analysis and set it to the then Commerce Secretary, YT Shah, pointing out how we can build on the strength of Kandla.

The basic thing I realised was that the investors did not know that KAFTZ existed. It is jocularly said about advertisement in business that doing business without advertisement is like winking at a girl in the dark. You know what you are doing but the girl does not know. In those days, 'Vividh Bharati' in All India Radio was the most attractive means of reaching a large number of people at a low cost. I had a sympathetic support in Mr Raghavan of DAVP (Directorate of Advertising and Visual Publicity). We launched an advertisement campaign through Vividh Bharati. I made a point to go to Mumbai which is the nearest big commercial city and operate from the office of SEEPZ from Nariman Point so that I could meet the prospective investors. I went all over the country to talk to the various chambers of commerce telling them about the opportunities in Kandla. I could persuade the Government of Gujarat to extend the sales tax exemption scheme and the capital subsidy up to Kutch because it was a backward district. The net result was that at the end of three years, when I left in 1977, the number of industries had gone up from 9 to 35, the exports from ₹1 crore to ₹4 crore and the number of people from 500 to 1,500. These numbers look very small for this period of time, but in those days the numbers meant very significant progress in the KAFTZ. One of the reasons for sending me to the KAFTZ was that the industrialists of the zone had come to such a pass that they met the then Chief Minister Ghanshyam Oza and said that they would give the keys of their factories to him because they could no longer operate in the KAFTZ.

To get anything done you require confidence. I was once addressing a gathering of nearly 8,000 students organised by the Chinmaya Yuvak Kendra at Trissur in Kerala on 2nd October 2001. Swami Tejomayananda, the current chief of the Chinmaya Mission quoted an observation by Mark Twain about success. When Mark Twain was asked about the secret of success, he replied that it was a combination of ignorance and confidence.

When I spoke I made this the basic theme of my talk because I find that really a combination of confidence and ignorance can bring very good results. So far as the confidence is concerned, how does one get confidence? I am a great believer in God. If you believe in God, the great advantage is that you know that things can never go wrong. You will never be down. Even if you are down for a day, you are going to be up and above the next day. Even if for some time you are in the dumps, you are going to rise again. The observation of Lord Krishna in the fourth chapter of the *Bhagavad Gita* that whenever evil flourishes, He comes in the form of good to conquer the evil, is also probably a message that can be taken as a message of optimism and hope. After all if we give up hope, we are not going to succeed. One of the reasons for the Chinmaya Yuvak Kendra to organise the conference was that while Kerala probably has the highest levels of literacy, it had also the maximum number of suicides. Why is that people are losing confidence in themselves? It was to make young minds appreciate the secrets of success and give a message of hope that this conference was organised. People who were successful in different fields like E Sreedharan who built the Konkan Railway and as well as the Delhi Metro, and Anil Sachdeva, an HRD expert were the invitees along with me, to address the students. I told the students that if you have faith in God, you basically get a sense of confidence that things would never go bad.

Equally important is the need for keeping your integrity intact. The integrity would be financial integrity, moral integrity and intellectual integrity. If you have this integrity, you will know that nobody can blackmail you. Another bonus is that if you have integrity, you will be able to walk your talk. Once again I quote Mahatma Gandhi as an ideal role model. The combination of integrity and faith in God gives immense confidence to any person who has experienced it.

I happened to spend my life in the Indian Administrative Service which is a generalist service. In these days of specialisation, people question whether there is need for a generalist service at all. Out of the 100 crore people of India, except the 5,000 IAS officers, everybody else is a specialist because only the IAS is called a generalist service. The great advantage of a generalist service is ignorance itself. I have been telling openly that the secret of success of the IAS is ignorance. How can ignorance be a source for success? If you are ignorant, you will raise issues that experts would not raise. It is only an IAS officer like me, who in 1993 could have raised this question "why should we wait for two years to get a telephone in the year 2000, why not in two days?" It is the raising of such questions that makes people think and if you combine it with the RAMA process and particularly the Michelangelo Approach, you will find that you will move towards solutions.

After all to get anything done, you must have a plan and you must have a feasible plan. But how will you still overcome the problem of ignorance? It is nice to raise the question but then you have to find solutions, and that means – you have to pick other people's brains. The significance of modern management has been dramatically highlighted by Jack Welch in his book *Jack: Straight from the Gut* where he talks about the immense potential in the human being.

My experiment in trying to use ignorance as a point of strength, and at the same time to overcome the weakness of ignorance in tackling real issues came from McNamara.

(vi) FIGHT CORRUPTION: ROADBLOCK TO EFFECTIVE GOVERNANCE

India is rated as one of the most corrupt countries in the world. It is a country of one billion plus people and is the largest democracy in the world. India has 29 States, some of which are bigger than many countries and 6 Union Territories, which are directly administered by the Central Government. The issue of fighting corruption in such a vast country is indeed a challenge. As I look back on my four years as the Central Vigilance Commissioner (CVC), I hope that just as Hong Kong was able to fight corruption through the remarkable work done by ICAC (Independent Commission Against Corruption), a large country like India will also be able to overcome corruption, if a systematic effort is made.

As I look back, I find that the strategies and the methodologies I evolved to fight corruption, have brought some successes but we have miles to go. I can say with Robert Frost, "The woods are lovely, dark and deep, but I have promises to keep; and miles to go before I sleep and miles to go before I sleep and miles to go before I sleep."

India was ranked 68 out of 85 in the Corruption Perception Index of Transparency International for the year 2002. The Corruption Perception Index has become a reference point for measuring corruption at the international level. I took upon myself, when I was appointed as the CVC, the challenge of trying to see whether the rank of India can be pushed up from the position of 68 to at least around 40. I did not succeed but I think the initiatives I took and the various legal and administrative measures I have suggested, if adopted, will go a long way in achieving this desirable goal. The rank of India from 1998 to

2002, when I was CVC, was 68 out of 85 in 1998, 73 out of 99 in 1999, 69 out of 90 in 2000 and 72 out of 91 in 2001.

The issue of corruption has been a subject of debate in the public life of India, almost practically since Independence in 1947. One of the major corruption scandals, which arose in the late 50s, during the time of Jawaharlal Nehru as the Prime Minister, was the so-called Mundhra Scam. This was a stock market scam where funds of the government were apparently misused by some unscrupulous speculators through the Life Insurance Corporation of India to fix the stock market. The then Finance Minister, Mr TT Krishnamachari had to resign and corruption became a major issue of national concern. A committee under former freedom fighter, Mr K Santhanam was appointed to go into the issue of corruption and make recommendations. The Santhanam Committee submitted its report in 1962. In 1964, as recommended by the Committee, the Central Vigilance Commission was set up. It was to be a single member body, headed by the former Chief Justice N Srinivasa Rao of the Mysore High Court (now called Karnataka High Court). The Central Vigilance Commission was not a statutory body and was supposed to advice the government on action to be taken in cases of corruption involving senior public servants of the Government of India and its organisations. From 1964 to 1998, there were ten CVCs. Apart from Justice N Srinivasa Rao, other CVCs were either senior diplomats or retired civil servants. The commission continued to be single member body and its basic function was to be an advisory body.

In 1998, there was dramatic change forced on the organisation of the CVC because of a judgement of the Supreme Court of India on 18th December 1997. This judgement was delivered in connection with a case relating to a major corruption and foreign exchange scandal called the Hawala Scam. The Kashmiri militants who were agitating for secession of Kashmir from India were getting funds through the Hawala route, which is the illegal money laundering route. One of such alleged money launderer was Mr Jain, who had a diary, which was seized by the police in the course of their investigations. From the diary of Mr Jain it came to light that not only the Kashmiri militants, but even senior people in business, politics and government were involved in the hawala scandals. A journalist, Mr Vineet Narain, filed a Public Interest Litigation (PIL) in the Supreme Court. The Supreme Court held that the investigative agencies of the Government of India namely, the Central Bureau of Investigation (CBI), which is like the FBI in the United States, should be shielded from external influences and another investigative agency of the government called the Enforcement Directorate (ED), which looks into foreign exchange violations and money laundering issues also was to be immunised from external influences. In order to achieve this goal, the Supreme Court directed the government that the Central Vigilance Commission must be made into a statutory body instead of being only an advisory body operating on the basis of an administrative notification. The CVC must be able to exercise supervision over both the CBI and the ED. The Court also directed that a committee consisting of the Prime Minister, the Home Minister and the Leader of the Opposition in the Lok Sabha, the Lower House of Parliament, must select the CVC. The CVC was to be given a term of four years and he could be removed only by the President. The CVC will be reporting to the President annually and would give a report which would be placed on the floor of the Parliament. The CVC will also head a committee for appointing as the Director, CBI and other senior officials in the CBI. Similarly, the committee will also recommend names for the panel of the Enforcement Directorate.

The government has to appoint only a person from this panel as the Director of the CBI or the ED. Once this person is either appointed as a Director, CBI or Enforcement Director, he cannot be shifted from his position without the permission of the CVC. The Government of India had to accept the judgement and implement it.

Under the Indian Constitution, the three main pillars of the governance of the country are the Judiciary, the Executive and the Legislature. The Indian judiciary has been a very independent organisation with rich traditions of fairness and justice. The legislature consists of the Parliament with a Lower House (Lok Sabha) and an Upper House (Rajya Sabha). In the 29 States of India there are Legislative Assemblies. The executive consists of the permanent bureaucracy (or the civil servants) and also the political executive of Ministers and the Prime Minister who are elected from time to time.

The root of corruption in India today can be traced to the fact that the operation of democracy through the political parties in India depends on 'black money'. Every political party needs funds and these funds are collected in cash. This means that there could be funds generated by evasion of taxes like customs, excise, income tax and sales tax, and also money got through corruption. As the entire political funding system is not transparent, the Indian corruption scene can be seen as a vicious cycle starting from political corruption leading to bureaucratic corruption, business corruption and the criminalisation of politics. If India is to become corruption-free, then the reform process has to tackle all the four elements of the corruption scene, namely, political corruption, bureaucratic corruption, business corruption and criminalisation of politics. It may be recalled that the reform in every organisation or society ultimately comes from within. Jesus was a Jew. Our social reformers like Raja Rammohun Roy or Vivekananda in the 19th century came from the society itself.

I joined the Indian Administrative Service, which is the premier civil service in India, on 16th May 1960. By the time I was selected to the post of Central Vigilance Commissioner, I had put up 38 years of service. I retired at the age of 58 from the post of the Secretary, Department of Electronics and was working as the Chairman, Public Enterprises Selection Board, post-retirement. My appointment as the CVC came as a big surprise not only to me but also to virtually everybody else. The manner in which I was selected also shows how the system works. The story I heard was that a lot of lobbying was done for the post of CVC. The selection was to be made by a committee consisting of the Prime Minister, the Home Minister and the Leader of the Opposition. There is a version that the Prime Minister in desperation said, "Are there not honest officers who are not lobbying?" A panel of such officers was prepared and I was placed at the top of the list and finally selected. The President of India gave me the oath of office on 3rd September 1998, for a term of four years.

I was hopeful and optimistic about India one day becoming corruption-free because, in spite of so much systematic corruption, the government honours the judgement of the Supreme Court and implements it. The CVC has become a stronger organisation to fight corruption, thanks to the directives of the Supreme Court. Throughout my career in the civil service, I have been adopting a simple strategy whenever I was given a new assignment. The Indian Administrative Service is a generalist service where an officer could be posted in a wide variety of departments of the government, which may have no direct connections at all. I worked as the Managing Director of the largest single stream Ammonia urea plant in the world, Gujarat Narmada Valley Fertiliser Company at Bharuch in Gujarat. I have been a Secretary, Department of Health, and Industries Commissioner and also worked in the departments of Atomic Energy, Electronics and Telecommunication. How does one learn to adjust and operate in such a wide variety of departments? One technique I adopted right from 1969 was the questionnaire, issued on the day I took over or within a week of my taking over to all senior officers in the organisation. For example, when I took over Department of Telecom, which had 4.5 million employees and 5,000 officers, I sent 5,000 questionnaires. The questions in the questionnaire were like – (i) What should be the objective of the organisation?, (ii) What could be done to achieve the objectives?, (iii) Where were we failing? – and suggestions about checking corruption, etc. I gave a time limit of one month and got the replies. This technique provided a basis to build a programme of action. When I took over as the CVC, I sent questionnaires to all the Secretaries in the Government of India and heads of the 240 public sector organisations who are within the purview of the CVC and the 27 CMDs of the Public Sector Banks. I also sent my questionnaire to those on the supply side of corruption, namely, the Chambers of Commerce and Industry. The three premier chambers are Confederation of Indian Industries (CII), Federation of Indian Chambers of Commerce and Industry (FICCI) and Associated Chamber of Commerce and Industry (ASSOCHAM). I recall having sent questionnaires to 913 people and organisations and I got about 25% response. Going through this process in itself was an educative one. I began by focusing on the system.

The Central Vigilance Commission gets a number of direct complaints from the public and references are also made by the various departments and organisations of the Government of India seeking advice of the CVC on whether in a particular case there should be a launching of prosecution or a departmental action? In the case of departmental action, what should be the type of action? Should we go for imposing a major penalty or a minor penalty on the public servant and if so, what should be finally the quantum of punishment? References are made both at the stage of launching of the inquiries and after the inquiries are over when the stage of fixing punishment comes. 97-98% of the recommendations of the CVC are implemented. Those, which are not implemented, are reported in the Annual Report of the CVC.

I began by focusing on the system aspects of corruption. The simplest point was whether the public had an idea of what to do when they faced demands for bribes from public servants. I directed that a simple notice board must be displayed in all the offices within the purview of the CVC. The public can complain by phone or letter to the Chief Vigilance Officers (there are 598 such CVOs in all the organisations within the purview of the CVC) or to the CVC himself. Addresses and telephone numbers were given. This simple step had a very good impact and the visibility of the CVC increased. The number of complaints every year went up from 2200 in 1998 to more than 17,000 in 2001.

Corruption is always rampant in government procurement processes because once the tenders are opened, there could be negotiations and scope for kickbacks. In order to strike at the root of this system, I issued a directive that once the financial bids are opened, there should be no negotiations with any other bidder other than the lowest bidder. This brought in a lot of discipline. I could issue this directive because I found out that one of the powers of the CVC was "exercising superintendence over the vigilance administration over the Government of India organisations". This included the power to give directives. Before issuing the directive, I also consulted all the senior Secretaries in the Government of India. In fact, in retrospect, this step of mine is considered as one of the good measures I initiated to clean up the procurement system.

Many a time, the vigilance function is looked upon as a function, which comes in the way of effective, pragmatic management decision making. In fact, when I took over as the Central Vigilance Commissioner, one of the first persons to congratulate me was Dr Bimal Jalan, the Governor of the Reserve Bank of India. He said that at the cutting-edge level, the decision making of the bank had come to a halt almost because of the sense of fear among the bank executives about the CBI. It may be recalled that in 1991 there was big stock market scam, known as the Harshad Mehta Scam and this had involved bank funds being used by speculators for fixing the stock market. Subsequent inquiries by the CBI into the matter have resulted in a situation where many bank officials were prosecuted. The main point urged by the bankers was that decision making in a commercial organisation like a bank is different from decision making in the government and it was necessary for the vigilance to take this aspect into account before deciding on cases of bank violations. The Indian Banks' Association had been demanding separate vigilance manual for banks. Ultimately, I took the initiative to call the bankers and the Indian Banks' Association, the RBI and the CBI. Two meetings were held to decide all parameters on how the manual should be written if we were going to have a separate chapter for banks. Within 90 days of my taking over, from 1st January 1999, a new chapter in the Vigilance Manual was added, especially for banks. This took into account the requirements of banks. The Governor, RBI appreciated this action and said that normally it would have taken about three years for such a chapter to be written but in fact this was done in less than two months. This was a very welcome development. Subsequently, in July 1999 a separate chapter for Public Sector Enterprises was also published. These steps brought a greater level of transparency and generated confidence in the minds of public servants.

My basic approach to the issue of vigilance was to see whether the CVC could emerge as a focal point for fighting corruption. There is a well-known story about a sadhu and three masons. A temple was under construction and a sadhu who was passing by asked one of the masons what he was doing. The mason replied that he was carrying the bricks. He asked the second mason the same question. The second mason replied that he worked for eight hours a day at the construction site of the temple and he was earning ₹25 per day. This was his means of livelihood. He asked the third mason the same question. The third mason replied that he was participating in the building of the temple.

Building a corruption-free and prosperous India is an exercise like building a temple. The Central Vigilance Commission plays an important role in trying to check corruption so far as the Government of India's organisations are concerned. The Commission can take a limited view like the first mason and look upon its function only as disposal of files and complaints received by it. Or it could take the attitude of the second mason and consider that the Central Vigilance Commissioner and Vigilance Commissioners, who happen to be retired people, get a well-paying job for a fixed term. The third option is that the Commission can become a catalyst and a focal point for organising a fight against corruption in the country, one major factor that is preventing India from becoming a prosperous and powerful country. The CVC has plumbed for the third option.

I evolved over a period of four years a three point strategy to fight corruption. The corruption temperature in any country or organisation depends on three factors. The first is the individual's sense of values. The second is the set of accepted social values. The third is the system. As the CVC, I focused on the system and saw what could be done to fight corruption. In focusing on the system, I followed a three-point strategy:

- Simplification of rules and procedures so that the scope of corruption is reduced.
- Transparency and empowerment of the public.
- Effective punishment of the corrupt.

On the issue of simplification of rules and regulations, the best case I remember is the issue of the hawkers in Delhi, which was reported to me on 18th June 2001 by the activist, Madhu Kishwar who runs the organisation Manushi. According to her, there were five lakh hawkers in Delhi who were paying a cumulative monthly bribe of ₹40 crore to the police and the municipal authorities in Delhi. I took up the matter with the Chief Minister and the Urban Development Minister and also participated in the Jan Sunvayee organised by Manushi. The matter was reported in the media and came to the notice of Dr Prodipto Ghosh, Additional Secretary in the PMO. He took my letter to the CM where I argued that while in the context of economic liberalisation, a person who wants to set-up an industry does not need any licence, then why should a poor man who wants to sell vegetables or run a cycle-rickshaw need a licence. The licensing system should therefore be abolished. Based on my letter and further discussions with me, a concept paper was prepared by Dr Ghosh and presented to the PM. The PM personally intervened in the matter on 23rd August 2001 and wrote to the Lt Governor suggesting a scheme for abolition of the licensing system for hawkers and cycle-rickshaw pullers and also a system for better regulation. It is perhaps a commentary on the state of affairs that the PM's directive is yet to be fully implemented.

Computerisation of banks is another system improvement I was able to push through to check corruption. When I became the CVC, only 10,000 out of the 65,000 branches of the public sector banks were computerised. Today 74% of banking business in the public sector banks is computerised. I must thank the bank managements and unions for their positive cooperation on this issue.

While it is important to punish the corrupt, it is equally important to protect the honest and innocent public servant. I therefore issued a total ban on 29th June 1999, on any action being taken on anonymous/pseudonymous complaints. The rationale is spelt out in the order. The second element of my strategy was transparency and empowering the public. It was the first example of the use of the Internet to fight corruption. This attracted worldwide attention. The Harvard University called me to make a presentation on e-government on 19th October 2000 in the Centre for International Development. Ninety-three per cent of the respondents to a *Hindustan Times* poll said that they welcomed the CVC's step. Eighty-three per cent respondents of *The Economic Times* poll said that it was a good deterrent measure. 70.5% of the people who responded to *The Pioneer* poll said that it was a good anti-corruption measure. The website became a useful instrument not only for publicising the names of persons who have been found guilty but also to follow up with the disciplinary authorities, and take action for implementing the decisions regarding punishment. The computerisation of the

CVC's data highlighted the fact that in September 2000, there were 170 cases where even after the completion of inquiry and major penalty recommended, no action was taken for more than five years. I took up the matter with the disciplinary authorities and pointed out that if even after five years no action was taken, it could only mean that either the department was inefficient or there was an attempt to protect the guilty. This had a good impact and the cases of delay came down.

The second element of my strategy was empowering the public. For this, the CVC published on the Independence Day of 2001, the Citizens' Guide for Fighting Corruption, which spelt out what the citizens can do to fight corruption. They can adopt a four-point plan.

- The first is to participate in the Vigilance Awareness Week, which is observed on Sardar Patel's birthday on 31st October for a week every year, from the year 2000. From 2001, 1.2 million NCC cadets are also participating in the Vigilance Awareness Week. This week is used to sensitise the public about the negative consequences of corruption and show that corruption is an anti-economic development, anti-poor and anti-national.
- The second action point would be for citizens to participate in suggesting to the CVC how rules and procedures can be simplified. The CVC can use its powers for giving directives for changes in rules and procedures. State Governments are not within the purview of the CVC and the CVC can at best be an empowered post office in the process for bringing change.
- The third element of the strategy for the citizen is to give information about those who have black money or benami property so that the CVC can ask the Income Tax Department or the CBI to conduct raids. From July 2001, this scheme was introduced and more than 900 applications were received of which 64 have been sent for

scrutiny to the Income Tax Department resulting in several successful tax raids.

- The fourth element of action for a citizen would be to participate in the trapping of corrupt public servants with the help of the police.

The Citizens' Guide for Fighting Corruption also pointed out four agencies, which can be used by any citizen to fight corruption. These are:

(i) Judiciary in the courts through Public Interest Litigation,
(ii) Agencies like the CVC,
(iii) Media, both print and electronic, to create public opinion, and
(iv) Direct action through NGOs like Lok Satta in Andhra Pradesh.

The Citizens' Guide for Fighting Corruption was widely welcomed.

The third element of the strategy is effective punishment. As mentioned earlier, the website and follow-up action has been used to speed up disposal of cases. It is a matter of satisfaction that 97-98% of the advice given by the CVC for punishment is accepted by the disciplinary authorities. Those 2% of the cases where action is not taken, according to the CVC's advice, are reported in the Annual Report of the CVC, which is placed before the Parliament.

As I see it, corruption in India is the result of a vicious cycle involving political corruption, bureaucratic corruption and criminalisation of politics along with business corruption. The root cause of corruption in India is political corruption. Our entire democracy is based on corruption. Every political party needs funds and they collect funds in the form of black money. Black money is the oxygen for corruption and corruption is the oxygen for black money.

I would suggest the following strategy:

Phase I

(i) Implement the Benami Transactions (Prohibition) Act, 1988.

(ii) Amend Prevention of Money Laundering Bill to cover Income Tax, Customs, Excise and Sales Tax.

(iii) Enact Corrupt Public Servants (Forfeiture of Property) Act as suggested by the Law Commission and pending with the government from 4 February 1999.

(iv) Amend the Income Tax Act on the principle of zero exemption. Exempt all income up to ₹2 lakh per annum. Levy a flat tax rate of 20% on all income above ₹2 lakh.

(v) Amend the Customs and Excise Acts on the principle of zero discretion.

Phase II

Introduce an amnesty scheme under which, within a period of three months, all those who have black money can declare the same and regularise the same by paying an income tax of 21%.

Phase III

Effectively implement laws passed in Phase I so that black money is practically eliminated.

- Hold the National Convention on Ethics in the government on the lines suggested by Dr CP Srivastava in his book *Corruption – India's Enemy Within*.
- Enact the CVC Bill after taking into account the comments of the CVC on the Parliamentary Committee's Report on the CVC Bill.
- Amend the Representation of People's Act so that the candidates against whom serious criminal charges have been framed in a court of law are prohibited from

contesting the elections till their name is cleared in the courts of law.

- For all sensitive posts in government and sensitive organisations like banks, PSEs, etc, introduce the matter which is now prevailing for selecting the Director, CBI. This will mean that neutral committees of experts will select the panels for filling up the sensitive posts. The government will appoint candidates to the sensitive posts from these panels. Once a person is appointed to a post, he will have a fixed tenure of three years.

In order to check corruption, there is a need to encourage whistle blowers. The Law Commission has recently drafted, in consultation with the CVC, the Public Disclosures Act for this purpose. This law also needs to be enacted urgently.

In the last few years the CVC has emerged as an organisation with visibility, credibility and effectiveness.

(vii) FURTHER REFLECTIONS ON CORRUPTION

Corruption is very much a part of the Indian work culture. I had an occasion to examine this issue at length and above all do something about it at the fag end of my career when I was appointed as the Central Vigilance Commissioner (CVC). After recalling my experiences as the CVC, I may now analyse the nature of corruption in India and examine measures to tackle this important problem.

I became the CVC on 3rd September 1998, after I had put in more than 38 years in administration. As I look back, this four-year tenure of mine as the CVC gave me an opportunity to reflect on one of the afflictions affecting our entire system of administration and public life. As I came to hold this post after a long innings of 38 years in government, I could also look at the issue of corruption from a larger perspective. When I became the CVC, the organisation was already 34 years old.

Justice N Srinivasa Rao, who retired as the Chief Justice of the then Mysore High Court, was the first CVC. After his five-year tenure, there were nine more CVCs appointed, successively in the next 39 years. Most of them were drawn from the bureaucracy. Eminent people like Shri MG Pimputkar (ICS), Shri RK Trivedi, Shri UC Agarwal, Shri GC Khanna, Shri Acharya, Shri CG Somaiya, Shri TU Vijayasekharan, Shri SV Giri have all been CVCs. In all there were ten CVCs before I became the CVC.

Talking on the same subject again and again, year after year, day in and day out for four years from 1998-2002, I was forced to think on different aspects and explore different dimensions of the issue of corruption.

As a part of encouraging an open and wide ranging debate on the issue of corruption, I readily accepted all invitations to seminars and discussions on the subject.

I estimate that I must have delivered at least one hundred lectures on corruption every year during the four years I held the post of CVC.

If you speak four hundred times on the same subject you yourself will die of boredom, if not your audience. Finding new angles and perspectives provided a nice intellectual challenge.

The first result of this lecturing effort was greater visibility to the organisation. Under the Indian Constitution the three main pillars of the governance of the country are the Judiciary, the Executive and the Legislature. The Indian Judiciary has been a very independent organisation, deeply rooted in fairness and justice. The Legislature consists of the Parliament with a Lower House (Lok Sabha) and an Upper House (Rajya Sabha). In the 29 States of India there are Legislative Assemblies. The Executive consists of the permanent bureaucracy (or the civil servants) and also the elected political executives of Ministers, Chief Ministers and Prime Minister.

The root of corruption in India today can be traced to the fact that the operating of the democracy through the political parties in India depends on 'black money'. Every political party needs funds and these funds are collected in cash. This means that there could be funds generated by evasion of taxes like customs, excise, income tax and sales tax, and also money obtained through corruption. As the entire political funding system is not transparent, the Indian corruption scene can be seen as a vicious cycle starting from political corruption leading to bureaucratic corruption, business corruption and the criminalisation of politics. If India is to become corruption-free, then the reform process has to tackle all the four elements of the corruption scene. It may be recalled that the reforms in every organisation or society ultimately comes from within. Our social reformers like Raja Rammohun Roy or Vivekananda in the 19th Century came from the society only.

My selection as the CVC was a greater surprise. I began my effort of educating the public about corruption and seeking their cooperation in fighting it, by focusing on the system aspects of corruption. The simplest point was whether the public had an idea of what to do when they faced demands for bribes from public servants. I directed that a simple notice board must be displayed in all the offices within the purview of the CVC. It appears that the people at large came to know that there is an office called the CVC to fight corruption only after this initiative.

For the present generation who begin their life with the ubiquitous mobile phones with the internet, this will come as a surprise.

Corruption is always rampant in government procurement processes because once the tenders are opened, there could be negotiations and scope for kickback. In order to strike at the root of this system, I issued a directive that once the financial bids are opened, there should be no negotiations with any other bidder other than the lowest bidder. This brought a lot of discipline. I could issue this directive because I found out that one of the powers of the CVC was "exercising superintendence over the vigilance administration over the Government of India organisations". This includes the power to give directives. Before issuing the directive, I also consulted all the senior Secretaries in the Government of India. In fact, in retrospect this step of mine was considered as one of the good measures I initiated to clean up the procurement system.

Perhaps in my career as the CVC, one of the toughest moments I faced was when I published the names of IAS and IPS officers against whom major penalty recommendations had been made. It so happened that there was a mistake. The name of one Suresh Kumar, who was dead and whose case was closed, was included and his wife threatened me with legal action. I apologised profusely and also took legal cover. Nevertheless, the publication of the names of the officers facing corruption charges on the website brought international recognition to the office of the CVC and me.

TIME and *Newsweek* magazines commented upon this development. It was the first time that the Internet had been used to fight corruption. The Harvard University called me on 19th October 2000 to give a talk at the Institute of International Development on e-governance. The IAS Association of Punjab passed a resolution against me and *The Indian Express* published a stinking editorial by the Editor, Shekhar Gupta calling me as 'Diet Seshan'. 'Icondemnyou.com' was the title of the article in which I was hauled over the coals. There was no alternative for me but to continue. I was clear that what I had done was right and when the mistake was pointed out, I apologised without flinching. I quoted Mahatma Gandhi who had also said that his initiative of Civil Disobedience Movement in the 1920s was a 'Himalayan blunder' after the Chauri Chaura incident. When I look back, I find that the website incident was perhaps one of the most defining moments of my career as the CVC as from that point onwards it became established that the CVC was an organisation which was trying to fight corruption. The visibility of the organisation improved tremendously.

It is an unfortunate development that in the 60 years and more since independence, India has became a corrupt country. In fact, corruption pervades in every aspect of life. The enormous damage which corruption is causing to India, as it does into many other developing countries, is the fact that has to be taken into account when we plan any activity for any project in the country.

We should explore the dynamics of corruption and try to relate it to social roots in the Indian culture, and also see whether there is a way out of the situation.

As we look at our country today, especially from the point of view of development, we find that India is a victim of social disease. Disease that is preventing India from realising its full potential. This disease is the disease of corruption. Corruption is the AIDS of our body politic. AIDS arises out of uncontrolled sexual behaviour. Similarly, corruption is the result of uncontrolled financial behaviour. This includes financial rape where the public servant exploits his position to extract bribes from the citizen and financial adultery where the citizen and the public servant collude to cheat the public exchequer.

Corruption is the lack of integrity – could be intellectual, financial or moral integrity. I shall focus on the aspect of financial integrity.

The negative consequences of corruption are well-known. Corruption is anti-national, anti-economic development and anti-poor. Nevertheless, there does not seem to be in the public at large a proper and adequate realisation of the dangers of corruption. Either we have given up hope of making our country a less-corrupt country or we have come to terms with corruption out of a sense of resigned cynicism accepting that corruption is a fact of life. The question, "Have we become immune to the issue of corruption in public life?" has become increasingly relevant, especially in the context of the recent elections in the states. We have had also the tehelka.com expose on 13th March 2001 followed shortly thereafter by the CBI raid on the Chairman of the Central Board of Excise and Customs, perhaps for the first time in the country. We seem to be living in a country where there is a scam a week, if not a scam a day. The city of Mumbai has seen scams in the stock market which seem to be occurring with sickening regularity, the latest being the Ketan Parekh case into which a JPC is inquiring. We meet corruption practically in every walk of life in India.

Corruption in any system or society depends on three factors. The first is the set of individual's sense of values, the second is the set of social values which are accepted by the society as a whole and the third is the system of governance or administration. There are two broad elements, which determine the extent of corruption or the lack of probity in public life. The social roots of corruption form the first element and the second is the system of governance. Let us begin with the first element.

India is a corrupt country. According to the Corruption Perception Index (CPI) published in 2000 by Transparency International, India was ranked 72 out of 91 countries, as can be seen from the following table (page 171).

We have wide differences in terms of social and economic development in different parts of the country. From a sociological point of view, the family is the basis of our society. The joint family and caste are only the extended versions of the family. The joint family might have been eroded in recent times, especially in the urban area but the kinship in the form of caste still prevails. Casteism gets a continuous boost because this seems to have become the basis of our entire politics. When I was young I recall leaders like Jawaharlal Nehru speaking about building India into a casteless and classless society. The classless society never evolved and instead of building a casteless society, we have today a caste identity based politics. From casting our votes in the first election in 1952, we have come to a stage of voting a caste in recent elections.

Corruption Perception Index 2001 – Ranking by Transparency

1. Finland	24. Belgium	47. Bulgaria	70. Venezuela
2. Denmark	25. Portugal	48. Croatia	71. Honduras
3. New Zealand	26. Botswana	49. Czech Republic	72. India
4. Iceland	27. Taiwan	50. Colombia	73. Kazakhstan
5. Singapore	28. Estonia	51. Mexico	74. Uzbekistan
6. Sweden	29. Italy	52. Panama	75. Vietnam
7. Canada	30. Namibia	53. Slovak Republic	76. Zambia
8. Netherlands	31. Hungary	54. Egypt	77. Côte d'Ivoire
9. Luxembourg	32. Trinidad & Tobago	55. El Salvador	78. Nicaragua
10. Norway	33. Tunisia	56. Turkey	79. Ecuador
11. Australia	34. Slovenia	57. Argentina	80. Pakistan
12. Switzerland	35. Uruguay	58. China	81. Russia
13. United Kingdom	36. Malaysia	59. Ghana	82. Tanzania
14. Hong Kong	37. Jordan	60. Latvia	83. Ukraine
15. Austria	38. Lithuania	61. Malawi	84. Azerbaijan
16. Israel	39. South Africa	62. Thailand	85. Bolivia
17. USA	40. Costa Rica	63. Dominican Rep	86. Cameroon
18. Chile	41. Mauritius	64. Moldova	87. Kenya
19. Ireland	42. Greece	65. Guatemala	88. Indonesia
20. Germany	43. South Korea	66. Philippines	89. Uganda
21. Japan	44. Peru	67. Senegal	90. Nigeria
22. Spain	45. Poland	68. Zimbabwe	91. Bangladesh
23. France	46. Brazil	69. Romania	

This organisation of our society based on caste and kinship and the differences in the state of development between the states provides a very strong rationale for corruption. Caste and nepotism become the basis for distribution of patronage. One of the Chief Ministers is reported to have replied when asked why he was favouring his relatives, "If I do not favour my relatives, whose relatives am I supposed to favour?"

This concept of standing by one's caste or family is also reflected in the sense of tribalism of the corrupt. In addition to the social bond provided by caste and family ties, the common financial interest is another cementing factor. We are largely an illiterate society with at least 40% of our people being illiterate. Hence, emotions dictate politics. Politics is the route for power in a democracy. So when the politics is based on caste and the voter at the emotional level takes the decisions, corruption probably becomes more tolerable.

I wonder whether one of the social roots of corruption in India can be traced to basic philosophy of Hinduism and Hindu ethos. Hinduism preaches the concept of tolerance. Any number of examples is given in the Puranas, where a sinner, having led a life of sin, can get redemption by taking the name of Lord Narayana in his last moments, as in the case of Ajamila. In social terms, this has come to be accepted. People who lived a life of sin, like the prodigal sons return to the straight and narrow path at some stage, usually late in life. The shloka: *Vridha nari pativrata vridha veshya tapaswani* probably represents the cynical acceptance of how people change in life from vice to virtue.

This concept of forgiveness and redemption in the evening of life is also reflected in another social tendency. We find a plethora of sadhus or spiritual leaders who have started preaching. Each sadhu has a band of well-to-do chelas. An analysis of the chelas and sadhus may probably prove the well-known statement that every sinner has a future and every saint has a past.

At another level, the very basis of Hinduism, which believes in rebirth, shows that every soul is given innumerable opportunities to improve on its onward path. There may be setbacks for sins committed but then virtue is also earned. This endless cycle of birth and death leads to the ultimate goal of *moksha*. The emphasis of our saints on getting out of the cycle of birth and death cycle also is an attempt to persuade people to come to the right path as early as possible.

Punarapi jananam punarapi maranam
Punarapi jananai jathare sayanam
Iha samsare bahu dustare
Kripaya pare pahi murare

Adi Shankaracharya had said this in *Bhaja Govindam*, reflecting the toils of repeated births and death.

As we trace the social roots of corruption in our country, we can identify that this eternal message of tolerance, the sense of forgiveness, the hope held for sinners to come to the right path, probably have also led to the tolerance of a sin like corruption.

It is perhaps Hinduism which makes most of us tolerant and this tolerance also gets translated as not making a rigorous and rigid choice once for all. I sometimes wonder whether even our Non-Alignment Policy has an atavistic connection with our attachment to the Hindu principle of tolerance and non-attachment. This is not only characteristic of Hindus but perhaps of all Indians. As Indians, therefore, we do not make any firm and rigid choices and we adopt a very tolerant attitude. This gets translated in the *'chalta hai!'* attitude which makes us compromise and be satisfied with less than optimum performance. This in turn, leads us to a lack of a killer instinct be it in the area of sports and any activity. This ensures that we do not cross the last mile and go for full achievement. We are perennially a country with future potential.

If we examine the roots of corruption, we will find that it arises perhaps from the extreme attachment of people to their families. Nepotism is natural in this situation. Corruption, as defined by the World Bank, is the use of public office for private profit. A person in an office feels that he should earn enough not only for himself and his lifetime but also for his children, grand children and perhaps for seven generations. That is probably the basic motive behind the enormous accumulation of wealth by the corrupt in our country today.

Equally important also is another psychological factor. Power is never demonstrated in the society unless it is misused. In certain communities, I understand, being as much corrupt as possible and amassing wealth is seen as a macho demonstration of his 'competence'. If this is the attitude, those segments of society, which did not have an opportunity to share the power cake in the past, may also rationalise that they must also be able to emulate those who had earlier enjoyed and misused their powers and amassed wealth by rampant corruption. Thus, a vicious cycle of corruption is launched where a society tolerates amassing of wealth and does not question how that wealth is accumulated.

This brings us to another important social roots for corruption, which probably is getting more accentuated in recent times, this is the spreading cult of consumerism. The electronic media has had a tremendous impact in creating a desire in the mind of everyone to have the best of the consumer goods even at the early stage of life. Newspaper reports regularly made out how domestic servants have been the agents of crime in many cases. Perhaps, it is this upstairs-downstairs syndrome or the ostentatious consumption of the well-to-do and the sense of jealousy created as a result among the deprived which leads to crimes. Consumerism and desire for an ostentatious life style tempts many to make money by hook or crook. Corruption is the result.

Evil social practices also promote corruption. One major social cause that promotes corruption is the dowry system. Every public servant wants to ensure that his daughter is married off well. There is continuous pressure for having a minimum level of dowry. This may be one of the reasons why one comes across cases where even public servants who have had a clean life towards the end of their careers become vulnerable to corruption. Dowry system is definitely one of the social roots of corruption in our country.

It is the social pressure in a competitive society for ensuring that the children get the best possible education. Right from the kindergarten to every educational institution, there is pressure of competition and education has become commercial. This has been further aggravated by the government policies about affirmative action resulting in a great incentive for self-financing colleges who charge a lot of donation fee and most of it is collected in black. Education pressure and corruption in the education sector is another social factor contributing to corruption in our system.

The elections from time-to-time raise a debate whether corruption is no longer an issue. In other words, is probity in public life relevant in India today? As I see it, the position is as follows. Probity can be looked at two levels. One is the corruption or lack of probity, which the common man meets at every stage in his day to day life. This is petty corruption and is more widespread. The impact in financial terms, of this type of petty corruption, may not be as high compared to the corruption at higher levels where massive deals and kickbacks take place or even policies are modified to suit certain vested interests. Nevertheless, the poor man is not bothered about deep corruption at high levels of society.

One feature of the developed countries is that at least the type of petty corruption, which the common man experiences in India, is absent in those countries. Corruption may exist at higher levels but the standards are apparently strict. For example, Vir Sanghvi in an article in the *Hindustan Times*, dated 13th May 2001, dramatically brought the difference in perception between when the lack of propriety takes place in Britain and India, taking the case of the passport of the Hindujas. This is what Vir Sanghvi said:

> "As the British example demonstrates, the only way to stamp out corruption is to begin with impropriety. Don't wait for the CBI to try and prove that a bribe has been paid they will never get the proof and the case will take 20 years to come to trial. Start with impropriety which is much easier to establish. The moment you see a minister handing out with dodgy businessmen, assume that he is crook. This may be unfair and perhaps he is only a naive fool, but it is the only way to stop corruption at the root. Follow a policy of zero tolerance;

> insist on the highest standards of propriety in public life and only then do we have any chance of preventing impropriety from becoming corruption. One instance should prove my point. If we had followed the British example with regard to the Hindujas, would we be in this mess today with the Bofors chargesheet? The answer is self-evident."

Vir Sanghvi has raised this issue about focusing on propriety as against the legality aspect of corruption. In Britain also, there was corruption and thanks to William Gladstone's four innings as the Prime Minister of the country when he brought the structural changes relating to recruitment in civil services, army, etc, that the country became a cleaner country. After all, education is also an important factor. According to an *India Today* study made in 1997, Kerala emerged as the least corrupt state. Probably this can be directly related to the increased literacy in that state and also the corresponding awareness of exercising their rights in Kerala.

Is probity in public life a middle class virtue? It is true that it is the middleclass that is the backbone of democracy. In banana Republics we have two classes, only the super rich and the abominable poor. Democracy, in its real sense, does not exist. In totalitarian systems, of course, there will be no democracy and there could be total exploitation. If democracy has to survive, the middleclass value of probity in public life will also have to be sustained. We have to find practical methods of introducing and maintaining probity in public life. It has been said that the Indian democracy is feudal. It is quite possible therefore that we take a tolerant view of the misbehaviour of the leaders because the king can do no wrong.

The corruption debate in Indian politics is viewed as only an attempt at one-upmanship. Even though it has affected some elections, by and large public memory seems to be short. For example, in 1973, in Gujarat, Chimanbhai Patel was thrown out of power based on the Nav Nirman agitation started by the students on the issue of corruption. But the same Chimanbhai Patel came back to power and died in office 16 years later. The total revolution started by Jayaprakash Narayan in Bihar seems to have had minimum impact. Although Bofors became a very decisive issue in the 1989 election, subsequently, whenever any party raised the issue of corruption, it was seen more as an act of political vendetta. In the process, even government agencies like the CBI are used by the powers that be to meet their political agendas. The initiation of a process of transparency in the selection of the Director, CBI was an attempt made by the Supreme Court in the Vineet Narain case, to insulate the sensitive investigative agencies from outside influence.

The issue of corruption has also figured prominently in the elections of 2001 where some of the candidates were either denied permission to contest election or were permitted to contest election even though they have been convicted in a court of law. In spite of the legal position, the voters have elected such candidates. Does it mean that for the common voter in India, probity in public life is not important? While one set of commentators have said that corruption and probity in public life does not matter in the view of the voters, a contrary view has also been advanced by people like Mani Shankar Aiyar. According to him the Tehelka tapes were an issue in the recent elections.

If probity in public life is not a sensitive issue what are the issues that distress and concern them? In some of the opinion polls conducted, issues like price of foodgrains, drinking water, employment, shelter etc, come higher as voters' priority than corruption.

From this development, one can perhaps draw two conclusions. The first is that so far as Indian politics is concerned, the voter knows that our entire political system is based on corruption. Every political party needs funds for running its activities, and this is collected in cash. This cash is basically black money. In this situation, therefore, the voter considers that all parties are equally corrupt. The only difference may be that some are more corrupt than others or some have been exposed, while others have not yet been exposed.

There seems to be total lack of awareness about the damages of corruption or lack of probity in public life in the well-being of the people. The voter who considers drinking water or shelter or schools or employment opportunities as higher priorities is perhaps not aware that if there was no corruption, these issues can be tackled more effectively and the benefits would be much more than what they have got. Rajiv Gandhi indicated at one stage that only 15 paise out of every rupee reach the beneficiary in the anti-poverty programmes. If corruption was checked, perhaps another 40 paise worth of benefits will flow even assuming 45 paise may be the overhead connected with administration and delivery mechanism.

The second conclusion from the election results could be that the voters are not bothered much about the high level corruption but they are more directly and visibly affected by the corruption at the cutting edge level of administration which they experience every day. Probably this discontent, frustration and anger gets transmitted to the ruling party and gets translated as the anti-incumbency factor. It is possibly corruption at the higher levels involving large funds either not known to them or even if they are known they discount it. In fact, one of the journalists close to a leader, who was very popular among the poor, told me once that when the issue of bribe came up, the leader told the hesitant parties who had come with money to bribe him and that they need not worry. If they went outside and said that they have bribed the leader, nobody would believe them for the simple reason that the public know that the leader was rich enough and was not dependent on the bribes from the parties concerned. Secondly, even if they gave proof that the bribe was paid, the poor will rationalise the act of the leader by saying the money was taken for doing some benefit for the poor. Such is the impact of the personal charisma that the public condones corruption at higher levels in our democracy.

Another reason for tolerance of corruption by our public can be traced to the Hindu concept of *prayashchit*. If a person at a higher level is caught accepting bribes and even if a mirror punishment is imposed, the public seems to think that he has atoned for his sins and he should be given another chance. This is also reflected in Vir Sanghvi's observation above about our being too tolerant of impropriety.

We have evolved in our country red tape ridden elaborate systems leading to enormous delays in many public offices. This probably makes the common man consider paying a bribe as speed money is a part of the system. So long as he gets his rightful dues, he considers the bribe given as speed money as an additional tax which is inevitable. Particularly in the business community I find that there is a perception that one has to take a long-term view of the business. If one starts fighting the bureaucracy at the lower levels, the cost for fighting the bureaucracy at the lower levels, the cost for fighting for probity in public offices or fighting against corruption leads to more loss in business. In fact, we find a very peculiar equation in India. With 6% as the conviction rate in our criminal courts, corruption is a low-risk, high-profit business for those who can afford to be corrupt. At the same time, with the enormous clout of the bureaucracy, people outside the system, be they NGOs or businessmen, find that if they want to take on the system, the risks in terms of loss of profit is much more than the gain, which may be mostly in terms of psychological satisfaction.

Then there is the aspect of 'National Character'. Rajaji, the eminent leader of our freedom movement in the book *Rescue Democracy from Money Power* (Bharatiya Vidya Bhavan), makes very perceptive observations about probity in public life. He says:

> "National character is the keystone on which rests the fate and future of our public affairs, not this or that 'ism'."

"National character, again, depends on and in fact is individual rectitude. Movements for the encouragement of personal rectitude, for purifying individual character, are therefore not irrelevant in the context of politics but are vitally connected with our hopes in respect of national affairs."

"National character is the keystone of national affairs. It locks the bricks together like the key stone in the arch. If the keystone is not there, the arch goes to pieces and tumbles down. It is the improvement of individual character that goes to make the uplift of national character which in turn becomes the keystone in the arch of national prosperity." (p 81)

"Gandhiji, it has been often stated, wished to spiritualise politics. He firmly held the view that we cannot keep politics and morality apart. Indeed he wanted politics to be re-built based on a true and reliable foundation, viz, individual honesty." (p 82)

"If the parched field of Indian policies and administration has to get fresh green life and grow, we need the monsoon of purity in national character. And the monsoon consists of little drops falling and uniting to make the rain. Individual purity of character alone can revive the parched field." (p 82)

"When will the people of India wake up, wake up to the need to work hard, to the need to be honest in all matters and in all walks of life including manufacture and trade? Character, which includes efficient work and truthfulness and purity of mind, is the keystone of the arch both in individual life and in national life. Politics, economics, administration, education, health and hygiene and a score of other things, all call for good character in the individual. Individuals make or mar the nation." (p 82)

I think, basically most of us are selfish. When we face a problem, we are interested in finding immediate solutions, it may sometimes involve breaking the queue or breaking the rules or sometimes it may involve a financial advantage. How many of us insist on a regular receipt when we buy things with the sales tax duly added? In order to save on sales tax, cash transactions have become more a rule than an exception. Perhaps, the scope of corruption also in such department is also correspondingly higher.

The second element responsible for corruption in our country is our system of governance. Our democracy is based on corruption because all political parties have to collect funds in cash, which is black money. Further corruption in our system flourishes because of certain systemic aspects. It is this system that has resulted in a ₹58,000 crore of Non-Performing Assets (NPAs) in our banking sector, a VDIS scheme which rewards the tax evader by levying a 30% tax while punishing the honest tax payer with a 40% tax, and so on.

What do we do in such a situation? The easiest option is not to do anything, accept the reality and take a cynical view to live with corruption. It will be similar to the situation where an astrologer advised a worried client that he was having all the problems because in his horoscope Saturn, Jupiter and Mars were in very harmful places and this might continue for the next three years. Hopefully, the client asked: "What will happen after three years?" The astrologer told him that he would get accustomed to it! Perhaps the majority of the people in the country are adopting this advice.

When I suggest that out of the hundred crore people in the country may be five crore are corrupt and 95 are not. I have heard cynical people say that the 95 crore people may not have got an opportunity to be corrupt! Once you give them an opportunity, they will also become corrupt. The question therefore to ask ourselves is, are we so bad?

The response of the public to the CVC's initiative in displaying the names of the charged officers on the CVC website showed that even now, in these cynical times, there is a sense of shame. The *Newsweek*, which carried a story on this, called it 'e-shame'. Perhaps even today public opinion can be mobilised. We must be able to make the best use of the media, both print and electronic, to convey the message about the need for checking corruption.

It is a good thing that the issue of corruption is becoming a global issue. I attended the Global Forum Against Corruption held at The Hague, Netherlands from 28-31 May 2001. The comment made by Mr TN Ninan, the Editor of *Business Standard*, who also attended the programme is worth noting in this context:

> "The wisecrack goes that everyone complains about the weather but no one does anything about it. I suppose the same thing could be said about corruption, on which Indira Gandhi famously explained away her own inaction: it was a global phenomenon, she said. Well that turns out to be true. Except that something is in fact being done about it on a global scale. Conferences are being held in quick succession to discuss the issue: one in The Hague earlier this week, which 1800 people attended; another soon in Prague, and then two more in South Korea before the end of the year. After working up of the remarkable team on the environment and human rights, the global conferencing community has discovered corruption as an issue on which corrective action is urgently required.
>
> Don't laugh and turn the page. This is serious business. It may take a while before the conferences leads to measurable action, but it seems pretty clear that we shall get there. Remember that the first major international conference on environment was held in Stockholm in 1972. From there to Kyoto was just over a quarter century. The human rights movement has gone from agenda item to action item in a much shorter period, and I suspect that this will be true of corruption as well. Though, what kind of action, and how effective it will be, remains unclear."

Educational system can be another major area where values can be inculcated and the need for integrity ingrained. I had taken up the matter with the Ministry of HRD in the context of the revision of the syllabus. Perhaps an open discussion especially about the nexus between corruption and its negative impact on social development has to be ingrained in the public. Once this value gets institutionalised, perhaps we would have made some progress.

When we talk of corruption in public life, do we mean only public life in the sense of politics or do we take the entire society and look into corruption in other parts of society like the business, education and bureaucracy? Corruption pervades practically in all sectors of our life and society today. Corruption seems to have become a way of life in our country because of the social causes, which we have identified. The next question is, where do we go from here? Do we accept the corruption as given or is there a way out?

It was Alexis de Tocqueville who said that the inevitable became intolerable, the moment it was perceived to be no more inevitable. Today, it is possible that people of India in their different capacities as voters or businessmen or citizens have come to accept corruption as inevitable. If we could persuade them that corruption is not inevitable, then we will be able to bring about a change.

There are two approaches to the whole issue of corruption. One approach which may be considered as pragmatic, realistic and worldly-wise is to accept that corruption is as universal as human nature and it is only the degree of corruption that can perhaps be controlled. The other approach is that corruption can be controlled and countries, which were once notorious for corruption, have been able to bring in greater probity in public life, thanks to committed and visionary leadership and changes in rules, systems and procedures.

Britain itself was not known as a corruption free country in the 19th century. This is what Dr CP Srivastava writes in his book

Corruption – India's Enemy Within (p 86). The suggestion of Shri Srivastava should be seen in the context of how one Prime Minister in Britain, WE Gladstone, was able to bring about probity in public life.

Other democratic countries have come out of a virtually intractable state of corruption by adopting and implementing with courage and determination, a carefully conceived programme involving fundamental changes in the electoral system as well as in governmental administration, especially in the public services. For example, the United Kingdom, whose public – notoriously corruption in the 18th century, made a transition across barely 50 years to a regime of extraordinary public probity. This was achieved primarily because of the visionary leadership of the liberal party under WE Gladstone, who first in his capacity as the Chancellor of the Exchequer in 1850s and later as Prime Minister, four times during the period 1868 to 1894, initiated a string of reform measures. The purpose of these measures was to abolish practices with payment of commissions in the army, to define and outlaw corrupt practices by state officials, to introduce competitive examination for admission to a non partisan civil service, to replace fees by salaries in public offices, and to set-up systems of financial scrutiny by Parliament.

In the twentieth century we have seen how the Independent Commission Against Corruption (ICAC), set-up in 1974 in Hong Kong, was able to bring greater cleanliness in public life at least till 1997 before its handover to China. World Bank quotes Botswana as a country, which has vastly improved its probity in public life. We have seen the enormous drive the leadership of Lee Kwan Yew who was Prime Minister for a long time, literally making Singapore a very clean country over three decades.

I, therefore, subscribe to the view that while it is true that India is a very corrupt country, it is nevertheless possible that the level of corruption in India can be brought down. India can also become like post-Gladstone Britain or post-Lee Kwan Yew Singapore. Success, it is said, is a self-fulfilling prophecy. So is also failure. In my job as the CVC, I take the stand that corruption can be controlled.

The advantages of removal of black money are obvious. The economy will become cleaner. As corruption goes down, economic development takes place. If India's corruption level goes down to that of Scandinavian countries, according to the 1999 UNDP (United Nations Development Programme) report for South Asia, GDP will go up by 1.5% and FDI by 12%. Now that the budget exercises are on, here are some ideas which government can consider for getting rid of black money substantially by an integrated approach. This approach involves three phases. In the first phase, government empowers itself with legal measures to tackle the problem of black money and also cut at the root of generation of black money. In the second phase which will last for three months, an amnesty is provided to all holders of black money to come out into the open and join the mainstream. The third phase is the stage where after the amnesty period is over, stringent action is taken to rid the economy of the menace of black money once for all.

Bureaucratic corruption is mainly due to the following five factors:

- Scarcity of goods and services
- Red tape and delay
- Lack of transparency in administration
- Legal cushions that have been created in the form of procedures and laws by which a corrupt official can engage the best lawyers and quibble his way to freedom.

Tribalism or *biradari* between the corrupt who protect each other.

A three-point strategy is followed by the CVC to tackle the issue of bureaucratic corruption. The first is the simplification of rules and procedures so that the scope of corruption is reduced. The second is transparency and empowering the public. The third is effective punishment.

The CVC has the powers to exercise superintendence over the vigilance administration of the various ministries of the Central Government or corporations established by or under any central act, government companies, societies or local authorities owned or controlled by the Central Government. This power of superintendence empowers the CVC to give directives even in policy matters and definitely in procedures. The CVC therefore, focuses on procedures, which are likely to lead to corruption and try to modify them. One example is the corruption in government procurement procedures. On 27th November 1998, the CVC issued a directive that in government procurement procedures, once the tenders had been opened, there must be no post tender negotiations except with the lowest bidder. This has brought a lot of transparency and some check on corruption in government purchase operations.

The second element of the strategy of the CVC is to bring in greater transparency in the system. Perhaps for the first time in the world, the CVC published the names of charged officers on a website. These are officers who were facing departmental inquiries and who have been proved guilty after a due inquiry. This was almost an exercise in serendipity. Serendipity is a word coined by Horace Walpole in 1754 after *The Three Princes of Serendip*, a fairy-tale. Serendipity means the faculty of making happy and unexpected discoveries by accident. The Central Vigilance Commission has had an experience in serendipity after it launched on its website the names of the charged officers who were either facing prosecution under the Prevention of Corruption Act or departmental action for a major penalty like dismissal.

The action of the CVC was basically motivated by a desire to communicate the correct facts of action against public servants. The general perception of the public was that publicity is only given about middle level or junior officials. The fact is that contrary to public perceptions, action is also taken against senior persons but somehow this aspect does not get reflected in the media.

The display of names of the senior officials of the Government of India, including IAS and IPS officers, on the website of the CVC in January 2000 proved to be a classic example of serendipity. While the basic objective of the CVC was to meet the long-standing demand of the media for information about senior officials facing corruption charges and inquiries, once the information was put on the website, the reaction was an exercise in serendipity. The public at large welcomed the measure. Ninety-three per cent of the people in a poll conducted by the *Hindustan Times* welcomed the measure.

Some of the people who figured on the website were also occupying sensitive positions. It is a normal government principle that if a person is facing a vigilance inquiry, he should not be placed in sensitive posts but in practice this was not being followed. This is an important reason why corruption flourishes in our system. This aspect was highlighted immediately by the website. Lack of transparency of the departmental operations helped people facing vigilance inquiries, to occupy sensitive posts. Placing the names of the charged officers on the website, introduced an element of transparency. Questions were raised in the public at large about people who are facing inquiries occupying sensitive positions. There was another somewhat unexpected development. An impression grew that the very fact that the names were figuring on the website meant that those persons have already been condemned to be corrupt. In fact, one paper went to the extent of saying that the CVC has started an Icondemnyou.com website. All that the CVC had done was to extend to the departmental inquiries the practice, which is as old as the Indian Penal Code in criminal cases.

In criminal cases when a person is accused, he is legally innocent till proved guilty but so far as court proceedings are concerned, the name of the accused is in the public domain. While, even in a serious criminal offence like murder or theft, the accused does not protest that his reputation has been damaged, the moment the CVC published, on the website, the names of officers, who were facing prosecution cases under the Prevention of Corruption Act or departmental action for major penalty, a hue and cry was raised saying that with this very action the CVC had already condemned the innocent public servants! One of the IAS Associations went to the extent of passing a resolution against the CVC stating that here after departmental authorities will not be willing to take a sympathetic view of the officers facing departmental action.

It was interesting to see that while under the law no defamation has been caused by publicising the names of the charged officers, the general perception appeared to be that the CVC website was a sort of a rogues gallery, which it is not, legally or technically. In spite of the fact that we have become very insensitive and cynical on the issue of corruption, the website publication seems to have caused some stirring of the conscience in our society. The perception was that public servants would avoid getting their names published on the website of the CVC. This was confirmed in a poll taken by *The Economic Times* in which 83% respondents said that the publication of the names of those charged officers on the CVC website will have a deterrent effect.

There was a third benefit, which flowed from the website. Some of the persons whose names were on the website said that even though their names were there, they had not been even served with a charge sheet. This highlighted another dimension about how corruption flourishes in our system. This is the element of delay in departmental inquiries. It is quite possible that innocent persons may also become subjects of vigilance inquiries. If the departmental inquiries are delayed, the results are totally contradictory so far as the honest and the corrupt persons are concerned. In the case of an honest person, he becomes a victim of mindless departmental procedure. His career may be ruined, thanks to the delay in getting his name cleared. On the other hand, in the case of a corrupt person, delay provides a cover of respectability because he can continue to maintain that he was innocent till he was proved guilty. The CVC was able to use the website initiative as a device by which monthly reminders to all the departmental authorities could be sent so that the disposal of the cases could be expedited. The intention of the CVC is to see that within six months all departmental inquiries are completed so that honest persons can get their names cleared and the corrupt punished without delay.

Yet another benefit is the apparent launching of a virtuous cycle in other areas of government where transparency can be introduced to improve the quality of governance. If the names of the charged officers facing departmental inquiries can be publicised, why not disclose the names of the wilful defaulters in the banking system? The Governor of the Reserve Bank of India has announced that the Reserve Bank is examining this issue. Similarly, in the case of the non-banking financial institutions also there were reports that the Department of Company Affairs is thinking of publishing the names of defaulters.

An interesting development is that while people are willing to complain, they are willing to go ahead and do the sting operation. Interestingly in a study conducted in six cities in December 2000, by the Centre for Media Studies, New Delhi, made the following observations:

> "Nearly half of those who avail services of most often visited public departments of government in the country had the first hand experience of giving bribe at one time or other. In fact, as high as two-thirds of people think that corruption in these offices is real. However, one-third think corruption is more often exaggerated. And yet, 80% of people are passive and hardly 20% had ever complained about such corruption to any.
>
> It is interesting that while 50% of the people reported that they had bribed, only 20% took the trouble of complaining. This also highlights the need for sensitizing the public about the dangers of corruption. Interestingly the

National Cadet Corps which has got about 1.2 million cadets have also decided that from this year, 2001, the vigilance awareness week will be observed by the NCC also."

We have explored so far the social roots of corruption, the present situation of corruption and possible approaches to become free of corruption. Have we become immune to corruption in public life? The answer a priori may be yes. But if we probe below this surface, we will find that the sense of immunity is the result of a defeatist and cynical approach. Many accept the situation of corruption but are not happy. It is interesting and curious fact that even corrupt politicians, when they came to power talk of fighting corruption and providing corruption-free government. The reason for this is the fundamental opposition to corruption as a way of life at least at the conceptual level. Many may feel a sense of helplessness but if we remember the eternal call of the *Kathopanishad*, which Vivekananda used to invoke, we will not feel so despondent. The message is: Arise, Awake and Stop not till the goal is reached:

Uttishthata Jagrata Prapya Varan Nibodhata!

(viii) ROOTS OF THE INDIAN WORK CULTURE

Each nation has its own characteristics and approach to life. Given the same situation, people will react differently depending upon their nationalities and culture. Dame Kettle in her book on 'European History' gives an example to bring out this aspect. An Englishman, a Frenchman, an American, a German, a Pole and a Russian were asked to write an article about the elephant. The Englishman went immediately to the jungles of India, shot an elephant and wrote a book with photographs about 'How I Shot My Elephant'. The Frenchman came out with a book *The Love Life of the Elephant*. The American wrote a book *Launching Elephant Incorporated*. The German made a thorough research and published a thick three-volume set entitled *An Introduction to the Study of the Elephant*. The Russian entered into his room with a bottle of vodka and wrote, "The Elephant: Does It Exist?" The Pole wrote a book, *The Elephant and the Polish Question*. This was at the time in the 19th century in Europe when the Polish question was of major diplomatic issue to be resolved.

The work ethic of the country, to a large extent is determined by its culture which determines its national attitude. Lee Kwan Yew used to talk about Asian values to explain how South East Asian countries were able to observe better discipline and compete effectively especially on the export front. One of the obvious advantages the Asian countries, including India, enjoy over the developed countries of the West is that the family is still a viable social unit in Asian countries. The counterparts of the old people who depend on the social security systems in the West depend still on the family network in Asia. Perhaps even this social feature may be weakening today. Sometime back there was a report that in Himachal Pradesh the court had to pass an order to see that the children took care of their old parents. Nevertheless, the dominant influence of family ethos is a significant fact of the Indian society today.

Richard Tawney wrote a book *Religion and the Rise of Capitalism* in the '30s, to explain how religion affects the work ethics. The vigorous growth of the American economy can be traced to the protestant work ethic. In the '70s and '80s a lot of management books were written about the Japanese culture and how a tendency for conformity and a desire for consensus building was the secret of their success. We have already seen how Lee Kwan Yew traced the success of the South Asian countries to the Asian values. In India, the dominant religion is Hinduism. Even though many Hindus may not really practice the religion seriously or understand its underlying philosophy, certain attitudes are very common.

What ultimately makes things happen in India? What is the nature of Indian work culture? The *Bhagavad Gita*, is considered as the essence of the Indian approach to life. The *Bhagavad Gita* is a many-splendoured multi-dimensional book. As in the story of the six blind men and the elephant, each person can find the meaning he wants in the *Gita*. Coming to think of it, it is not only *Bhagavad Gita* but our whole attitude of life itself depends on our perception. Let us take any object, like a mango, for example. A hungry man will look upon it as an object for satisfying his hunger. A painter may like to paint a still life of the mango. A Botanist may analyse how better quality mangoes can be derived. If he is a molecular biologist or expert in genetics he may like to understand the genetic code of the mango. A chemist would analyse the chemicals that constitute the mango. Each person looks at every issue from his perspective. This realisation about how each person looks from a different perspective or how even the same man may look at an issue from different perspectives is important. Before we launch into any attempt to understand the Indian work culture with a view to utilise such understanding to get anything done in India, we must keep this aspect in mind. Edward de Bono in his book *Six Thinking Hats* focuses on this aspect. According to him, the black hat is for criticism, yellow is for optimistically welcoming everything, and so on.

The issue of making things happen in India may be looked from different angles. The most familiar quote is from the second chapter of *Bhagavad Gita* where Lord Krishna says, "Do your duty and do not worry about consequences" – *Karmanye vadhikaraste ma phaleshu kadachana*. For any modern manager, this would appear to be a totally contrary advice for getting results. If each person does his duty and never bothers about consequences, how are we going to achieve our objective at all? Every action has to be done, according to any modern manager, to get results.

Management by objectives is a technique that became popular after Peter Drucker's book *Managing for Results*.

Sometimes, I wonder whether the inefficiency, which we find in India particularly in large government organisations is because consciously or unconsciously every one of us is acting on the advice of *Bhagavad Gita* – doing our duty and not bothering about the consequences! Nevertheless, one who has a deeper knowledge of the *Bhagavad Gita* knows that this is not the right interpretation. This was not the idea Lord Krishna had in mind when he advised Arjuna. What he meant was that one should work with full vigour and discharge one's duty but leave the ultimate consequence to God. An excessive obsession with the result may dilute or distort the way we work to achieve the goal. The ethical dilemma of means and ends cannot be correctly resolved if we are obsessed with results. I think that is the same advice that Longfellow gave, "Do thy duty that is best, leave unto thy Lord the rest."

After that bird's eye view about the values underlying cultures of the United States and South East Asia, we can now try to analyse at some length the roots of our own culture. An analysis of Indian culture is necessary to get an idea about the Indian work culture. "Is there a single dominant value which can be considered to be the decisive characteristic of the Indian culture?"

I had said elsewhere that whatever is said about India is true and the opposite is also true. How can there be such a contradiction in the cultural analysis? This arises because of the tremendous impact on India of its history and tradition. The Indian capacity for synthesis and managing contradictions has been commented upon by many others. Dr Radhakrishnan was very articulate in highlighting India's capacity for synthesis. Others like Jawaharlal Nehru have highlighted India's capacity for tolerance. This capacity for tolerance and synthesis perhaps is what enabled India to survive as a nation and although external cultural influences were there, India did not lose her identity nor Hindu religion its unique identity.

Mahatma Gandhi had rightly said that he would like the winds of culture to blow through the windows but he would not like to be swept off his feet. Probably he was only articulating the essence of Indian approach to life and Hindu culture, when he made that comment. As we explore the major features of the Indian culture in order to understand its impact on the work culture, we realise that our success – and failure can indirectly be traced to the strengths and weaknesses of our culture.

For me, the most significant attitude of the Hindus is their extreme tolerance. As a result, we tolerate inefficiency and corruption. The *'chalta hai'* (it will do) attitude prevails. Probably in any other country if there is so much corruption, there would have been a people's revolt. We have seen for example, in Philippines how Joseph Estrada had to leave the post of President in favour of the Vice-President Gloria Macapagal Arroyo because of 'the people's power'. In India, people sometimes show their resentment to corruption during elections. It has become common to talk about the anti-incumbency syndrome because ruling parties are generally defeated in the elections. Nevertheless by and large we are an extremely tolerant society. Probably this culture of tolerance also will explain why our cities are not clean, why our services are poor and why we put up with a lot of inconvenience as citizens. Surprisingly, I read somewhere that in the World Happiness Index India ranks much higher than the developed countries.

Probably this is the result of a sense of cynical resignation. There is a story of a man who had a lot of difficulties and who went to an astrologer for advice. In India, anyway one aspect of our work culture is a tremendous respect and faith in astrology. We find that religion holds its sway even in well-run companies. When things go badly the first thing the workers in an Indian company would like to do is to perform a 'Satyanarayana Pooja'. Annually there are celebrations, the 'Ayudha Pooja' during Navaratri and also the 'Vishwakarma Pooja', Vishwakarma the divine engineer celebrate worship of the instruments. Auspicious days are selected carefully for launching new projects and even starting the operation of new machines. I have myself broken coconuts many times against the machines as a part of the ritual.

In the story of the man who went to the astrologer for advice, the astrologer studied his horoscope and said that for the next three years he would have lot of difficulties because of the position of planets like Sani, Rahu and Ketu. Anxiously the man asked what would happen after three years. The astrologer replied, "By that time you would become accustomed to all this bad luck!" Sometimes, I wonder whether we as Indians generally have become accustomed to poor performance and blame it as a matter of luck. We are not sufficiently motivated to change this situation. The civil society movements of 2009 by Anna Hazare followed by Baba Ramdev in 2010 and the Aam Aadmi Party (AAP) led by Arvind Kejriwal in 2012 showed that from 2009 the long suffering civil society of India dramatically sent a signal "Enough is enough". In fact the 2014 General Election to the Parliament and many State Assemblies were based on the issue of good governance and fighting all round corruption in public affairs.

There have also been attempts to understand the Indian work culture in terms of India's spiritual and cultural heritage. For example, when it comes to general administration, our history provides very valuable guidelines and principles for good governance. In practice unfortunately, they are not much remembered and much less practised.

Vedanta is basically the quintessence of the Vedas. The origin of the word 'Veda' is also traced to 'vid' which means knowledge. Vedanta can be looked upon as being related to knowledge. It ultimately leads to the spiritual side of knowledge. Swami Parthasarathy in his book *Vedanta Treatise* says, "Vedanta literally means the end of knowledge." It is a systematic knowledge which explains the relation between man and God. A knowledge that is founded on its own authority. Vedanta trains you to think for yourself; to analyse, investigate and realise the essence of life; not to rely on outside forces to do your thinking; not to submit yourself to blind faith, superstitious beliefs and mechanical rituals.

Knowledge of course covers a wide spectrum. Vedanta represents knowledge of a spiritual nature. At the same time our current economy with the world becoming a global village is also known as a Knowledge Economy. Management of both commercial and non-profit organisations in the knowledge economy would need knowledge. But the question is, "Is the knowledge as represented by the Vedanta needed?"

Before we explore the connections between Vedanta and Management, taking for the moment that it represents the spiritual knowledge and realizing the fact that management relates to the temporal and physical world, we can also have a look at the relationship between the matters, temporal and spiritual. There was perhaps a time as human civilizations evolved, everything in the world around us was looked upon as being imbued with a spirit. At a very crude level, in the early stages of development, there were animists who thought that every object around us had a spirit. Many traditional tribal societies and aborigines believe in Shamanism or witchcraft, which basically accepts that there is a spirit in everything we see and also everything is motivated and guided by that spirit.

However, as we trace the evolution of modern societies, we find that there evolved a distinct separation of functions. This is dramatically seen in British history when Henry VIII rebelled against the Pope. Eventually, spiritual and temporal matters got separated. Secularism is a very powerful and emotional word used by the politicians today to garner votes. The meaning of secularism itself is being debated endlessly. Nevertheless, the point is that in our day-to-day life matters, spiritual and which are Vaidika, are separated from what are temporal or Laukik. By discussing Vedanta within the context of management, are we trying to combine Vaidika with Laukik?

Any student of Management who has seen the trends in the last 40 years will find that from time to time there seems to have been an intersection of management concepts with spiritual or non-material concepts. In the late '60s and '70s when Japan began to give tough competition to the Americans, the whole focus of the management experts, especially in the United States, was on how the Japanese focused on quality, which incidentally is a non-material value, though it has material manifestation also measured in terms and quality standards. Quality was the basis on which the Japanese gave a tough fight in the market to the Americans; but then while trying to explain the success of the Japanese, the cultural issue of how the Japanese society was moulded by the teachings of Buddhism and Shintoism. These emphasised that the community was above that of the individual's interests. On other hand, the American and the Western societies in general were very stridently individualistic. Attempts were thus made to explain the success of Japan in terms of the ethos of Japan and its society.

In the late '70s and early '80s and up to the '90s we saw the success of the Asian tigers which included Singapore, Taiwan, Hong Kong, Thailand, Indonesia, South Korea and Malaysia. That was the time when Lee Kwan Yew started talking about 'Asian values' being more important and a significant factor behind the success of the South East Asian Tigers. The issue of success in the market place, based on values was recognised.

The subsequent collapse of some of the South East Asian miracle economies, thanks to cronyism and corruption in the financial sector. Post-1997, perhaps also can be seen as another demonstration of the intersection between the society values and management practices and how values like Nepotism, the primacy of the family over that of even the society can lead to disasters in management.

The basic lesson of the Vedanta is to look beyond our existence and try to find a meaning to our existence. One lesson of the Vedanta has been summarised as *"Atmano mokshartham jagat hitaya cha"*. As an individual, one should try to attain *moksha* or liberation from the cycle of births and deaths and so far as the rest of the world (society) is concerned, one must try to do good to the world. A manager therefore, can think in terms of his own development on the spiritual side and at the same time ensure that his own organisation is beneficial to the society. The ultimate purpose of existence *moksha*, has the advantage of helping every manager to realise that beyond the day-to-day hassles, success and failures, etc, which all lead to stress, there is a more permanent and a more long-lasting purpose or object in life. If a person is oriented to Vedanta and is aware of at least the purpose of life as Vedanta teaches, the minimum benefit he would have is a mental equipoise. This in turn would help him not to become over-stressed and tension ridden. There are any number of experts who point out that if an executive is very much under stress and that too distress negative (bad) and not eustress (good and beneficial), then his results are going to be sub-optimal. So, one advantage of a Vedantic orientation may be to share some of the ideals of the *Stithaprajna* as described by Lord Krishna in the second Chapter of *Bhagavad Gita* and take the world as it comes. *"Vihaya kamanyaha sarvaan pumaamscharati nispruhaha nirmamo nirahankara sashantimadhigachathi"* – meaning a person who is rooted in Vedanta is bound to be mentally detached and at the same time have peace, which gives him strength.

The *Stithaprajna* according to Lord Krishna can also be a contrarian thinker. In these days of highly competitive environment, probably a capacity to swim against the current may be one method of generating new ideas. *"ya nisha sarvabhutanam tasyam jagarti samyami yasyam jagrati bhutani sa nisha pashyato muneh"*, says Lord Krishna in the second chapter which means when others are sleeping, the *Stithaprajna* is awake and when others are awake, he is sleeping. So, creativity can be another strength that comes from an orientation rooted in Vedanta.

A third issue is that a Vedantic orientation can help a manager to look beyond the immediate present and take a long-term view. It is true, as Keynes pointed out, in the long-run, all of us are dead. But many a time in a competitive environment, that too which is time-based competition, losing the long-term perspective can be counterproductive. Take for example, the excitement about dotcom companies in the year 2000 and the mad rush of both the venture capitalists and the stock market into the dotcom and technology stocks. There has been a corrective market response since then (the dotcom bust). Apart from contrarian thinking, a Vedanta-based mentality will also help a person to take a long-term view so that one does not act in haste and regret at leisure.

The ultimate lesson of Vedanta is a continuous quest for improvement. It is the concept of moving towards perfection. The concept of perfection or Poornatva is given in the Upanishad talks. Once we reach perfection every part attains perfection. *"Om poornamadah poornamidam poornaat poornamudachyate poornasya poornamaadaya Poornamevaa vashishyate"*. Today all the discussions about total quality management or ISO-9000, point out that we cannot have quality in our products unless it is part of the whole process of manufacturing. The spirit of quality is nothing but the pride of the artisan in his art, and the quest for perfection. A competent manager who is imbued with the basic lesson of Vedanta, which is again, striving upward towards *moksha*, will also try to bring in this approach of continuous improvement or KAIZEN in every act. To that extent he can be a better manager with the focus on quality.

Perhaps there are other dimensions of Vedanta, which I am missing, but at this stage, I would like to raise another issue. How many managers, even if they are brought up in our Hindu religion, are aware of the importance and real message of the Vedanta? Normally, we live our life on the principle "get on, get honour, get honest". It is a mad rat race for success. Particularly in these days of consumerism, our whole orientation is towards success in our material world and acquisition of material goods. Who has the time to look into the spiritual matters?

Even if we take our Indian tradition of the four stages or *ashramas* in life, we find that we move from Brahmacharya, Grihastha to Vanaprastha and Sanyasa. Perhaps, spiritual matters become important only in the Vanaprastha and Sanyasa stage. But managers are most likely to be in the Brahmacharya or the Grihasthashrama stage. How are we going to ensure that these basic values, which are useful for success in management, are inculcated in the Indian managers? This in turn would mean that there is need for speakers and leaders like Swami

Parthasarathy who can make this knowledge of Vedanta available to the public and at the same time we should also think of using the modern media to see how some of these basic values can be inculcated. As Central Vigilance Commissioner, I moved separately to see how in education and training programmes we can have a capsule on the values of ethics in business and administration. Perhaps a similar strategy of bringing in a module of Vedanta and spiritual values can be made part of regular management training programmes so that the Indian managers can take advantage of the cultural heritage, we are fortunate to have. It is already true that some organisations like the Centre for Human Values in IIM (Kolkata) or the Symbiosis Institute in Pune are introducing such courses. Having such institutionalised arrangement in management programme may be one method of ensuring that the Indian managers are able to fully benefit from our heritage.

Drawing upon the spiritual roots of India, going back thousands of years to the Vedanta and Upanishads, Swami Vivekananda gave a call for the regeneration of India – "Arise, awake and stop not till the goal is reached." *"Uththishtatha, Jagrata, Prapya Varannibhodhata"* (*Kathopanishad*, 1:3:4)

Aurobindo Ghosh carried on that spiritual tradition and showed how human beings can rise above themselves. He identified that basic purpose and significance of life as follows: The earliest preoccupation of man in his awakened thoughts and, as it seems, his inevitable and ultimate preoccupation – for it survives the longest periods of scepticism and returns after every banishment – is also the highest, which his thought can envisage. It manifests itself in the divination of Godhead, the impulse towards perfection, the search after pure Truth and unmixed Bliss, the sense of a secret immortality. The ancient dawns of human knowledge have left us their witness to this constant aspiration; today we see a humanity satiated but not satisfied by the victorious analysis of the externalities of Nature preparing to return to its primeval longings. The earliest formula of Wisdom promises to be its last – God, Light, Freedom, Immortality....

Mahatma Gandhi again drew his inspiration from the spiritual strength of India. His technique of Satyagraha was a concept which was based on the concept of Ahimsa and was able to throw out the British whose empire, was at one time, such that the Sun never set on it. In Rabindranath Tagore we have another spirit of renaissance, this time in the field of art spanning literature, language, painting and music. All of them symbolise the spirit of renaissance, drawing upon our ancient roots or classical insights to tackle the problems of modern life.

In a way, they also symbolise the other optimistic message of Hinduism, so beautifully enunciated by Lord Krishna in the fourth chapter of the *Gita*,

Yada yada hi dharmasya glanir bhavati bharata
Abhyutthanam adharmasya tadatmanam srjamy aham
Paritranaya sadhunam vinashaya cha dushkritam
Dharma samsthapanarthaya sambhavami yuge yuge.

When evil tries to triumph over good, the Lord comes again and again in every *yuga* to protect the good and punish the evil. It is obvious that our Indian culture does not believe in the pessimistic projection of the second law of thermodynamics which says that we always go from order to disorder and that entropy is always increasing.

History has two fascinating aspects. The first is the perennial chain of changes as history marches through time. The second is the constant presence of certain features. These include values, which are the basis of moral or ethical conduct. Some have tried to identify the common dynamics underlying history. Many have traced the onward march of history from different angles. Arnold Toynbee saw in history the continuous recurring theme of challenge and response. A civilisation progresses if it is able to rise and meet the challenge it faces, and decays if it fails. There is a process of growth, achievement and then decay. Alvin Toffler looked at the technological changes in terms of generations and the pace of change. He discovered that the pace of change itself is becoming so fast, that in the 20th century mankind started experiencing what he called 'future shock'. He went on to analyse further the waves of growth and change in mankind. First came the agricultural wave, then the industrial wave and then the post-industrial wave. Communists look at the march of history in terms of dialectical materialism.

Indian culture has had a head start in understanding the fascinating aspects of human life. The Vedanta and the Upanishads represent our ancient seers' continuous search for knowledge guided by logic. They also achieved great leaps forward in perception because of their mystic powers. We are the fortunate inheritors of a great tradition, the Vedantic tradition, which looks at life in this world and tries to find its underlying meaning. The quintessence of Vedanta has a dual dimension. The *Rigveda* lays down the dual purpose of human life: *Atmano mokshartham jagat hitaya cha*. We look forward for the emancipation of our souls and also the welfare of the world.

Shri Aurobindo is one of the brightest stars in this rich Indian tradition of spiritual development. The Vedantic concept of self-realisation was articulated beautifully by Shri Aurobindo as follows: Existence is not merely a machinery of Nature, a wheel of law in which the soul is entangled for a moment or for ages; it is a constant manifestation of the Spirit. Life is not for the sake of life alone, but for God, and the living soul of man is an eternal portion of Godhead. Action is for self-finding, for self-fulfilment, for self-realisation and not only for its own external and apparent fruits of the moment or the future.

Another concept, which has been cherished through the long history of our cultural and spiritual existence is the concept of welfare of all human beings. *Bahujana sukhaya bahujana hitaya cha* – the welfare of the many and the happiness of the many. In fact, this concept of the happiness of the many has also been transformed into the area of public administration as the basic principle. Kautilya says in his *Arthashastra* :

> "In the happiness of his subject lies the king's happiness, in their welfare his welfare. He shall not consider as good only that which pleases him but treat as beneficial to him whatever pleases his subject."
>
> *Praja sukhe sukham rajyaha prajanamcha hitehitam*
> *Natma priyyam hitam rajanaha prajanam cha hitam priyam.*

This ancient wisdom is also reflected in other parts of the country and in literature of other languages also. Two thousand years ago, Tiruvalluvar, in Tamil Nadu, spelt out in the 1330 verses the three *purusharthas* of existence – dharma, artha and kama. In his chapter on artha, like Kautilya's *Arthashastra*, he also dealt with the characteristics of a well-run administration or shall we say the ethics of good administration. For instance, when talking about the responsibility of a king, Tiruvalluvar says: *Murai saithu kapatrum mannavan makkalukku iraiyendru vaikkapadum*. The king who administers justice and protects his people would be considered as God. The responsibilities of running administration have also been spelt out by others who have looked into the concept of good administration.

If there is one principle that is fundamental to ethics in administration in India, it is the principle of dharma, the principle of doing the right things, the principle of justice. The *Brihadaranyaka Upanishad* points out the basic principle of the responsibility of the king is to protect Dharma. This is because it is only by protecting Dharma all citizens get equal opportunities and the weak will not be exploited and harassed by the strong.

> *"T'adetat kshatrasys kshatram yaddharmaha*
> *Tasmaddharamatparam nasty atho abliyan*
> *Baliyamsamanshamsate dharmena yatha ragna evam"*

Justice M Rama Jois in his Shri Bhau Rao Deoras Lecture Series, gave a talk entitled 'Reforming Our Polity on the Basis of

Dharma'. In this talk he has provided valuable insights into the concept of Dharma. This is what he says:

> *"Tyajedekam kulasyarthe gramasyarthe kulam tyajet*
> *Gramamjanapadasyarthe aatmarthe prithivim tyajet"*

From most ancient times, as a part of Dharma, one of the ideals placed before individuals was that for a higher or greater interest, lower or personal interest should be subordinated. This idealism is incorporated in a verse in *Hitopadesha*; it reads:

> "Subordinate the interest of an individual for the sake of the family, of the family to sub-serve the interest of the village, of the village in the interest of the state, of the worldly interest in order to attain eternal bliss." (Mitralabha, 150)

Replacing the last which is concerned with the other world by the words, *"Rashtrathe Swartham Tyajet"* brings forth the ideas to be followed in the nation's interest.

Dharma is a Sanskrit expression of widest import. There is no corresponding word in any other language. It would also be futile to attempt to give any definition to that word. It can only be explained. *Mahabharata*, the great epic which is acclaimed as 'Manava Kartavya Shastra' (code of duties of human beings) contains a discussion on this topic. On being asked by Yudhishthira to explain the meaning and scope of dharma, Bhishma, who had mastered the knowledge of Dharma replied thus:

> *Tadrisho ayam anuprashno yatra dharmaha sudurlabaha*
> *Dushkamha pralisankhyatum tatkenatra vysvasyathi*
> *Prabhavarthaya bhutanam dharmapravachanam kritam*
> *Yasyat prabhavasamyuktaha sa dharma iti nischayaha*
> (Shnti Parva, 109-9-11)

It is most difficult to define Dharma. Dharma has been explained to be that which helps the upliftment of living beings. Therefore, that which ensures welfare (of living beings) is surely Dharma. The learned Rishis have declared, that which sustains is Dharma.

Kama Parva (Chapter 59, Verse 58) eulogises Dharma in the following words:

Dharanat dharma mityahu dharmo dharayate prajaha
Yat syad dharanasamyuktam sa dharma iti nischayaha

Dharma sustains the society, Dharma maintains social order, Dharma ensures well-being and progress of humanity, Dharma is surely that which fulfils these objectives.

Jaimini, the author of celebrated *Purvamimamsa* and *Uttaramimamsa* explains Dharma thus: Dharma is what is indicated by the Vedas as conclusive to the highest good.

Sa hi nisreyasena purushamsamyunaktiti pratijaneemahe
Tadabhidhiyate chodanalakshno artho dharmaha

(Jaimini, 1-2)

Madhwacharya, the Minister to Hakka and Bukka, founder kings of Vijayanagar Empire, in his commentary on *Parashara Smriti*, has briefly and precisely explained the meaning of Dharma as follows:

Abhyudaya nisreyase sadhanatvena dharayati iti dharmaha
Sa ha lakshana pramanaabhyam chodana sutrair vyavasthapitahan

Dharma is that which sustains and ensures progress and welfare of all in this world and eternal bliss in the other world. Dharma is promulgated in the form of commands – positive and negative Vidhi and Nishedha.

Therefore, Dharma embraces every type of righteous conduct covering every aspect of life essential for the sustenance and welfare of the individual and society and includes those rules which guide and enable those who believe in God and heaven to attain *moksha* (eternal bliss).

The Upanishads say very clearly that there is nothing beyond dharma. The same concept of dharma is also reflected by Tiruvalluvar – *Irai kakkum vayyakam ellam avanai murai kakkum muttacheyim*. The king protects the world and if he acts according to justice or dharma, then the justice itself will protect him. *Dharmo rakshati rakshitah* again reflects the same principle that if a person rules according to dharma, that dharma itself will protect him.

If we explore the roots of ethics in public administration, we find that we have a rich tradition. From our literature we find that there is a harmony between the individual and social goals in our tradition. It is this harmony that provides a meaningful basis for ethics in public administration. Every individual has to strive to achieve *moksha* – *Aatmano mokshartham*. But at the same time his other responsibility is the well-being of the many – *Jagat hitaya cha*. In fact, the goal in life for the individual, as well as society has been ultimately distilled in the concept of dharma through thousands of years of our rich cultural heritage.

The *Bhagavad Gita* is in fact the quintessence of Indian thinking on the spiritual front. It also is an eminently practical guide for our secular life. The centrality of the dharma is also emphasised by Lord Krishna in his famous observation in the third chapter of the *Gita*: *Swadharme nidhanam shreyah paradharmo bhayavahah*. Each person has his own dharma and he has to live up to his dharma. It is better to die rather than give up one's dharma. If everybody practices the concept of dharma, then that in itself brings a sense of self-discipline. In a society where there is self-discipline, automatically there will be peace and prosperity. Unfortunately, this is an ideal situation and does not exist. There are people who are bad and we have to punish the bad people if we want to maintain the peace and prosperity of the society.

Manu is very clear on this subject. Everybody has a tendency to enjoy the material goods in life. It is only the fear of punishment that ensures order. There is hardly an individual in this world who on his own is pure in his conduct. The King or the Sovereign's power to punish and teach the people the righteous path, and the fear of punishment by the king yields worldly happiness and enjoyment.

> *Sarvo dandajitho lokohdurlabho hi suchirjanaha*
> *Dandasys hi bhayat bheetobhoghayaiva pravartate*
>
> (Manu VII – 222)

Tiruvalluvar has also beautifully described the same concept of punishment. The process of the King removing the bad elements from the society, is like the farmer removing the weeds from his field to protect the crops – *Kolayil kodiyarai venduruthal pain kuzh kalai kathathanodu ther*. The concept of dharma as the foundation for public administration is obvious.

Before we proceed further, it is worthwhile to have a look at the dynamics of ethics in public administration. This will help us to identify the basic elements that shape the ethics in public administration. We can then appreciate how while changes may be taking place in society due to various factors from time to time over centuries, the values remain constant. As values remain constant, the principle of ethics also remain constant. As they remain constant, we all stand to gain by looking at the classical insights on ethics in public administration, so that we can improve our current practice.

As a society evolved, it is realised that the behaviour of people have to be regulated if the society as a whole has to survive. The welfare of a society is the result of co-operation between its members. No man is an island. The Ten Commandments evolved because if everybody was indulging in stealing or murdering or coveting his neighbour's wife, no orderly society is possible. The Ten Commandments reflect the values which a society cherishes so that they become guidelines for action. The values are the fundamental principles which are essential for a good orderly society. Practising those values in terms of code of conducts gets translated into morals or ethics. As the values of society remain the same, the ethics also in principle remain constant. This is the underlying dynamism of ethics in public administration.

It is interesting how each age has to discover the principles from time to time. We are in the age of globalization. We are supposed to be living in materialistic times. But even here the old principles of honesty being the best policy is being rediscovered. For example, in an article in *India Today* of July 2000, Kaushik Basu, Professor of Economics in Cornell University points out how an individual's honesty is reflected in the prosperity of his community. In the intriguing article titled 'Truth About Lying', this is what Prof Basu says:

> "Lying and honesty are intriguing subjects that have engaged philosophers for centuries. Social scientists took very little interest in them. This has suddenly begun to change. It is a much more mundane concern with lying and honesty that has been engaging economists and political scientists in recent times, but it's a concern of some pervasive importance."

Social analysts, notably Francis Fukuyama and Robert Putnam, have argued: "societies with a high level of trust – i e where people tend to be honest, adhere to promises and respect contracts – tend to prosper. So, faster growth is not just a consequence of appropriate economic policy, savings rate, human capital and fiscal deficits but, somewhat surprisingly, the level of honesty in the citizens."

This is one area in which the Indian citizens can do with a little bit of brushing up. The damage usually gets done early, when children are taught that 'honesty is the best policy'. As they grow up, they realise whoever taught them that lesson was not quite honest. There are many situations in life where a quick lie, a broken promise or a reneged contract can bring in gains.

Collectively, people may have a interest in being even more honest and trustworthy that what selfish rationality calculus requires. This is not always easy to understand. Let us begin by nothing that people use group characteristics to judge individuals. Thus, people hold views as to how trustworthy Indians are and how punctual Latinos are; about the ethics of the Protestants and the materialism of the Calvinists; about how dependable the Japanese are as business partners and about how untrustworthy such and such people are (let me leave the identity of this last group to the reader's imagination); of how good south Indians are as tenants and how bad.... Once again, dear reader, let me, leave this to you.

Something similar happens in the domain of corruption and dishonesty. Each such act hurts the nation or the community that one belongs to, but since that hurt does not enter the individual's calculations (especially so when the individual is selfish) people tend to 'over-indulge' in corrupt and untrustworthy activities. Hence, nations where people are habitually (that is, not prompted by rational optimization) more honest, will tend to get more investment, trade and business.

Most economists direct their advice at the government or to the politicians to act in certain ways or to the bureaucrats to carry out certain responsibilities. This new research in economics on the role of trust is a reminder that some of the responsibility lies with ordinary citizens.

We have seen how values lead to evolution of codes of ethical conduct. In the context of public administration, what will be these values? The first, of course, is the concept of dharma or righteous behaviour. When the British came and we inherited the British system of administration, we became familiar with the concept of the rule of law. The rule of law is nothing but the rule of dharma. As *Brihadaranyaka Upanishad* says, the law is above the king himself. In fact, it is necessary that we realise this and try to shape our system in such a way that the principle of dharma or law is re-established. In the Indian context where today we have a democracy, we will be able to establish the rule of law only if we ensure the law makers do not become law breakers or law breakers do not become law makers in the first instance.

The above analysis gives an idea about the work culture. How the culture of every country may be different and work culture is the subset of the national culture? The question is, for getting things done from the point of view of a leader or a manager, is the culture deterministic? Is it possible to overcome culture? Before proceeding, we will have to look into two aspects. The first is, how to understand the work culture so that one can take advantage of it for getting things done. This can be done perhaps by an understanding of the language and the proverbs.

Going to the roots of Indian culture by trying to understand the basic principles of Hindu scriptures may appear to be an indirect approach to understand the work culture of Indians. A simpler method is to understand the significance of the proverbs in the Indian languages. The proverbs represent the distilled essence of wisdom of a community and an area. When we talk about Indian work ethics, we should also realise that the work ethics is not uniform. It also changes from place to place. Generally India is looked at from a broad cultural point of view in terms of North and South. In the context of economic development especially after the liberalisation process introduced since 1991 there is an increased realisation that probably the divide is not between North and South but between the West and the East. The West consisting of States like Maharashtra, Gujarat, Karnataka, partly Andhra Pradesh, Punjab and Haryana seems to be more pragmatic and action-oriented, whereas the East seems to be slow and underdeveloped. Nevertheless, we cannot condemn any particular area as being beyond redemption. The traditional culture and background will definitely bring a difference in attitude and approach to work. I always found that to understand the culture of a place, knowledge of language is useful. The proverbs are of particular significance.

To look upon life itself as a game is perhaps an ancient Hindu concept. We talk about 'Ishwara Leela'. The entire world is seen as a game of the Gods. Coming to recent times, the ideas of business as a game, war as a game have been popularised in institutions preparing people for facing the onslaught either in the market place or in the battle field. The Rubic Cube which was only a pointless game became a craze for some time and made the investor a millionaire.

Perhaps in all of us there is the child still alive and we crave for games. In the field of psychology, Eric Berne in his book *The Games People Play*, indicated the many situations which can be viewed as a game. A common parlour game which all of us play in India is the "Isn't it awful" game. How many conversations either in cocktail parties or drawing rooms, you find start with some member saying that things have deteriorated, be it the field of prices, education, standards or administration. Everybody then joins the chorus bringing out his experience or his perception of how badly things have been going. In fact, in many a conversation, we hear that everything is going to the dogs. I suspect that the dog in our country must be pretty fast and though things are going to the dogs, all these years, these have not yet caught up with the dogs.

As I look back, I find that many an administrative situation is also a sort of a game. I feel that perhaps if this attitude is cultivated there will be more display of sportsmanship. This in turn may lead to the concept of fair play, chivalry and better observance of the rules of the game. However, a little reflection will indicate that it is not only in administration that we are looking at games. Perhaps in any given situation in life, the scenarios unfold in a predictable manner most of the time and this pattern has been noticed. As every scenario is a bit of experience and we learn from experience, the lesson of the game is ultimately encoded in folk wisdom. The proverbs in our language contain a lot of sound common sense but they can also be looked upon as a shorthand description or as thumb nail sketches of standard sets of scenarios which we have come across in life.

I hail from Tamil Nadu and my mother tongue is Marathi. When I was allotted to Gujarat after joining the IAS, I did not know a word of Gujarati. I had to learn the language from scratch.

If one has to be an effective administrator, one has to learn the local language. The British I found had realised the importance of learning the local language. The British definitely had the uncanny skill of focusing on the really sensitive, even subliminal aspects of human behaviour. One method of learning the language is to get a good novel and start reading so that one can enjoy the book and learn the language as one goes along. Another way is that one should learn the proverbs because every proverb has in a capsule form, the conventional folk wisdom of a particular ethnic or linguistic group. For an administrator, learning the proverbs and using them effectively can be one method of establishing instant rapport and communication. The proverb comes very handy to communicate the essence of a given situation. It is much more than that. The use of the proverb is a signal to the people one is dealing with, that even though one is an administrator, not belonging to the state, one has entered into the spirit of the community and started thinking in the native idiom. This also certainly contributes to a better exchange of ideas and builds a certain degree of camaraderie and rapport. For success in administration I found that this was very essential.

Using the proverb to describe administrative situations also has the advantage of labelling a given situation. Once you have labelled a situation, the quest for solutions also becomes easier. It could also have another advantage, namely that the situation one is confronting is not totally hopeless or unusual or unprecedented. The very fact that society has come across such situations in the past and has encapsulated them in proverbs gives a certain amount of solace if one is really in a helpless situation. As I grew into my career, I came across different proverbs. Some of them I learnt as the events unfolded; some I learnt elsewhere in local gatherings and used effectively in discussions. Here is a selection of those.

One of the basic scenarios that strikes any officer when he enters service is the manner in which events snowball from a small insignificant beginning. Many a time an insignificant event has a series of consequences mainly because of wrong perceptions. I once went with a Block Development Officer, ND Shah, to a village where there was a local dispute arising out of a petty problem and a series of misunderstandings. Shah came out with the following proverb, which described how things snowballed due to misconception: *"Va vavathi naliun kasyun te joine Kutaru Basun Koi kahe mejoyo chor tyan thayo chor bakor"* which means that because of a mild breeze in a house some tiles got rattled. Hearing the rattle, a dog barked. Somebody said, "Oh, I have seen a thief." Soon there was a great hue and cry.

Years later I realised that the press is always on the lookout for sensational things. When there is no news, the journalistic code probably required that it should be invented. Bad news makes a good copy. As a result we find that there is a lot of sensationalism especially in the language press. But the Gujarati has a word for this sort of exaggeration: *'Kaagno vaagh banavao'*. In other words, making a tiger out of a crow. Probably, this is more appealing to the native perception than making a mountain out of a mole hill.

As I started learning the language, I also noticed that the expressions vary. For instance the language spoken in the western part of Gujarat called Saurashtra is different from that spoken in South Gujarat or for that matter Kutch or North Gujarat. The Gujarati has a proverb for that: *"Bar Gau E boli badalai"* (one Gau is 2.5 miles or 4 kilometres). Hence every 48 kilometres the language changes. How realistic a perception! In the olden days when communication was poor, language evolved catalysed by the distance. Each language developed local nuances and idiosyncrasies, a highly interesting development to any student of linguistics.

But in administration ultimately the results are more important. A management Guru like Peter Drucker can talk about managing for results. I always feel that administration and for that matter management is like sex. Ultimately, everything depends on your performance. You may read a lot, you may write a lot, you may go for consultancy but ultimately your success as an administrator or a manager depends on your performance. The Gujarati mind has a clear perception of this accent on results. In 1970-72 I was a Member Secretary of a Commission of Inquiry into the system of Octroi. The Chairman was the late Maldevjibhai Odedra. A seasoned political leader, he was full of folk wisdom. We went about talking to various Municipal Presidents and Corporation Chiefs about the possibility of abolishing octroi. The point to be made was that after all octroi is a source of revenue and if the government could provide an alternative source of revenue, there should be no objective to it. Maldevjibhai used to communicate this in a simple proverb: *"Amare to roti sathe nisbat chhe, tap tapi sathe nathi"* (our interests are in getting our bread, not in the noise that accompanies the kneading of the dough and shaping up the *roti*).

Years later I have used this expression very effectively in negotiations with labour unions. Many a time labour disputes arise on petty matters. It is more about form than of content. There is another version for this proverb which also uses the childish expression *'mum mum'* for *roti* and probably make it even more musicical: *"Mum mum sathe nisbat chhe, tap tap sathe nathi"*. This has helped to relieve tension in many a negotiation I had with the unions.

There is also an intrinsic value behind this. Drucker again points out how in management or for that matter in administration what is important is doing the right things and not placing the emphasis on the procedures about doing the things rightly. Unfortunately, in many organisations we find that the emphasis is more on the form than on the content, more on observing the correct procedures than doing the correct thing.

This obsession with process instead of results is likely to lead to a situation where one is very busy may be working beyond the normal eight hours but the results are very negligible. Again there is a good Gujarati proverb to describe this situation because Gujarat is a place where the successful businessmen (success being measured very solidly against the bottom line) are honoured. A businessman who is only merely busy and does not produce profits is no good. The experts on management by objectives would say that we should look for key results and not the activities. This comes out in the following proverb: *"Painin pedash nahi ane kalakni navrash nan"*. In other words, there is not an income of even a naya paise and yet there is no leisure even for one hour. In fact, it can also be characteristic of many people who are poor in time management. Such people remain excessively busy but are very poor when it comes to tangible effective results.

Anyone who has been in administration is aware of the tremendous respect given for precedents. Even for doing the right thing, we always look for precedent. If some action or some policy is to be taken for which there is no precedent, there is generally a great deal of hesitation and fear and reservations are expressed especially when it comes to any expenditure in which the Finance Department is to give approval. There is the ultimate bureaucratic exercise in self-delusion. "This is an approved subject to the condition that it will not be taken as a precedent." (I am still to understand how you can take an action which is known subsequently and plead that this action should be deemed not to have taken place and should not be quoted as a precedent). Perhaps this is on par with the situation where we talk about crossing bridge when we come to it because how to cross the bridge without coming to it is a possibility I have not been able to visualise. Anyway, the fear of precedence is not only in administration but in other situations in life also. The following Gujarati proverb brings it out beautifully: *"Doshi mare ani beek nathi pan jam ghar pesijaye to?"* In other words, one is not afraid because the old lady is dead or going to die but what if the god of death, Yama, comes to know the location of our house? There could be further deaths.

People who would not like to rock the boat would sail along quoting precedents are 'a dime a dozen' in administration. These officers take the neutral stand that they do not want to be identified with having taken any decision. After all there are Public Accounts Committees and Public Undertakings Committees and so on not to speak of regular inspection by superiors. They, therefore, adopt an absolutely neutral stand or path of least resistance. There is a Gujarati proverb for such 'passengers' in administration which was used by one of my officers while describing one of my predecessors in office. When I asked him how it was in those days, he said, "Sir, master *mare pan nahi bhanave pan nahi*". In other words, my predecessor was like a teacher who will neither beat the students nor teach them. I wonder how many such masters are there in administration.

Talking of teachers there is also another Gujarati proverb, which I have come across. When we try to get funds for genuinely useful projects, it is quite a common experience that genuine demands may be turned down by the finance department on the ground that there is a fund constraint, yet some fancy projects tend to get the clearance due to extraneous factors. This again is expressed in the Gujarati proverb: *"Gharna chokara ghanti chate ane upadhaynathyan ate"*. In other words, while the children of the household are starving and are licking the Ghanti (mill) in which the flour is made, the flour itself goes to the teacher. Of course, this relates to a period long before the teachers started agitating about their rights and taking to the streets. The same concept is also expressed in another Gujarati proverb: *"Gaine dohine kutrine pivadavo"*. In other words, you milk the cow and use the milk for feeding the dog. Of course, many a pet dog enjoys this facility but when you think of the hundreds of children in our country who do not get a glass of milk, in the pampering of pets by the rich, you will find this proverb very relevant. One feature that will strike anyone concerned with the way the files are handled is the amount of excessive deliberation and nothing that goes on producing very minuscule results. The Gujarati proverb *"dali dali ne kuldi ma bharya"* is an expression which also comes out in the expression *"kodyo dungar ane nikalyo undar"*. The result is incommensurate with the efforts made. The first proverb means that one goes on grinding, the net result is so small as to go into a very small vessel. The second is about digging a big mountain and ultimately coming out with a mouse.

Many a time, a file is lot and no section or department owns it. This is similar to the washerman's dog, which belongs neither to the house nor to the washing ghat *"Dhobino kutaro na gharno na ghatno"*. In spite of all precautions in the bureaucratic jungle, many a time one is likely to commit a mistake. Once the mistake is made, there is always a fear that one should not repeat it. The story of Tenali Rama's cat, which was scalded by hot milk and became so scared of milk that it never came near it, is reflected in the Gujarat proverb *"Doodhno dajelo chas fukine pive"*. A person who has been scalded by the milk will try to even cool buttermilk first before drinking it.

We also have situations in bureaucracy as anywhere in life. There is always the game of passing the difficult buck to others. *"Balthu ghar Krishnarpan"* is a proverb for such situations. There is the basic concept of making a gift out of a burning house. Of course, when there is a fire even good things are destroyed with the bad. In a jungle when there is a forest fire even the green trees are burned away along with the old trees. The Gujarati proverb *"Suku begu leelu pan bale"* bring out this idea.

Finally, we are all faced with the problem of finance. Many an idea, however excellent gets killed at the beginning itself because of a lack of funds. The Gujarati proverb *"Kuvama hoi to havadaman ave"* brings out this concept. Unless there is water in the well, you cannot get water in the bucket. Of course talking of a well, there is another proverb which emphasises the need for preventive action. There is no point in digging a well once the fire has started. *"Aag lage tyare kuva dhodava"*, brings out this idea.

Coordination is another problem in administration. Many a time, we have committees in which different members pull in different directions. Of course, Parkinson said that if you do not want to commit yourself, committee yourself. The internal tensions and the problem of the Chairman or Convenor is neatly brought out in Gujarati by the expression *"Dedkani panch shere bhare"*. This is the odd situation where one is trying to weigh five seers (say 5 kg) of live frogs. What with the jumping frogs, the balancing scales will be nerve-wracking experience! I was struck by the odd smile – the nearest I could think of was Pickwick observing the situation of a truckload of monkeys with their tails burnt off!

We have also seen the tendency among officers to be particularly harsh on those whom they know. This is a weakness of many of the honest officers who bend over backwards to prove their honesty being harsh on those who are friendly with them. The Gujarati proverb *"Olkhito sepoy be danda vadhare mare"* brings out this idea. The known policeman will beat more. One could go in this manner with innumerable proverbs.

The point is that for every bureaucratic situation there is a proverb. After all, life in a bureaucracy is a part of life. The interesting point is that many of the situations we have come across have their parallel elsewhere also and the situation has been condensed in the form of a proverb. I think proverbs serve two purposes. Once you are able to relate a proverb to a given situation, it helps you to identify the situation. It also gives the mental satisfaction that after all the more things change, the more they remain the same. That of course is a French proverb.

Understanding of a culture, particularly through proverbs is useful. The proverbs contain the distilled essence of wisdom. They are also useful in effective communication and establishing instant rapport. After all, if you want to get anything done, first you will have to communicate your ideas. The proof of the management is getting things done. Effective communication becomes important and understanding the culture in a way helps to establish the right rapport.

We have tried to examine the roots of Indian culture with a view to assess its impact on the Indian work culture so far.

However, we must be aware that there is nothing rigid about this culture.

The world today has become a global village. There is a very close exchange of ideas today and as a result there is a trend for a greater degree of homogenisation of culture. Thanks to the dominance of the US and the impact of information technology. English is fast becoming the universal language. Perhaps by the year 2050, 50% people of the world would be speaking that language thanks to the internet, and Satellite Television. Cultural influences are also becoming uniform. In this context, does it still make sense to talk about the work culture and ethic of a nation or an ethnic group?

Perhaps it is unavoidable. When an Indian is shifted to outside the country, he is able to adjust to the prevailing environment and succeed. Contrary to the general impression that Indians are easy going, I feel that Indians are really extremely hard working. That is why whether it is in United States, Europe, Africa, or the Middle-East, they have flourished.

One of the stories I often repeat is an anecdote about Dr V Kurien who brought the milk revolution in India and made India the largest producer of milk in the world. He is from Kerala. When he went to Kerala once, he was asked why he had not done anything in Kerala and worked in Gujarat and elsewhere? Dr Kurien replied that the problem in Kerala was that there were too many Malayalees.

Kerala incidentally is almost 100% literate. The people are more rights-conscious than others. However, when they go to the Middle-East the same Kerala labours are one of the most obedient ones. This is because in the Middle-East there is no scope for forming unions and launch agitations. When an Indian is put in the work environment outside India, he is able to adjust to the environment.

Is the work culture immune from change? It is not. It was Rajaji who by a beautiful simile (metaphor) pointed out how human nature can be changed. He said: "The charcoal in our kitchen is carbon. The graphite we use in pencil in schools is carbon. The diamond we use in our jewels is also carbon. If a lifeless substance like carbon, depending upon temperature/ pressure conditions can be low value charcoal, middle value graphite and high value diamond, how much greater is the potential of a human being who is a sentient one?"

The basic fact to appreciate is, that while the work culture can be the product of history and circumstances, there is no determinism about work culture. Work culture can be changed.

Even within India, there have been successful cases of a new culture being imbibed which goes against the general perceptions about Indian work culture. The Calcutta Metro for example is a case in point. Kolkata, like any other Indian city, is dirty and generally there is not much attention given to public property. It is again typical of the Hindu approach. We would like to keep our own house very clean but when it comes to public places, we make them dirty. Perhaps this may be a universal human trait and can explain the classic example of the tragedy of the commons. Some of our holiest places are also the dirtiest. (We do not know whether it is because all the sins are washed by the pilgrims in such places). Nevertheless, the Metro Railway in Kolkata is a shining example of a public place, which is being used by nearly 3,00,000 passengers per day, but is kept literally spick and span.

How has this miracle come about? One reason may be that the access is initially controlled. There are no hawkers and shops on the platforms. So, the platforms are not dirty. But still this cannot explain fully the remarkable degree of cleanliness of the Metro. The real reason I think is that by some psychological process every Kolkatan feels that he "owns the Metro" and keeping it clean is a matter of pride for him. A sense of ownership has developed in the citizens of Kolkata. That is the secret behind the miracle of the clean Metro in Kolkata.

At an individual level, I have been able to establish a culture of cleanliness in the offices where I have worked. I removed 30 tonnes of paper from Sanchar Bhavan with its 14 floors when I became Chairman, Telecom Commission in 1993. Earlier, when I became Secretary, Department of Electronics, I moved into a new building called 'Electronics Niketan' on January 31, 1992. My experience with the Electronics Niketan itself is an example of how to get done in India and also how we can build a better work culture measured in a very limited way in terms of cleanliness of the work environment. The secret is whether the boss is really committed to the value of cleanliness and walks his talk. In fact, I literally did walk all over Electronics Niketan in the early days of 1992 to send a signal on the need for clean office environment and apparently the message went home.

When I became Secretary, Department of Electronics in June 1990, the Department of Electronics was in eight different offices with the main office of the Secretary at Lok Nayak Bhavan near Khan Market. At a cost of ₹20 crore Electronics Niketan was under construction.

Incidentally, the building was not called 'Electronics Niketan' when its foundation stone was laid. The name chosen was 'Electroniki Mukhyalaya'. The name was so Sanskritised that by the time the building was ready, people expressed fears that Electroniki Mukhyalaya will in course of time will be transformed into 'Electroniki Murkhalaya'! We had to select another name. I had a very committed Chief Engineer by name Krishna Kumar, who later on became Director-General of CPWD. He wanted a name, which was not the usual *'bhavan'*. There are so many government offices called Bhavans in Delhi. You cannot throw a stone in Delhi without hitting one bhavan or other. Both of us chose the name Electronics Niketan inspired by Rabindranath Tagore's Shanti Niketan. But as luck would have it, majority of our officers were unhappy with the name. They wanted the standard Bhavan, 'Electronics Bhavan' as the name.

When I explained to them why we wanted the name Electronics Niketan, they hesitantly expressed the fear that Electronics Niketan may remind people of Nari Niketan. Nari Niketan is the place where destitute women go for refuge. I converted even this fear into a virtue by pointing out that for India's electronics industry, Electonics Niketan would become a last refuge. We can say in a modified form what Lord Krishna said in the *Bhagavad Gita*. The Lord said that man should surrender himself to God by giving up all religions – *Sarva-dharman parityajya mam ekam saranam vraja*. I suggested that Electronics Niketan would say to the electronics industry Sarva Department parityajyam, Electronics Sharanam vraja!

The 40,000 sq metres Electronics Niketan building was totally air-conditioned. I wanted to ensure that cleanliness was maintained. We therefore engaged contract labour for the cleaning. There were silent protests. In fact, the Labour Ministry had issued instructions that contract labour should not be engaged for a work of perennial nature like cleaning. Anyway, we stuck to our guns and the culture of cleanliness was maintained.

I had always held that unless the top officers personally supervise, the culture of cleanliness will not be developed. Every day, at least in the initial year, I used to go round the entire building with my Chief Engineer Krishna Kumar particularly to see whether the rooms and toilets were clean. If the toilets were clean then we can be sure that the rest of the office will be clean.

I also wanted that there should be some elegant artificial flowers and greenery in the offices to cheer up the atmosphere. We spent about ₹5,00,000 in getting them. There was a fear that these would be stolen. Because of the constant rounds we used to take in the initial stage, stealing did not take place. Even after years if any one visits Electronics Niketan today, the first comment they make is that it does not look like Government office! This is indeed a great compliment.

When I was the Managing Director of the GNFC, I used to spend a lot of time on housekeeping. I focused on greenery and controlling pollution. I used to say that when people visit GNFC, the world's largest single stream Ammonia-Urea Plant producing 1,350 tonnes of Ammonia and 1,800 tonnes of Urea per day, they should wonder whether they were seeing a chemical plant or a botanical plant. My practice of going round and particularly checking cleanliness in the toilets helped a great deal.

One of the problems we had was the maintenance of cleanliness in coal handling plant. Thanks to the nature of coal and the people using the toilets, the toilets were bound to become dirty. I told my engineers that people would be dirty and coal would not be clean. They must be able to design toilets which are people proof. Our engineers rose to the challenge. Instead of white tiles normally used in toilets, they went in for Kota stones. Instead of porcelain fittings, they went in for stainless steel fittings. If one visits GNFC plant, one will find that the toilets are clean and the housekeeping is remarkable and a global standard.

This experience highlights two basic facts about work culture. A lot depends upon the top management and the people in the organisation. In the ultimate analysis, work culture is dependent upon the leadership of the organisation. The second fact is that there is no substitute for effective monitoring.

Yet another example of a new work culture being brought in an Indian environment was when Maruti started their operations under the visionary leader, V Krishnamurthy. Maruti was able to bring India the same Japanese work culture of quality and commitment. Unfortunately, after many years, the Japanese work culture seems to have yielded to the Indian culture. There were strikes also in the Maruti in the '90s. Nevertheless, the fact remains that it is possible to have a culture of cleanliness, efficiency and productivity, if the top management pay their attention to these aspects and walk their talk.

An important aspect of the work culture in India is the impact of corruption. India is a country which is perceived to be very corrupt. We had examined the Indian corruption scene elsewhere. In spite of India being a corrupt country, there are companies which have stood up for their values of integrity. Tata Infotech is an excellent example. Once an executive of this company came to me with a complaint that a particular official of a particular department to whom they were trying to sell computers demanded a bribe. The company policy was not to bribe. I advised them to stick to their principles. Incidentally, later on that very officer was trapped, suspended and sent to the police lock up in a corruption case.

From what has been said, it will be obvious that the Indian work ethics can be modified for the better. Indians themselves work better and adjust themselves to the work ethics of the countries wherever they go and work outside India. Within the country, there have been successful cases where a better work ethic has been introduced.

(ix) DEALING WITH FAILURES

It is a cliché to say that failures are stepping stones to success. From my experience I find that many a time failures can also open new windows of opportunity, which we may not anticipate in the beginning. When I was Managing Director, GNFC, one of the projects I was chasing, was a small ammonia plant, which can use the surplus synthetic gas capacity available in the gasifier. This would have been a plant that could produce about 150 tonnes of ammonia per day compared to the main plant of 1,350 tonnes of ammonia. Nearly for two years we pursued the case and ultimately the government rejected the whole proposal. We still had the surplus synthetic gas capacity and the ammonia potential. Once our proposal was rejected, we were forced to explore in what other ways this ammonia potential could be used. We then hit upon the idea that the ammonia can be used in nitro-phosphate plant. This in turn could help us to build a plant to make nitric acid and further go down in the chemical chain. We could also consider going in for formic acid and acetic acid. We therefore worked on this alternative strategy and product mix. Today GNFC is really making its profits not so much from the main fertiliser Urea, but from other products like methanol, acetic acid, and so on. A failure can indeed be the starting point for a new road to success.

In fact, many others have used this formula of converting failure as an opportunity to open a new window for success which has also been successful. In the book *The Amul Story*, Ruth Heredia has described the strategy adopted by Dr Kurien to make 'Operation Flood' a success. This indeed arose out of the initial setbacks he had in the concepts for dairy development he was following.

Sometimes, a failure may only mean that the idea you were trying to pursue was a little ahead of time. When I was Director, Geology and Mining in Gujarat, I found that irrespective of their seniority and experience, Assistant Geologist, Geologists and Senior Geologist were all doing the same type of work. There was also a feeling among Senior Geologists that their leadership potential and experience were not being recognised and exploited. This demoralised them. Further, the nature of geological work is such that the surveys go on for eight months and in the monsoon everybody had to come to the headquarters to write their reports. This also was providing an opportunity for a lot of politicking. I proposed the concept of regional offices of the Directorate so that senior geologists could be entrusted with the supervision of geological surveys in different regions. They can provide guidance to the geologists and assistant geologists working under them in their region. This was in early 1974. There was tremendous resistance to the scheme. I had gone round the state and selected offices and also arrangement for solving the housing problem, which would be faced by the officers and staff who would be shifted away from headquarters. 1974 was the year when Gujarat had experienced the Nav Nirman agitation against Chief Minister Chimanbhai Patel and there was President's rule. The administration during President's rule wasn't ready to face another mini agitation in a department like Geology and Mining. The government did not support my idea. Fortunately around this time, I had also an opportunity to go on deputation to the Government of India as the Development Commissioner of the KAFTZ. I left Gujarat without my reorganisation plan being implemented.

What is interesting is what happened after two years. Sometime in 1976, Mr Makarand Desai, the then Minister for Industry, who was in charge for Geology and Mining, sent for me and wanted my advice on how the regional offices could be set-up for the Directorate of Geology and Mining and the scheme of decentralisation which I had proposed in 1974 could be implemented. This only shows that if there is a good scheme, sometimes one may not succeed because of other conditions, or conditions prevalent at that time and the timing. But there is no need to lose heart. As Victor Hugo says, nothing is more powerful than a idea whose time has come.

I have also had the unhappy experience of total failure after the initial success because of change of circumstances. The Gujarat Narmada Scooters project is a case in point. In GNFC, we had already decided in 1983-84 that we should emerge as a multi-sector, multinational industrial giant. When the Government of Gujarat suggested whether we could take up the issue of revival of Girnar Scooters in Ahmedabad started by the Gujarat Small Scale Industry Corporation, we plunged into it with great enthusiasm. I had an excellent team of officers led by Mr Kanak Trivedi, our GM (Marketing) who was a committed, imaginative and energetic marketing wizard. The first decision we took was that if we tried to revive the scooter plant in its original place, we would face two disadvantages. The first was the physical infrastructure. According to our estimates at least 28,000 sq m plant was necessary to set-up a 50,000 scooters per annum production. We had to put up a modern plant with all the facilities and not try to revive the existing plant without the modernisation. The second important problem we faced was that, Girnar Scooters had a highly demoralised staff. What was needed was for us to bring a programme for cultural change. I have described elsewhere – successful cases of bringing in changes in organisational culture by people like V Krishnamurthy, who in SAIL, was able to use organisational development interventions and bring about changes in a substantial way. In fact one of the officers who underwent the course in SAIL told me years later that when they were going for these OD intervention programmes they used to joke that they were going for 'a cultural programme'. But the remarkable effect of the programme was that middle level managers in SAIL had a change of mindset. This was probably an important factor that was behind the success of V Krishnamurthy as CMD of SAIL.

We thought we could also bring about a similar change. We had an excellent HRD expert in Anil Trivedi, who applied the concept of transaction analysis in Gujarat and was able to bring a change in the cultural attitudes of the employees. I still remember the Diwali of 1986, when the wives of the workers in the Scooters project came and thanked us. Their husbands who were drunkards and who were ill-treating them had undergone a total change in character. Their attitude and behaviour had changed for the better under Anil Trivedi. We had exposed these workers for training in the ITI at Baroda. Simultaneously, the construction of the factory at Valia in Bharuch district went apace. In 144 days, a 28,000 sq m modern factory for manufacture of scooters was put up. Chief Minister Amarsinh Chaudhary commented that in 144 days we did not have cotton or groundnut ripening, but here a factory had ripened within 144 days! We not only put up the factory but also arranged for the township and shifted the six hundred families of workers to Valia.

I was transferred on 30th April 1987 and by that time the factory had already been set-up. Narmada Scooters was already in the market. We had set-up the modern metrology lab and were looking forwards to a bright future. Unfortunately, the change of management brought a change of mindset. The enthusiasm and the commitment with which the whole project was being pursued did not continue. I was sorry to see the Gujarat Narmada Auto Limited end up as a failure.

Two questions arise: (i) Was this failure due to an inherent mistake of strategy? (ii) Was the failure due to a lack of dissonance in culture?" Probably experts can have different views. Nevertheless, as a person who has been connected to the project, I still feel that if we had continued with the same zeal and commitment, we would have overcome the competition and today probably GNAL would have overcome the competition and have been a significant player in the two-wheeler scene. We were even thinking in terms of going in for three wheelers and also got the prototype made in Japan. Unfortunately, all this came to naught.

I, therefore, come back to the basic point about work ethics and culture and the main management challenge of getting things done in India. Unless there is commitment, no project will succeed. It is a sense of commitment and vision, which kindles the imagination and makes things happen. The example of the Reliance project in Patalganga where a repair work, which was to take two months was done in 11 days, shows the type of commitment and the magic that it can work. The same thing was seen in the early days of GNAL but unfortunately the change of management resulted in a failure.

A question may be raised whether consistency, which is the virtue of the donkey, is what is expected when disaster stares in the face. As we have seen in the case of the small ammonia plant, if the alternatives are available they can be intelligently used and then exploited. I will give another example.

For nearly two years I pursued another project. This was for the manufacture of the seamless steel pipes used in oil drilling.

India was importing ₹100 crore worth of these tubes every year. Our project would have an import substitution angle. I located Mr VV Ratnam who was the expert with BHEL on a similar project in Tiruchirapalli to bring him to GNFC. We worked hard. Ultimately, a very impossible condition that GNFC must be able to supply seamless steel pipes at a cost comparable to the landed cost of the imported pipes without any countervailing duty was imposed. As a result the project had to be abandoned. By then I also had built a team for implementing seamless steel project. What do we do? We could have let go the manpower and closed the chapter. We did not do that. We went in for a major diversification in electronics. Ratnam proved to be a very quick study. We were able to implement a project for manufacture of glass shells for television picture tubes. This was a ₹200-300 crore project. I tied up the technology with Owens-Illinois and Ratnam continued to lead this.

But after I left, the project was handed over to Videocon. Although initially they had problems, ultimately, Videocon found in the glass shell project a successful venture. In fact Mr Raj Kumar Dhoot the Chief Executive in-charge of this project in Videocon had many times expressed to me his happiness that Videocon benefited from the glass shell project. Many a time, failure may not lead to abandoning of a project. It can provide an opportunity if not in the same line as in the case of the small ammonia plant of GNFC but a new opportunity for using the manpower for a better project as in the case of the seamless steel pipe project of GNFC.

(x) DYNAMICS OF WORK CULTURE

As I see it, the expression 'work culture' represents the framework of values, which people in an organisation cherish as far as their work is concerned. Ultimately, it is the values we cherish that lie at the root of our behaviour. Values are nothing but the principles, which we hold dear. If we want to understand the Indian work culture, we will have to explore the values, which the Indian holds dear at the work place because it is these values which are going to decide the attitude to work.

While individuals may vary, in any community, there are certain common values that are cherished. We have already seen how Kaushik Basu in his article, 'Truth About Lying', in *India Today* in July 2000, explored why suddenly economists are interested in values.

Organisations are a collection of individuals. While individuals may have their own values, when we examine the work culture of an organisation, it is the values cherished by the people in the organisation as a group that decides the culture of that organisation. Is there any difference between individual's values and collective values in an organisation? That is a point that has to be also gone into. It was the cynical Machiavelli who pointed out in *The Prince* that the individual's value may not be the same for a Prince who has to handle the affairs of the state. In our own Indian context, the concept of "Dharma" has been articulated for the ruler as well as every member of society.

The dynamics of work culture is the result of a mix of six factors. Basically the following can be identified:

1. The individual's sense of values.
2. Organisational culture.
3. The tradition of the place.
4. The cultural background of the entrepreneurial group.
5. The conditions under which the industry operates (as in the case of software).
6. Government policies, which affect work

We can begin by examining first the values of an individual. At this stage it will be worthwhile to examine how my own values have been formed. My framework of values are based on what I have learnt from my parents. My parents were very orthodox religious people. Right from childhood, some of the values of integrity, truthfulness and devotion to God, etc, were inculcated in us as children by my parents.

We also had, in our family, a tradition of supreme integrity as exemplified by my maternal grandfather C Balakrishna Rao, who was the Chief Engineer in the erstwhile State of Travancore in the twenties. He was the man who designed and implemented the water supply system to the city of Trivandrum. He not only completed that project, without time-overrun but also without cost-overrun. One of the contractors apparently offered a bribe of ₹3 lakh, which was very large amount in the 1930s. My grandfather cleverly ensured that this amount went to the coffers of the government and also saved money in the project. These are the family traditions, which probably motivates a person like me.

In our official career, the seniors and colleagues with whom we work also influence us. Two officers have influenced me a lot in my career. The first is Mr LP Singh (ICS), who was the Secretary in the Home Ministry in 1960s, when I was the Under-Secretary in that Ministry. Mr LP Singh was known for his devotion to work and the long hours he put in. His attention to detail was remarkable. His philosophy was that if a person was negligent in small matters, he was likely to be so in larger matters as well. In my life I have never worked as hard as I did when I was Under-Secretary in the political division of the Home Ministry in 1965-68.

The second person who influenced me a lot is Mr LR Dalal (ICS). He was a total contrast to Mr LP Singh. While LP Singh was an intellectual and wanted in every file the process of decision making and policy making to be reflected step-by-step and articulated, LR Dalal was a man of action. He was a person who followed the theory of 'shoot, ready and aim'. He was always for getting things done. The pressure of working under him probably taught me the need for getting results quickly and not delaying things.

As a result, I think, I have developed a unique combination of thoroughness in work with speed in action. Nevertheless, when the chips are down, my policy is, "Between perfection and speed, vote for speed." Other officers have also influenced me to some extent. SM Ghosh (IAS, 1951 Gujarat cadre), with his capacity for limpid, logical elegant and stylish articulation in English; M Sivagnanam (IAS, 1952 Gujarat cadre), who was the Chief Secretary of Gujarat, for his computer-like memory and SJ Coelho (IAS, 1957 Gujarat cadre) who was a great executive in implementing projects. The values I imbibed from these seniors, probably, are reflected in my work. I suppose the seniors with whom we work influence each one of us, in this way. The impact of LP Singh and LR Dalal probably is at the root of my approach to getting things done as a bureaucrat. LP Singh helped in honing my capacity to analyse every situation intellectually, make a SWOT analysis and develop a strategy based on building on strengths, overcoming weaknesses, exploiting opportunities and guarding against threats. It was LR Dalal who gave me the instinct for action, which many a time is more effective and helps to overcome analysis paralysis.

We can understand the dynamics of work culture, if we look at the various elements that affect the work culture. We have so far focused on the values based on tradition and religion and also the experience of the society as reflected in the proverbs. India is a huge country with each region having its own culture. What is true of Gujarat may not apply to Kerala or Bengal. The second important factor is the cultural background of the entrepreneurial group. The third is the organisational culture. In this, we can look at the organisational culture at the micro level of the organisation and the culture of the sector. For example, the software industry has grown as a globally competitive sector in India and it is worth exploring the reasons for its success.

When it comes to organisational culture, individual leaders play an important role. Many have commented upon this. Perhaps one of the best examples of successful leadership by an individual who has been able to bring his stamp and effect organisational change is V Krishnamurthy who was able to bring his own stamp of entrepreneurial vision and an efficiency oriented culture even in the public sector when he headed BHEL, SAIL and later on Maruti. The individual's roles is always most important.

Management in the ultimate analysis means making things happen. It is said that some people make things happen, some people have things happening to them and there are some who have no idea of what is happening! To make things happen, a mere capacity to hold on to existing operations is not enough. What is required is leadership, a capacity to motivate people, develop a vision and ensure that all people in the organisation buy and share into that vision.

Business environment is constantly changing. If any organisation does not respond to the changing environment, it will go the way of dinosaurs. For 120 million years, the dinosaurs ruled the earth. But when 65 million years ago there was a catastrophe caused perhaps by an asteroid striking the Earth, the environment changed drastically. The dinosaurs and a lot of other forms of life disappeared because they could not adjust to the rapid changes in the environment. The change in the environment need not be so catastrophic. Even mild gradual changes can take their toll, if an organisation does not adjust itself. If the organisation does not change as the environment changes even imperceptibly then there is a danger of the organisation suffering what has been called the 'boiled frog syndrome'.

It is said that if a frog is placed in a bowl of hot water, it will jump and save itself. But if it is kept in a bowl of cold water, which is gradually heated, the frog remains insensitive to the changing temperature and can be boiled to death. This is the boiled frog syndrome. In short, if organisations do not take notice of the changes in the business environment that are taking place and adjust themselves, they are bound to fail.

Being sensitive to the emerging business environment, therefore change is the basic requirement for any leader of an organisation. The leader is expected to provide a vision and show initiative, in not only articulating the vision but also in communicating that vision to everybody in the organisation so that they buy into it. Effective communication means a capacity to simplify and exaggerate. This is also called charisma. This is the basic dynamics of leadership.

Being sensitive to the changing environment therefore is the first requirement for a business leader today. As we look around the environment, five trends appear to be important in the emerging business scene. The first is the phenomenon of globalization. The end of the cold war resulted in the many countries opting for the market-driven model of capitalism. Even the communist countries were shifting towards the policy that in economic matters market dynamics will prevail. The concept of the state controlling the commanding heights of the economy was given up. In practical terms, for the business leaders of today this means that competition is going to be severe. Before 1991, when the liberalisation process began, there could be national barriers for trade and one could operate in an effective seller's market. In India, we have seen the permit licence raj give undue benefits to the producers. However, in the post cold war era there has also been another phenomenon of a greater fillip to global leading to greater globalization. Globalization means that four elements of the economy namely, physical capital in terms of plant and machinery, financial capital in terms of money invested in capital market, technology and labour move across borders very fast.

The increasing competition therefore in the domestic market itself means that innovative methods will have to be found for facing competition. That brings us to the second trend, namely the erosion of the concept of lifetime employment and emergence of a tribe of what can be called technological mercenaries. The challenge before every enterprise is to attract and retain talent because it is the talented people who can come up with innovative products and services to capture the attention of the customer and retain him. In fact, in an article in the *Economist* of 4th December 1999, this emerging challenge faced by big companies from start up, who are more mobile and agile and who are more innovative, was highlighted.

Innovation has become the buzzword of American management. Firms have found that most of the things that can be outsourced or re-engineered have been (worryingly, by their competitors as well) the stars of American business tend today, to be innovators, such as Dell, Amazon and Walmart, which have produced ideas or products that have changed their industries.

A new book by two consultants from Arthur D Little records that, over the past 15 years, the top 20% of firms in an annual innovation poll by *Fortune* magazine have achieved double the shareholder returns of their peers. Much of today's merger boom is driven by a desperate search for new ideas. So is the fortune now spent on licensing and buying other's intellectual property. According to the Pasadena-based Patent and Licence Exchange, trading in intangible assets in the United States, rose from $15 billion in 1990 to $100 billion in 1998, with an increasing proportion of the rewards going to small firms and individuals.

And therein lies the terror for big companies that innovation seems to work best outside them.

Attracting and retaining talent is therefore an important issue. The increasing trend of globalization has also brought into focus another trend namely the trend for greater transparency, integrity and accountability in management. The word 'corporate governance' has recently acquired significance because of the importance of this aspect to especially foreign investors. In the highly globalized context, the investors want to be sure that the companies in which they invest are not only management competent, but also follow ethical standards. That brings us to the reason why many leaders today are also emphasising the integrity dimension.

The fourth trend in the environment is the increasing use of information technology. Though the dotcom bubble might have burst and we are not witnessing almost euphoric references to anything dotcom, the fact remains that perhaps after the invention of the telephones and electricity, the information technology is also having a comparable impact on the way business is conducted. The Internet has emerged, as a new medium of commerce and one impact of this is the phenomenon of disintermediation. Secondly, the Internet can be a new shop window providing greater reach to the existing enterprises and also at the same time could be a new shop in itself. There are dotcom companies like Amazon.com, which exist in the cyber space and are doing a new type of business.

The IT has also brought increased velocity to business. Competition apart from the phenomenon of speed also calls for a focus on the customer. This will mean that quality focus has to be on quality and productivity but above all the competition is also becoming time-based. The phenomenon of just in time is already two decades old but Internet probably adds a new sting to the whole competition. Technologies like enterprise resource planning are also adding a new dimension to the speed with which the business is conducted.

Equally important is the fifth dimension, namely the activism of ecologists and green warriors to business. So it will not be possible to continue business purely for monetary goals. The social impact of the business has also to be taken into account.

In short, the five trends, which define the emerging business environment, are:

(i) Globalization
(ii) Challenge of attracting and retaining talent
(iii) Increasing emphasis on corporate governance
(iv) Significance of information technology; and
(v) Activism of the environmentalists

In this environment, what will be the principal elements of leadership? Perhaps, we can go back to the management icon, Jack Welch and take note of what he says:

> "The world of the 1990s and beyond will not belong to 'managers' or those who can make the numbers dance. The world will belong to passionate, driven leaders – people who not only have enormous amounts of energy but who can energize those who they lead."
>
> "I simply dislike the traits that have come to be associated with 'managing' – controlling, stifling people, keeping them in the dark, wasting their time on trivia and reports. Breathings down their necks, you can't induce self-confidence into people. You have to get out of their way and let it grow in them by allowing them to win, and then rewarding them when they do. The word manager has too often come to be synonymous with control – cold, uncaring, button-down, passionless."

We have in India also emerging models of business leaders. One such is Azim Premji of Wipro. I heard Azim Premji describe in a talk, the challenge of building a world-class enterprise in India and the lessons that could be learnt. He summarised the lessons in five terms. The first is the need to develop a vision. Without a vision people perish and organisation also will perish. The development of a vision is probably the most important role of the leader and his awareness about the sensitive-changes taking place in the environment is helping evolving and articulating the vision.

Next to the vision comes the need for values. As mentioned earlier, Jack Welch has also pointed out the need for integrity and values. Jerry Porras and Jim Collins point out in their book *Built to Last*, that visionary companies which live for more than 50 to 100 years which is indeed much beyond the normal life span of 15 years of ordinary companies, are those who always stood by certain values and practised them.

For example, 3M have been known for their passionate emphasis on the value of innovation. IBM was known for focusing on marketing and caring for the customer. Every successful and excellent company has stood by certain values which is the soul of what is today called brand equity.

The third aspect highlighted by Azim Premji is developing leadership within the organisation. Perhaps, one of the most important challenges of leadership is not only for the leader to be effective and lead the company, but also generate leadership within the organisation. Again one can go back to the track record of Jack Welch and see how from GE, many executives have come and gone to lead other enterprises. In the Indian context, perhaps BHEL and NTPC give examples of such leaders who could go and lead other companies. Nurturing leadership within the organisation itself becomes the challenge in today's context.

The fourth aspect emphasised by Premji was the aspect of innovation. We have already seen the significance of innovation in today's dynamic market, whereas Andrew Grove says: Only the paranoid may survive. Finally, the social responsibility of an organisation should not be forgotten. This is where, I think, the leader of an enterprise must be able to look beyond the balance sheet and the impact his organisation has on the society and see how the company does not forget its social responsibilities. The emerging anti-globalization forces although may be scattered and weak now, but there could be situations in the future where a purely commercial approach of an enterprise may meet with stiff-resistance in specific cases.

We have seen so far the emerging trends in the business environment and the areas where the leader should focus. There is however certain important eternal values which every leader has to nurture. The first is absolute integrity. If a leader does not have integrity, he cannot have credibility. If he does not have credibility, he cannot lead. People may listen to him for the sake of politeness but they may not follow. The second is the capacity to develop a vision and, if necessary, a bifocal vision which looks at both the short-term and the long-term developments. The third skill needed is communication because unless the leader is effective in communicating, he will not be able to succeed.

Ultimately, the leader will have to learn to walk its talk. There should be no difference between what he preaches and what he practices. After all, as the *Bhagavad Gita* says, the way the leaders behave, others follow. Others also imitate the techniques they adopt:

Yad yad acarati sresthas; tat tad evetaro janah
Sa yat pramanam kurute; lokas tad anuvartate

From a practical point of view, I find that the work culture is determined by three factors. The first and perhaps the most significant is the individual's sense of values

The second is the set of values cherished by the society.

There is a Hindi proverb, which says that one owl is enough to spoil a whole garden. One drop of poison is enough to spoil a whole can of milk. One person with wrong values can threaten, distort and destroy the culture of an organisation. In fact, some of the organisations, which have nourished, for example, good labour relations and an atmosphere of mutual cooperation may lose all their peace and culture of goodwill because one determined trade union leader can spoil the entire atmosphere. It is worthwhile looking at the role played by militant unions in destroying the overall prosperity and welfare of the organisations. Some states in India like Kerala and Bengal are known for militant labour. Even though in the post-Cold War and post-Deng Xiaoping period, which ushered an era of liberalisation, the state governments in Kerala and Bengal, have also been making the right noises to attract expected investment, the net result however is that they have not been able to attract the investment. This is because ultimately when it comes to a question of investment, the investor must have a confidence that militant trade unionism will not destroy his industry. What will be the industrial environment in which his organisation will have to function? The individual's sense of values is one factor that determines the work culture.

The third factor is the organisation's culture, which depends upon the values cherished by many people in the organisation. I mentioned earlier about the militant labour destroying organisations and coming in the way of the economic progress of the country. Apparently, the militant labour may still feel that they are right in their own way. When you come to think of it, every human being is right in his own perception. We make our decisions because we decide that what we do is the best under the circumstances. The capacity to learn from experience is perhaps not given to everybody. This is probably what distinguishes the wise from those who are otherwise.

In determining the organisational culture, social values play an important role. While there is the fundamental unity of Indians as belonging to the same culture, there are significant regional diversities. We are, after all, a multi-ethnic, multi-lingual country. The nature of the culture in different states is different. We have seen the general perception about the work culture in Kerala and Bengal. Incidentally, the same Keralites when they go and work outside their state and abroad like Middle-East are the most obedient of workers. Perhaps there is a difference between the individual Keralite, in his approach to work and the collective ethos of the Keralites. A Keralite working in Kerala in a highly militant union dominated atmosphere may not be able to give his full productive work. Nevertheless, the same person when transplanted outside his state, within the country or abroad, can bring greater devotion to work.

On the other hand, Gujaratis have a pragmatic approach to life. Their entrepreneurship is well-known. Gujaratis have built some of the leading industrial houses. The dramatic development, for example of Reliance, led by Dhirubhai Ambani, in the large-scale sector or Karsanbhai Patel of Nirma, in the small-scale sector, are classic examples of the Gujarati entrepreneurial spirit flourishing in spite of the permit licence raj. It may be recalled that the permit licence raj was considered to be the era where the initiative of the entrepreneur was stifled. Nevertheless, both these companies have been able to flourish in spite of this atmosphere, mainly because of the drive of Dhirubhai Ambani and Karsanbhai Patel. The pragmatic approach to business is also carried on in government. I have spent nearly two-thirds of my career in Gujarat, and in that period, a substantial number of years in the industry sector. What struck me was that by some process of cultural osmosis, even the bureaucrats who come from outside the state have become part of the Gujarat's entrepreneurial culture.

The joint sector enterprise, incidentally is a peculiar Gujarat government concept. The Gujarat Narmada Valley Fertilizer Company (GNFC) is an example. GNFC could be many things to many people. The composition of share capital was such that the Government of Gujarat owned 26%, 25% by Gujarat State Fertiliser Company (GFSC) of which again 49% was owned by the Government of Gujarat, the rest was owned by other financial institutions and the public. The GNFC had a large number of shareholders after its public issue in early 1981 with more than 4,20,000 shareholders. How do we classify GNFC? Is it public sector or private sector? When I went to the Government of India, I could argue that it was a public sector enterprise because it was under the control of the Government of Gujarat. After all, the state government de facto appointed all the Directors of the Board. However, when I went to IFC, Washington, I used to argue that GNFC was a private company because its shares were quoted in the Stock Exchange. GNFC, thus, could enjoy the best of both worlds. This is a very clever device operated by the Government of Gujarat.

I wonder why many other governments, and particularly the Government of India, did not adopt this strategy. In the Government of India, we are also struck not only with the concept of public sector but if equity is more than 51%, the enterprise is considered as a State, thanks to Article 12 of the Constitution. The Government of India, thus, ended with giving to the public sector employees the best of both the worlds, ie the benefits of better pay and perquisites as employees of a commercial enterprise and at the same time enjoying guarantees of protection of service like the government servants. The management of public sector enterprises of the Government of India lost on both counts – their commercial flexibility was stifled and they had the additional burden of the status of 'state'.

In a way, the Gujarat Government reflects the ethos of the people of Gujarat. The Gujaratis are very practical minded people and successful because they are commercially enterprising. My favourite Gujarati proverb is *"Hame roti sathe nisbad che taptapi sathe nahi"*, which means, "I am concerned with the roti and not the process by which it is made". The noise which is made when a chapati is beaten into shape, is the tap-tapi. The proverb also represents Gujaratis focus on results. I was the Controller of Accommodation in Ahmedabad nearly four decades ago. My job was to fix the rent for houses, which were requisitioned. Many widows who were landladies met me in this context. They argued how the rent of requisitioned houses should be fixed. For the landladies, the most important factor was the rate of return. They always discussed about percentage of return. *Aa man ketla taka che?* (what is the rate of return on this?) was the frequent question.

That exposure to the practical approach of the Gujaratis has been of immense value to me. At a more elevated macro level, I always wonder at the fact that the key person who led the Indian freedom movement critically and succeeded in winning independence was Mahatma Gandhi. He was a Gujarati. The person who united India, and was known as the Iron man of India, Sardar Vallabhbhai Patel was again from Gujarat. Incidentally, the Father of Pakistan, Muhammad Ali Jinnah also hailed from Gujarat. The famous Amul experiment, which made India the largest producer of milk in the world, happened in Gujarat. Perhaps it is the practical approach of the Gujarati, which get things done. Another great Indian from Gujarat who strode both the world of science and business was Dr Vikram Sarabhai, the Father of Indian Space Science and the successor to Dr Homi Jehangir Bhabha, the Father of Indian Atomic Energy efforts. On the industrial side, the remarkable achievement of Dhirubhai Ambani and the fantastic growth of Reliance as a dominant company showed not only the traditional Gujarati enterprising spirit but also how a company with vision would forge ahead in spite of the permit licence raj focused on a culture of leveraging the capital market. Karsanbhai Patel who built Nirma and gave a run for their money to the multinationals is another example of Gujarati entrepreneurship. In 1970-74, when I was the Director of Geology and Mining in Gujarat, Karsanbhai was a laboratory technician in our department. His remarkable success in industry is a classic example of the striking human spirit of enterprise.

It is remarkable that whether we consider the period before independence or after it, when it comes to the issue of getting things done or achieving results, the contribution of people from Gujarat has been very significant. Is there anything special in the culture of the people of Gujarat? Each community and state in India has its own culture. It is the culture of a people, which shapes the work ethic and operational efficiency. The starting point for making things happen in India is therefore an understanding of the Indian work ethic and culture.

At the same time, there is also another aspect of the Gujarati entrepreneurial spirit. This is the influence of values. For example, a sect like Swaminarayan is quite influential and this brings in a sense of values in business ethics. The permit licence raj and the culture of corruption that – India has developed has forced many business houses and entrepreneurs from not only Gujarat but other parts of the country also to adopt unethical practices. My own judgement is that by and large a Gujarati entrepreneur would stick to his ethical principles much longer and much more steadfastly than others.

The remarkable campaign of Narendra Modi who achieved a historic victory to propel the Bharatiya Janata Party to an all time record of capturing 282 seats in the 543 strong Lok Sabha and a 300 plus NDA led by the BJP in the 2014 general elections is a standing proof to convince all doubters and so-called secular intellectuals that the ideal combination of Hinduism, as articulated by the other Narendra [Vivekananda whose original name was Narendra Dutta], the discipline of a genuine RSS Pracharak and the values of a Gujarati will work wonders not only in business but also in a vast multi-ethnic multi-lingual India also. No wonder, Gandhiji, Sardar Patel and Jinnah hail from Gujarat.

I know I am making these observations based on my individual perception. Perhaps a rigorous academic may want these perceptions to be substantiated by a field study. This in itself can be an exercise for future academicians to see whether there is a region-specific value and cultural variation when it comes to the work ethic in the country. I do not know whether such an exercise has been done so far.

At this stage, as we are looking at the dynamics of the Indian work culture, it is better to note the broad features. Bengalis by nature are very art-minded and highly intellectual. Perhaps, the appeal of communism there is very strong because of its intellectual sophistication. At the same time, there is the well-known fact that there have been very few Bengali entrepreneurs. Other entrepreneurial communities like the Marwaris and Gujaratis have developed many industries in Bengal.

In fact an American author, more than 20 years ago, made a study of the Marwari community as one of the most enterprising of the business communities in India. The Marwari community has a very strong religious bent. While they may be very good in taking hard and sharp business decisions, the religious orientation also perhaps has a bearing on their approach to business.

Apart from the nature of the entrepreneurs and their religious background, the levels of development in the different states also determine the work culture. For example, in Tamil Nadu, Karnataka and Andhra Pradesh, there is a great respect for authority. To some extent we can expect better discipline among the workers because of the traditional respect for authority, which, communities in this part of the country have.

The more underdeveloped the state, greater is the influence and respect for the civil service. Perhaps, this is true in states like Orissa, Uttar Pradesh, Bihar, Madhya Pradesh and Rajasthan. However, in some of these BIMARU States, particularly Bihar, we are witnessing in recent times a total social change and the collapse of the governance itself. The weaker sections in these parts are now focusing on first getting respect rather than striving for development as one of their leaders is supposed to have said. So these approaches also probably determine the level of work culture in these states.

When India started on the path of planned development after independence, the public sector was visualised as a means of developing the backward areas and achieve balanced regional and economic development. However, what has happened is that even though heavy investments were made in some of the most backward states like Bihar, the development has not spread to the hinterland of where these public sector enterprises are located. These public enterprises are remaining as islands of prosperity in a sea of poverty.

There are states in India where the law and order position is not very happy. Militancy is dominant. How do enterprises operate in such places? Of course, many enterprises may just quit and try to find alternative places to do their business, if they can find such places. Otherwise, they will be forced to operate by coming to some sort of an understanding with the militant agencies. This issue of militancy in certain parts of the country will have to be taken into account when we consider the overall work culture in India.

Behind every case of militancy we will find that there has been a culture of corruption, which has precipitated the crisis. Because of corruption, the state loses its legitimacy and the militancy is looked upon as a lesser evil. I understand that in some of the North Eastern states, the militants also know who are the corrupt officials and executives. They kidnap or demand ransom only from such people. The honest people whom the militants know do not have the money to spare are spared from their activities like kidnapping and ransom. Probably, we are witnessing in these places maintenance of certain equilibrium between the good and the bad elements in the society irrespective of the formal legal boundaries of legitimacy and illegitimacy.

In addition to the regional balance, the work culture is also determined by other factors. In recent times, India has made some impact in the area of software development. What is the secret of India's software success? India's exciting success in Information Technology (IT), particularly software exports has been realised even by our political leaders. As the then Prime Minister Atal Bihari Vajpayee said: "IT is India's Tomorrow". Have you ever wondered what is the secret behind India's success in IT?

Prof CK Prahlad, in a talk delivered a few years ago gave away the secret casually. He said the baggage of the traditional old industries does not burden the IT industry in India. I am afraid that this fact is not fully realised and all sorts of reasons are attributed for the success of India in IT, especially in terms of software exports.

The first important fact to be appreciated is that in IT, merit and merit alone, counts. It is true that in our country the policies after independence have been very much geared towards social justice, reservation, affirmative action and so on. While they might have brought a lot of social benefit, the net result is that India is not fully utilizing the brainpower it has in the communities, which are not favoured under the affirmative action and so on. While they might have brought a lot of social benefit, the net result is that India is not fully utilizing the brainpower it has in the communities, which are not favoured under the affirmative action programme. Software, which is open to global competition, is based on the iron rule that ultimately success depends only on merit. This has provided an opportunity for India's brainpower to assert itself. India's tradition in abstract thinking in mathematics, familiarity with English and the Indian's multilingual ability have provided the competitive edge in terms of merit. The fact is that India has merit and this merit was not suppressed so far as software is concerned.

The second reason is that even if people are willing to work, our labour laws and the trade unions have ensured that maximum remuneration is got with minimum effort. Productivity based incentives in our industries have mostly been an exercise in consistently reducing the standards of performance required so that while one can on paper show that we have performance-based incentives, in reality, our productivity is way below the global standards. That is why, when it comes to global competitiveness, we are almost at the tail end, ranking 40 out of 53 countries, according to the World Competitiveness Index.

In software, fortunately, the dead hand of trade unions and the militant labour culture has not penetrated. In an interview to *The Times of India* on 13th July 2000, Mr NR Narayana Murthy, the current icon of success in the new economy, spelt out beautifully the philosophy of the software engineers. He said software experts would have to live, dream and breathe software.

> "Certainly I live, dream and breathe strategies for making a software company more and more successful. Our offices are open 24 hours a day, you get breakfast, lunch and dinner. We have created an environment where it is possible to live, breathe and dream software all the time. A few generations will have to work 20 hour days and 18 hour days. That is a small sacrifice that we have to make so that our children and our grandchildren will get a better quality of life, so that no child in India will be without access to education, shelter and food."

Contrast this with the attitude of the traditional industrialists of the old economy. They have thrived in the four decades of permit licence raj by wheeling and dealing. Nearly $100 billion of India's black money is in foreign banks. The old economy leaders would like to enjoy holidays abroad, and the employees would like to enjoy, the benefit brought to them through the labour aristocracy's demand.

That brings me to the third reason for India's strength in IT. Software is focused on creating wealth, whereas all the political rhetoric since independence has focused on eradication of poverty. In this age of globalization perhaps, having failed in our socialist strategies to eradicate poverty, we should give an opportunity to the opposite philosophy of creating wealth. Software is a classic industry where wealth is created with enterprise and merit alone without having to depend on family background or contacts. In the old economy, bankers would look for safety in investment whereas in the new economy, venture capitalists and angle funds, rush where the old bankers would fear to tread.

There are some who consider that the Indian IT industry succeeded because government did not mess up with it. In fact, one of the jokes going around is that our Indian girls are beating the world hollow in the beauty contests for Miss World and Miss Universe because the Government of India does not have a Ministry of Beauty! Fortunately, this argument is not valid for IT. The Ministry of Information Technology (MIT) in its earlier avatar as Department of Electronics had struck a strategic alliance with the industry and provided critical infrastructure like earth stations for high speed communication and the right policy package. Everyone in the IT industry is aware of this fact though those outside this sector may not be aware of the critical role played by the Department of Electronics.

Finally, is there a danger that the new economy and India's IT strength also will ultimately become a victim of politics and trade union movement? Fortunately thanks to the liberating effect of IT and concepts like Small Office Home Office (SOHO) operations this danger can be avoided. Software and IT are primarily designed to give full opportunities for individuals to flourish. When the individuals have got opportunity to flourish, I do not think they will succumb to the charms of the herd mentality or mob psychology, which underlies much of politics or the trade union movement.

The challenge before us is that while we can think of applying IT in the old economy in a purely technical sense of computerising manufacturing operations in the old industries or applying IT in management of the old industries, can we also bring some of the unspoken but very real factors of merit, commitment and a vision of creating wealth, which are driving the success of IT to the old economy?

The next aspect which determines the work culture in the system is the policy adopted by the government for the permit licence raj in the light of the socialist approach of the commanding heights of the economy being controlled by the state, led to a high degree of labour inflexibility which badly affects the entire productivity and competitiveness of the Indian industry. We still seem to be in a period of transition so far as introducing labour flexibility is concerned. Even though the Finance Minister announced in the budget of 2000-2001 that Part VB of the Industrial Disputes Act will be amended, so that companies employing up to 1,000 people can downsize without requiring prior permission, action on the ground has not taken place. This is because of the lack of political will.

In India, political will is exercised only under two conditions. The first is when there is no alternative (TINA). The second is when there is a vote bank advantage. Organised labour is still perceived to be a strong vote bank and hence the prevailing culture of labour in flexibility.

The prolonged permit licence raj for more than four decades also has built in a culture among the Indian industry of operating in a sellers' market. The customer is the last priority. In fact one of my Gujarati friends said that the person who dies out of difficulty is the customer: *Kashta se jo mar jata hai wo customer hai*.

The 1991-liberalisation policies have brought a change but still the tendency of the industry is to seek protection. This protection is sought to be achieved in terms of countervailing duties and other forms. For example, the perceived threat of import of second hand cars was successfully met by the automobile industry in India, which persuaded the government to put such high tariff walls, that hardly any import could take place. Nevertheless, the decade of liberalisation policies following 1991 have brought an increased degree of competition in the Indian industry. The Indian industry is trying to adjust itself.

Family controlled companies dominate the private sector. Some of the forward looking companies among them had gone in for getting the advice from the multinational consultants like McKinsey or Arthur D Little and are trying to restructure themselves. They are also trying to bring in professionalism. For example, Eicher led the way by Mr Lal stepping away from direct management. Companies like the Tatas and Larsen & Toubro had gone in for professional management quite some time back. What is interesting is the attempt being made to bring in professional management in the family controlled companies, which probably constitute more than 95% of the Indian private sector.

So far as the public sector is concerned, the work culture has been very much shaped by the governmental culture.

The public sector companies are like super Draupadis. Draupadi had to manage only five husbands, but PSES have to cope up with seven! These are Board of Directors, Administrative Ministry, Committee of Public Undertakings, Public Accounts Committee, Central Vigilance Commission, Comptroller and Auditor General and the Central Bureau of Investigation. Added to that is the provision in Article 12 of the Constitution, that the public sector will be considered as a "state". This therefore, has resulted in a situation where the public sector is many a time indistinguishable from the bureaucratic system of government.

Now exercises are being made after the process of liberalisation to bring in greater initiative. I was the Chairman of a Committee, which looked in to the guidelines issued to the public sector with a view to enhance the autonomy of the public sector. I found that there were 832 guidelines prescribed for the public sector undertakings. These had virtually stifled the initiative of the public sector. On the recommendation of my committee, at least 696 guidelines were scrapped.

Nevertheless, the fact remains that if we want to build a better work culture in the public sector of professionalism, we have to introduce a code of conduct by which there would be an arm's length relationship between the public sector and the administrative ministry in the Government of India.

As chairman of the committee on guidelines for the public sector enterprises, I had suggested the following code, but no action has been taken so far on this by the government:

1. **The objective of the code** is to prescribe standards of integrity and conduct that are to apply to all the executives and employees in the PSEs and the officers and employees of the administrative ministries concerned with them. The principles stated below, underlie and supplement the rules and laws regulating the public and private conduct of the executives/officers and employees in both the PSEs and the administrative ministries.
2. **Objectives of the public sector enterprises:**
   (a) The role of the executives/officers is to assist the PSE to achieve its objectives as spelt out in the charter constituting the setting up of the enterprise.
   (b) Respect for human rights solely in the public interest while making recommendations or exercising administrative authority. He or she must maintain the highest standards of probity and integrity.
   (c) In relation to the general public, the executives/officers and employees in the PSE/administrative ministries should conduct themselves in such a manner that the public feels that the decisions taken on the recommendations made by them are objectives and transparent, and are not calculated to promote

improper gains for the political party in power or for themselves or for anyone else. This would particularly be significant as far as the customer of the public service are concerned. This will apply also *mutatis mutandis* to the officers and employees in the administrative ministry concerned with the PSE.

(d) Executives/officers and employees of the PSEs/ administrative ministries should not seek to frustrate or undermine the policies, decisions and actions taken in the public interest by the management by declining or abstaining from action which flows from the management decisions. Where following the instructions of the superior authority would appear to conflict with the exercise of impartial professional judgement or affect the efficient working of the enterprise, he or she should set out points of disagreement clearly once in writing to the superior authority or seek explicit written instructions. This will apply also *mutatis mutandis* to the officers and employees in the administrative ministry concerned with the PSE.

(e) Where an executive/officer or employee of the PSE has reasonable grounds to believe that he or she is being required by the superior authority to act in a manner which is illegal or against the prescribed rules and regulations, or if any legal infringement comes to his or her notice, he or she should decline to implement the instruction, and would also have a right to bring the facts to the notice of the Chairman/ Managing Director of the enterprise or the Secretary of the administrative ministry concerned. It shall be incumbent to examine the issue carefully and take action appropriately. This will apply also *mutatis mutandis* to the officers and employees in the administrative ministry concerned with the PSE.

The religion, region, caste, language or the executive will have no influence on the working in his official capacity.

3. **Conflict of interest and peer pressure:**
   (a) Executives, officers and employees in the PSEs/ administrative ministries should refrain from decisions in respect of which they have reason to believe that they are calculated to benefit any particular person or party at the expense of the public interest.
   (b) Every executive, officer or employee in the PSE/ administrative ministry shall disclose any clash of interest when there is conflict between public and private interest, or he/she is likely to benefit from any act of omission or commission while discharging his/ her functions.
   (c) Executives, officers and employees in the PSE/ administrative ministries should be alert to any actual or potential conflict of interest, financial or otherwise and should disclose this to their superiors, whether the conflict covers them or their family members.
   (d) Executives, officers and employees in the PSE/ administrative ministries should maintain their independence, dignity and impartiality by not approaching politicians and outsiders in respect of service matters or private benefit. They should exercise peer pressure to dissuade those who do so within the organisation and set in motion disciplinary proceedings against such persons.
4. **Accountability and responsiveness to the public:**
   (a) Consistent with accountability to the superior officers and ministers in accordance with provisions governing PSE/administrative ministry, the executives, officers and employees in the PSEs should also practise

accountability to the people in terms of quality of service, timeliness, courtesy, people orientation and readiness to encourage participation of, and form partnership with citizen groups for responsive management.

(b) Executives, officers and employees in the PSEs/ administrative ministries should be consistent, equitable and honest in their treatment of the members of the public; with particular care for the weaker sections of society and should not even be or appear to be unfair or discriminatory. Decision in pursuit of discretionary powers should be justifiable on the basis of non arbitrary and objective criteria.

(c) Executives, officers and employees in the PSEs/ administrative ministries should accept the obligation to recognise and enforce customer's right for speedy redressal of grievances and commit themselves to provide services of declared quality and standard to customers.

(d) Executives, officers and employees in the PSEs/ administrative ministries should respect the right of public to information on all activities and transactions of the organisations except where they are debarred in the public interest, from releasing information by provisions of law or by valid instructions.

5. **Concern for value of public asset and funds:** The employees in the PSE/administrative ministry should avoid wastage and extravagance and ensure effective and efficient use of the public money within their control. In cases of disputes or grievances, efforts must be made to resolve them quickly. No unlawful stoppage or disruption of work or damage to the assets of the PSE should be resorted to.

6. **Non-abuse of official position:** Employees of PSEs/ administrative ministries have a responsibility to make

decision on merits. They are in a position of trust. They must not use their official position to influence any person to enter into financial or other arrangements with them or with anyone else. They must not abuse their official position to obtain a benefit for themselves or for someone else, in financial or some other forms. This will apply also *mutatis mutandis* to the officers and employees in the administrative ministry concerned with the PSE.

7. Continuous improvement through professionalism and teamwork.

It shall be the duty of every employee of the PSE/administrative ministry to continuously upgrade his/her skills and knowledge, strive for creativity and innovation and nurture the values of team working and harmony. He/she should promote and exhibit public and private conduct in keeping with the appropriate behaviour and standards of excellence and integrity. He/she should support the juniors in the latter's efforts to resist wrong or illegal directives and in abiding by the Code of Ethics. At the same time, they should reward good work and punish any dereliction of duty and obligations based on objective and transparent criteria.

The code of conduct has remained a dead letter because the government took the convenient stand that this code of conduct was beyond the purview of the committee's terms of reference, which related only to the issue of the guidelines. After all, the guidelines were being reviewed because there was need for operational efficiency to be introduced. If we want our public sector to develop a better work culture, such a code of conduct is absolutely necessary.

The issue of corporate governance is being very much discussed these days. Corporate governance shapes the organisational work culture. It has become a buzzword especially in the context of globalization. The dramatic collapse of the South East Asian economies in 1997 perhaps, highlighted the need for corporate governance. In India particularly in the decade of liberalisation, we have been witnessing a large number of scams in the financial sector, which indicates very poor corporate governance.

The basic question we face is whether the post-reform corruption scenario in India has changed. Some offices, which had a key role to play in the control regime, have been abolished. We can safely say that so far as these offices are concerned, corruption has ceased to exist because the offices themselves no longer exist. The DGTD and the Controller of Capital Issues come to mind. However, as regards the other offices, allegations of corruption seem to take a different dimension.

One of the consequences of the post reform scenario is the focus of government on the coming up of policies, which relate to disinvestment of government investment in public enterprises and also giving up monopoly of government services like telecommunications. It is in such process changes, where allegations of corruption have been made.

Economic reforms represent a conscious shift from socialism to capitalism. Nevertheless, what we have, as C Ram Manohar Reddy pointed out in an article in *The Hindu*, is corrupted capitalism. According to him, in the aftermath of the East Asian Crisis of 1997, crony capitalism was blamed for the failure. What is beginning to mature in India is a different and a larger phenomenon that lends to another but less attractive alternative term, corrupted capitalism. In this uniquely Indian phenomenon, which unlike in China, Indonesia and Russia is blessed by the established democratic process, political corruption and market capitalism thrive by feeding each other. Capitalism grows not through competition in the market but by excluding competition through large-scale corruption of the policy makers and administrators in high places. This is what changing the rules of the game in the new sector. Likewise, the stunting of the public sector, the sale of state assets to preferred buyers and the provision of subsidized finance to favoured enterprises all for a price have been giving a new meaning to capitalism, Indian style in the 21st century.

A look at the role of corporate governance and public governance in shaping the work culture will not be out of place here. Public governance describes the way a country is governed. Every country has a system of governance operated through a framework of laws. For example, India is a Democracy. According to the Constitution, there are three main pillars of governance. These are: (i) the legislature, which makes the laws, (ii) the judiciary, which interprets the laws, and (iii) the executive – consists of both the permanent bureaucracy and the elected political executives – which enforces the laws.

Corporate governance, on the other hand, refers to the value framework, the ethical framework and the moral framework under which a business enterprise takes its decisions. Till the collapse of the South East Asian economies in 1997, corporate governance was not a buzzword. Corporate management was all the rage. Good corporate management means using the physical resources, financial resources and human resources to get the best results in terms of profitability, productivity, market capitalisation and so on. Corporate governance became an issue because the South East and Asian economies which were booming and some of the countries were called 'tiger economies', suddenly faced a setback starting with the melt down of the currency in Thailand followed by Indonesia, Malaysia and South Korea. The main cause for this was identified as crony capitalism and lack of corporate governance in the financial sector.

The issue of corporate governance has become increasingly important especially in the context of globalization. Globalization involves the movement of four elements of the economy across national border. These are:

- Physical capital in terms of plant and machinery
- Financial capital in terms of money invested in emerging market
- Technology
- Labour

This investment of financial capital in emerging markets calls for the ethical dimension apart from the purely efficient dimension in enterprises. Investors globally want to be sure that the enterprises in which they are investing not only run competently but also ethically.

Hence, the focus on corporate governance.

At this stage, it will be worthwhile to have a look at what Kenneth Blanchard and Norman Vincent Peale say in their book *The Power of Ethical Management*, about the concept of ethics in the business context. The authors have articulated what has been called the three way ethical check. The ethical check questions are as follows:

- Is it legal? Will it be violating either civil or company policy?
- Is it balanced? Is it fair to all concerned in the short-term as well as in long-term? Does it promote win-win relationship?
- How will it make me feel about myself? Will it make me proud? Would I feel good if my decision was published in the newspaper? Would I feel good if my family knew about it?

These ethical check questions provide a good reference point to decide on ethical issues, which arise in the contemporary Indian management. The authors have also provided the following five principles of ethical power for organisations.

Purpose: The mission of our organisation is communicated from the top. Our organisation is guided by the values, hopes and a vision that helps us to determine what is acceptable and unacceptable behaviour.

Pride: We feel proud of ourselves and of our organisation. We know that when we feel this way, we can resist temptations to behave unethically.

Patience: We believe that holding to our ethical values will lead us to success in the long-term. This involves maintaining a balance between obtaining results and caring how we achieve these results.

Persistence: We have commitment to live by ethical principles. We are committed to our commitment. We make sure our actions are consistent with our purpose.

Perspective: Our managers and employees take time to pause and reflect, take stock of where we are, evaluate where we are going and determine how we are going to get there.

I think, the experience of excellent companies and visionary companies shows that in the ultimate analysis, both the values and the ethics do matter. In the book *In Search of Excellence*, Peters and Waterman, the authors pointed out how one of the characteristics of excellent companies was "hands on value driven". While the managements are hands on and decide on day-to-day matters, they have also not forgotten their values. Similarly in their book *Built to Last*, Jerry Porras and Jim Collins pointed out that ultimately the visionary companies, the companies which lasted much longer 50 to 100 years compared to the normal lifetime of 15-20 years of the standard companies, one main characteristic was their core values which irretrievably linked with their company practices and procedures. In other words, the long-term basis for success appears to be internalisation of ethical values and ensuring that these are woven irretrievably into the company policies and practices.

We may now examine the nexus between public governance and corporate governance. Corporate governance depends upon two factors namely, the attitude and the values cherished by the management of the business enterprise and the external environment in which the business operates. The external environment in which the business operates would include the legislation relating to the functioning of business enterprises, covering the entire spectrum from registration of companies, their structure, and settlement of disputes, laws relating to the capital market and punishment for bad practices like insider trading and so on.

Public governance on the other hand is broadly connected with the running of the government of a country and ensuring that the rule of law prevails. There has to be fairness and transparency in the system of justice. If the public governance is not conducted on healthy lines and if there is corruption, then there is no fairness. Corruption, as the World Bank defines, is the use of public office for private gain. If the public servants are going to exploit their position for private gain then the quality of public governance suffers. If the quality of public governance suffers, corporate governance then becomes more difficult. It can definitely be said that the management of an enterprise can still be ethical and try to maintain its internal corporate governance. If the environment in which it operates is not clean, then it may not be successful or even if successful, it will find it very difficult to operate.

The issue of corporate governance has its own dynamism. This will be obvious from the fact that, thanks to globalization there are many multinational companies that have their own internal sense of values. One of the most vocal and articulate leaders in business has been Jack Welch. This is what Jack Welch says about integrity:

> "Excellence and competitiveness are totally compatible with honesty and integrity. The A student, the four-minute miler, the high-jump record holder – all strong winners – can achieve those results without resorting to cheating. People who cheat are simply weak."
>
> "A professor gave a hypothetical case to his business school students. He said, if you were running a business for a larger company and were about to book a $50 million order, but to do so, you had to deposit $1 million in a Swiss bank account to an agent, would you do it? Approximately 40-50% said

they would. I was shocked! Shocked! I told the students someone was teaching them the wrong things. This was not one of those cases where you had to interpret the law, this was a simple bribery case."

"In the end, your integrity is all you've got."

(*Jack Welch Speaks*, John Wiley & Sons Inc., New York, pp 35-36)

In India, there have been excellent business leaders like Mr Narayana Murthy of Infosys and Mr Azim Premji of Wipro who have built world-class enterprises. Both these business leaders are also placing a very high value on the principles of business ethics. What Mr Narayana Murthy said in a talk to the students at Wharton School of Business is worth noting:

> "The Infosys value system can be captured in one line – the softest pillow is a clear conscience. A company's value system is the guiding light in its hours of darkness. It builds confidence, peace of mind, and enhances enthusiasm during tough times. The importance you attach to your value system is reflected in the cost you are willing to incur for your beliefs and convictions. At Infosys, we have stood firm whenever our value system was tested. We knew that talking short cuts that compromise our values would be detrimental.
>
> One of my strongest beliefs is that corporations have an important duty to contribute to society. No corporation can sustain its progress unless it makes a difference to its context".

Public governance can also bring in greater discipline for better corporate governance by nurturing the appropriate external environment in which an enterprise operates. Right now in India, we have the Stock Exchange Board of India (SEBI), to regulate the stock exchanges. We also have the Companies Act for governing the operations of business enterprises. Based on the experience gained, the rules and regulations relating to business are being constantly revised. In this year, there have been a series of scams relating to the stock exchange and a Joint Parliamentary Committee is going into this. Based on the past experience, corrections have to be made.

The increasing globalization and removal of trade barriers, thanks to agencies like WTO, is also adding one more dimension to better corporate governance through introduction of uniform standards. For instance, in India we are examining the issue of GAAP – Adoption of Generally Accepted Accounting Principles. Perhaps acceptance of such standards will bring in course of time, a uniform set of practices for corporate governance.

The thrust for greater uniform standards has got a boost, thanks to the increasing use of information technology. The Internet and the increasing use of information technology are opening new horizons for business. Simultaneously, the potential for cyber crimes, which can be committed internationally is also being realised. To tackle cyber crimes, it becomes necessary to have international standards and international cooperation. This is also going to contribute significantly to evolution of systems and procedures, principles and regulation to see that healthy corporate governance practices prevail. One can hope that this, in turn, will have an impact on the public governance in different countries and this may happen to be a healthy impact.

Development of organisations like the WTO is also another step that is trying to bring in a set of uniform standards and approaches so far as treatment of the behaviour of business enterprises is concerned. To the extent, common standards evolve, either due to the operational needs, dictating adoption of uniform standards or the necessity for fighting common enemies like cyber crime promoting cooperation or the legal commitment entered into internationally by members of the organisation, WTO all point to a state where the public governance and the corporate governance are becoming increasingly inter-related. To the extent a country is more globally and closely linked with the global economy, this inter-connection also becomes stronger.

The judicial system has an important role to play ultimately in ensuring better public governance and corporate governance. There may be so many regulations, rules and procedures but ultimately when disputes arise, they have to be settled in a court of law. There could be, of course, alternative dispute resolution mechanism like arbitration but in countries like India it is the judiciary that has to step in and ensure that healthy practices prevail. The Information Technology Act, 2000 of India has the following interesting position regarding its jurisdiction:

> "Act to apply for offence or contravention committed outside India
>
> 1. Subject to the provisions of sub-section (2), the provisions of this Act shall apply also to any offence or contravention committed outside India by any person irrespective of his nationality.
> 2. For the purposes of sub-section (1) this Act shall apply to an offence or contravention committed outside India by any person if the act or conduct constituting the offence or contravention involves a computer, computer system or computer network located in India."

We have already seen how the basic framework of the Constitution in India depends on the three main pillars namely, judiciary, executive and the legislature. The basic structure of the Constitution is not to be tampered with. One of the areas that the judiciary has been very active is in pointing out whether any legislation that is passed or practised, principles and laws enacted to test are in tune with the basic structure of the Constitution. This is an important provision and to that extent the judiciary is clean and effective. It can be a guarantee for better public governance and better corporate governance.

Ultimately, both better public governance and corporate governance are an exercise in continuous learning. We learn from experience and try to avoid the mistakes. But when it comes to new types of crimes or new types of frauds, it is better to remember what Oscar Wilde said: "The thief is an artist and the policeman is only a critic". It does not mean that we should stop devising systems, which will be as effective as possible in ensuring that the better governance prevails. Ultimately, there are two elements for better governance. The first is the individual values of the people who are in running the enterprise and the second is the external framework of rules, regulations, organisations and systems. Perhaps a continuous effort at sensitising the people about the need for good corporate governance is required because, however, good may be the operational systems and procedures, if the people who are operating systems do not have the right values, we will not succeed.

(xi) OVERCOMING CULTURAL GRAVITY

There are many negative perceptions about the Indian work culture, which are based on common experience. The simplest and the most common is the Indian's approach to time management and punctuality. This may be because majority of us have not yet come out of Alvin Toffler's first wave of agriculture. We are a feudal society. Hence, we take a relaxed view of time. Perhaps, this is also a legacy of the permit licence raj. The experience of many businessmen and industrialists who want to do business with the government is that when the panjandrums of the babus give an appointment, they are rarely held on time. There may be exceptions to the rule. By and large, lack of punctuality is the rule. There is a psychological reason behind this. The permit licence raj gave a sense of empowerment to the decision-makers at the bureaucratic or the political level. Getting an appointment itself is many a time a problem. This provides an excellent opportunity for corruption.

It was Francis Bacon who observed that free accessibility is the remedy to corruption. I have found from my experience that if one is accessible freely, this element of corruption can at least be eliminated. Throughout my career, I practised the principle of being accessible to all and getting appointment to meet me should not be a problem. But this is not a general trait. This lack of accessibility has also led to a culture where a person in authority proves his importance by being not readily accessible and if accessible and appointment given, not keeping up the appointment in time. In India, my experience is that status is inversely proportional to punctuality.

This perhaps is a reflection of the feudal culture, which prevails in many Indian organisations. It has been my experience, many a time, that when programmes are organised and I am invited as a Chief Guest, the organisers tell me to come 15-30 minutes late because at the appointed time, the people may not turn up. IST has been jocularly called not as Indian Standard Time but as the Indian Stretchable Time.

This attitude to time management also gets translated into an attitude for neglecting productivity. Time, perhaps, is the most valuable resource especially in this era of global competition. Time-based competition is the basis for success in the market place today. It is here that we find a combination of feudal culture and the legacy of the permit licence raj that have created an environment in which the Indian business finds it difficult to emerge as globally competitive. In one of the world competitiveness index studies out of the 53 countries studied, India ranks at 50. Part of this lack of competitiveness is due to the environment in which the Indian industry has to function. Corruption is an important aspect of the business environment. This has been explored in another chapter separately. Suffice to say at this point in the context of competitiveness, according to a study made by the Exim Bank, transaction costs add 5-25% to the cost of Indian goods and services, thereby making them less competitive on the global front.

The lack of concern for productivity is a more serious problem of the Indian work culture. This has never been a point of national focus. It is high time that the Indian Government and India as a country focus on this aspect of productivity. India is one of the countries with very low levels of productivity, practically in every sector. I wonder whether there is a prize for being the most wasteful country, we will, walk away with the prize. Wherever we look, we find there is enormous level of wastage and low productivity.

Let us start with our population. We are more than a billion strong. When it comes to economic development, if there is one key factor that is helpful, it is education. The South East Asian miracle of the '80s was attributed to education as the main factor. When it comes to employment, the educated earn much more than the uneducated, the skilled workers more than the unskilled workers. The more the income level, the more the purchasing power and the virtuous cycle of growth comes into operation. We are a country in which at least 40% of the population is still illiterate. We can look back and say that, perhaps, we have scored much more than many countries in terms of progress. Nevertheless, at the beginning of the 21st century, we have to compare ourselves with China, which is comparable in size. China perhaps has more than 80% literacy rate compared to India's 62%. In an age of knowledge economy, we carry the world's largest population of illiterates. We can see what a drag on productivity and progress thereof.

Our agricultural production probably is still stagnating. Again, when we compare with China, our productivity is much less than that country. Perhaps our productivity is about 1/3rd of the best productivity standards in agriculture. It is not only that we are not producing enough. Even whatever is produced is not stored and distributed effectively. Take for example, foodgrains or vegetables. We lose 10% of foodgrain or 22% of vegetables due to lack of effective storage. If we take the power sector, the distribution losses may be of the order of 22%. It is worth recalling that in Japan during the first oil shock in 1973, the focus was on energy conservation and they were able to save 33% of electricity without losing on GNP. On the other hand, if we look at our Indian industry, I am sure, for $1,000 GDP, our energy consumption level must be among the highest.

Productivity involves making optimum use of physical, financial and human resources and time. Perhaps, the most important resource in these days of knowledge economy and the global village is time. When we come to time, we find that perhaps we are again among the great wasters of this precious resource. Our bureaucratic systems are so slow moving and many have commented on the delays in our administrative system. Our judicial system is also enormously time consuming. A healthy debate about the judicial system is stifled by the fact that under the Contempt of Court Act, 1971, truth is no defence against the judiciary. Any serious person who is making a comment about judiciary, runs the risk of being held up for contempt of court. Nevertheless, in the course of this analysis, we will look at the judicial system also and see what can be done to improve the productivity of the judicial system in terms of removing the enormous delays that now take place therein. The Harshad Mehta scam took place around the same time as the scam in Singapore where Leeson of Baring's activities made the company go bankrupt. Leeson was punished within two years and had even finished his imprisonment in jail. It took seven years for first punishment in the case of Harshad Mehta to be pronounced. This, of course, is subject to further appeal. In the meanwhile, tragically, Harshad Mehta himself passed away.

The enormous delay in the judicial system affects productivity in one sense. For example, Justice Verma, former Chief Justice of the Supreme Court, in a talk on judicial delays mentioned that many a time, it is the businessmen and industrialists who do not want to pay government dues, for litigation. The cases drag for a long time. The delays in our judicial system ensures that litigation is a good investment for our Indian industry and business because even by way of interest, they will save much more than whatever the dues they would have otherwise paid to the government in time. On the other hand, if we see the reverse side of the coin, if the government were to get these resources and taxes paid in time, government will have adequate resources for keeping up investment for economic development. The delay in the judicial system, therefore, starts a vicious cycle, which goes to continuously reduce the productivity of our country stifling economic growth.

The legislature is an important part of our governance system. The sheer lack of productivity in our legislatures in terms of legislation enacted or contribution to effective governance is well-known. There have been reports from time to time about how little of the time of the legislature is spent on legislative or constructive work vis-a-vis that spent on sensational headlines of the day. The focus seems to be more on scoring political points which may be very much necessary in a democracy. Better governance of the country will be enhanced by effective and improved productivity in every sector of governance – judiciary, executive and legislature. We find that we have miles to go in this direction.

Unfortunately, the fact that productivity is a central issue which can be critical for better governance and better progress of the country has not caught the attention or the imagination of the nation. Other nations recognised the significance of productivity and have progressed. I have already mentioned that in 1973, Japan facing the oil shock by focusing on improving productivity of the power sector, both in terms of improved practices, energy audit etc, and in terms of legislation so that they could maintain the same GDP by consuming even 30% less energy. In 1989, I was in the United States and this was the time when Ronald Reagan was the President. The whole nation was worried about facing the Japanese competition and the national attention was on productivity. There were reports on the issue of productivity and, what is more, follow-up was taken which is reflected in the fact that in the 90s, the productivity of the American industry was better than that of Japan. Japan on the other hand, shifted into a long period of economic stagnation in the nineties.

In our country, it is high time that we focused on productivity. In this effort, the National Productivity Council should take the lead and start the process of sensitising the people at large about the need and significance for productivity.

I wonder whether some of the techniques adopted by the CVC, can be reproduced in the context of productivity. The CVC website at least brought a lot of awareness in the society about corruption at high levels and action being taken by the CVC. In fact, CVC became an agency that has been recognised. The number of applications received by the CVC has gone up by three times in the last years. The CVC then has focused on the system changes like the Prime Minister's directive to the Lt Governor of Delhi to abolish the licensing system for hawkers and cycle-rickshaws, the change in the policy of the Government of India regarding authorising agents or middlemen in defence procurement systems and computerisation of the banks up to the extent of 74% of their business by end of 2001. These are examples of system changes that have been brought, which may have an impact on checking corruption in the specific areas.

Can the National Productivity Council (NPC) think in terms of such a focused activity so that every year, the NPC can measure its contribution in quantitative terms? For example, the CVC costs ₹4 crore to the Government and because of the activities of the Chief Technical Examiner (CTE's) Organisation of the CVC alone, in the year 2000-2001, ₹8.75 crore was recovered and in the year 2001-2002, the recovery was more than ₹10 crore. In other words, the CVC has emerged not as a cost centre but as a profit centre for the country. The first question I would like to raise is, can NPC become a profit centre for the country, particularly, for the Government of India?

We can then take up this large area of governance and particularly the functioning of government. The year 2001 was declared as the 'year of e-governance'. I do not know the net result achieved but I have been seeing that initiatives have been taken at different levels. Today, we can think in terms of a cafeteria approach to see that information technology is used to improve productivity. In the west, particularly in the United

States, there has been the so-called productivity paradox of the information technology. Alan Greenspan said that because of the application of IT, America's inflation level is at least 1% less than what it would have been. Can we also focus on IT as an instrument for improving productivity of the functioning of the government at all levels and incidentally improving governance too? Improvement in the quality of governance would mean checking corruption as well. In this context, therefore, it is worth looking at the cafeteria approach to IT. So far, Governments at the Centre and States have worked on paper-based systems. E-governance means that government must be able to use IT extensively in all their functions.

The application of IT in government has been going on at different organisations for more than two decades. It was Rajiv Gandhi who focused attention on the use of computers, which started the process of application of IT in government. The tremendous success of India in software exports has sharply focused attention of even the political leadership on the potential of information technology. The Prime Minister has observed that IT will be India's tomorrow.

Between the grand vision of e-governance and its actual realisation, there is a big shadow. Generally, for implementing any policy, financial constraints are a major problem. Fortunately, the problem of the funds needed for investing in IT systems has been overcome by the broad acceptance of the policy of a certain percentage, say 3% of the budget being reserved for investment in IT systems. It is actually the government culture of secretary, seniority and corruption, which is coming in the way of rapid realisation of e-governance. There is also the problem of transition of any system, which is based on paper to the application of IT. Those who have knowledge of IT, do not have the domain knowledge of the organisation and those who have the domain knowledge, do not have the requisite knowledge of IT.

If we look at the current exercises going on about e-governance, we find that the progress is uneven. In this context, perhaps a cafeteria approach may be the most effective strategy to follow. We need not try to re-engineer the entire government systems and achieve the total replacement of the system of governance by application of IT. Depending upon the initiative of the champions in every organisation, we may try the different recipes which seem to be working in our country.

The basic strategy for achieving e-governance, therefore is obvious. There are strong cultural factors of resistance to e-governance but the hope is in the younger officers who are technology-friendly. A cafeteria approach by adopting a model that has been successful may be better rather than trying to achieve what has been done in Andhra Pradesh, which is perhaps the most advanced, so far as the application of IT is concerned. Mao Tse-tung said that banquet can be eaten only mouthful by mouthful. His words are very relevant today.

The third area in which we should focus is the area of corruption. In the age of the knowledge economy, it is necessary that India must be able to exploit its full human potential. The money we spend on R&D should ultimately be translated in terms of economic development. This will mean that we will have to tackle the issue of R&D comprehensively.

The problem, which we face today, is difficulty of getting bright creative youth for R&D. Who will come for R&D? The attractions available immediately for working for MNCs or private sector in the country or abroad are too tempting. We will face a severe manpower problem at the very fountain spring of technology, our R&D laboratories. These problems must be tackled by a package of solutions for development of technical manpower in India. The first is about the BSc science courses. I have two suggestions to make. The first is that we must make a computer course module a part of the input of every BSc course throughout the country, irrespective of the main course, be it chemistry, physics, geology or geography. This means everybody who comes out of the college would have been trained in computer science and IT. Today, while the need for the computer courses is being recognized, 25 years ago, the students after doing the 12th standard were going for learning typing. Today, they go for computer courses where they are forced to pay enormous fees by the mushrooming teaching shops, where the standards are also not uniform. Quite a few of them are holes in the wall operations. If computer science becomes a part of every student who gets a BSc degree you will find that the whole perception of the BSc course will change. More importantly, this country will have a vast number of students trained in computer science. An added advantage will be the domain knowledge of the different branches of science. We will thus be able to build a vast army of foot soldiers of technology in the emerging information age. We can thus provide for an explosive growth of IT that can take place in this country. What is more, the students will be saved from being exploited by many of the private teaching shops, which are charging very heavy fees. I am not wholly condemning the private companies. There are many good ones which are providing the manpower needed by our industry today. But when we think of a national strategy for scientific manpower, we should recognise that IT is going to be the key technology of the future. Even the political parties recognise this reality. The BJP's election manifesto for 1998 had a section on IT. The National Agenda for Governance mentions specifically IT as an area of priority.

The second suggestion I would like to make is that we should, like the National Science Foundation of USA, have a well-funded programme so that a bright student can think of taking science as a career and also become interested in R&D. This will tackle the problem about attracting bright youngsters in R&D as well as attracting bright faculty for teaching. The major problem is the problem of the bright students from the non-reserved communities losing the opportunity to learn technology. We have the formal education system of universities. We have private initiatives, private institutions which are almost run on commercial lines. We have in-company trainings. These three form the three streams of education today. I would suggest that we should have a fourth stream of education. This is the third idea. What I mean by the fourth stream is a stream of institutions set up by the industry to meet the specific needs of the industry. They must have full freedom in designing their curriculum, which will be up to date and as per the market demand. They can charge commercial rates of fees. But to enable the middle class and the poor students who may not be belonging to the reserved communities and who may like to take professional careers, banks and education trusts should come forward to give reasonable study loans. As these courses will be so industry-specific, once a person gets into these courses is bound to have an excellent well-paid career. The entire operation of running educational institutions will become a bankable proposition.

The fourth set of ideas deal with the third problem about creativity and encouragement of talent by IPRs. Without any further procrastinating, we should amend our patent act so that it is in tune with law in developed countries so that our patent has the same credibility as those in developed countries in the global market. Till this is done, I would suggest that we should at least improve the speed of giving patents. We must reduce the time taken for issuing a patent from the current six years to less than a year. Further, we must set up a venture capital fund of say ₹100 crore. Any promising technology by an Indian inventor must be assisted by this venture fund to take patents in the US and a dozen developed countries. It costs ₹5 lakh for a US patent and ₹50 lakh for the rest. In this way, Indian scientists and technocrats will be encouraged and we will have full IPRs protection. This will mean excellent returns in financial terms to the Indian scientist. This is one method of ultimately getting the right manpower.

Yet another problem is the issue of getting good faculty for teaching. The fifth set of ideas deal with these problems. I have already mentioned that if we can have something like the National Science Foundation and have programmes and funding schemes to encourage bright people to take the teaching career, it will be greatly helpful. Simultaneously, the fourth stream also will help in providing better faculty because the industry executives can be persuaded to come and teach in these institutions and on deputation. There should be a culture of the faculty from the education institutions going on deputation to industry get their financial rewards and also getting a hands on exposure to the industry. Such flexibility today is not possible in our present system. We will have to think of these innovative methods if we want to tackle the problems of scientific and technical manpower we are facing in the pragmatic manner.

How can this change be brought about? If, at the present pace of disposal, it is going to take 300 years to dispose off cases, the logical answer would be to enhance the infrastructure for judiciary covering all courts from the lowest to the highest by at least 150 times so that within a period of two years all cases will be disposed off. This number may appear to be mind-boggling. Where are the resources to come from?

The feudal culture has also led to a situation where managers may not openly come forward and express their views. In the Japanese culture, we have seen the importance of evolving a consensus. We do not know whether the Japanese managers openly express their views at least within their organisation. But so far as the Indian situation is concerned, the tendency may be to anticipate the wishes of the boss so much so that the situation as at the time of Alfred Solan in General Motors cannot arise in India. Solan consciously developed a culture of postponing of meeting to get difference of opinions developed but in India, this is very rare. Again, Jack Welch has highlighted how in the work-outs he went out of the way to make every person in his organisation speak out. In the Indian environment due to this feudal culture, expressing free opinions may be more an exception than a rule.

Another aspect of the Indian work culture is the lack of concern for physical cleanliness of the work environment. Many government organisations and public places are dirty. Here again, the feudal culture is reflected in the fact that the room of the boss and the top people would be much cleaner and more elegantly maintained than the rest of the organisation. This also has led to the concept of what SS Gill called our becoming "a nation of queue jumpers". The VIP culture is very much evident definitely in the government organisations and perhaps in the private sector too. Special privileges and in recent times, security has become a badge of status. Sometime, it was said that nearly 20-30% of the Delhi Police were involved in VIP security duty. They were not aiming high. Perhaps, years of permit licence raj had resulted in a 'Bonsai' mindset among our leaders and captain of industry.

I wonder whether the aspiration deficit is not only characteristic of the Indian companies but the nation as a whole. We are more than a billion strong nation. Nevertheless, in the comity of nations, China, which is of comparable size, seems to carry far more clout than India. China is accepted as emerging superpower. In fact, there is a view that the *raison d'être* of ASEAN is to contain the Chinese threat. Bill Clinton persuaded at the end of the Cold War that America should engage China. This perception also played a part in easing China's entry into the WTO. On the other hand, when it comes to India, we do not seem to be in the same class. Both Bill Clinton and Bill Gates may see India as an IT superpower but not in the military or strategic sense. The main reason for this situation is that when it comes to strategic matters in geopolitical terms, we are not able to convert our size to our advantage.

Take, for example the issue of defence and our capacity to defend ourselves with appropriate weapons. China is recognised as a nuclear power and is a member of the nuclear club much before we had our Pokhran blasts in 1974. After the second Pokhran blast in 1998, there was, for sometime a talk about India signing the CTBT. The pressure seems to have eased now as US itself did not sign the CTBT. While China, after its own nuclear tests, went ahead and emerged as an economic and a military power on its own in the superpower class, India seems to be still not realising its full potential. India seems to suffer from what I would call the Hanuman complex, before his celebrated leap to Lanka. He had a sense of diffidence and Jambavant had to tell him that he would be capable of crossing the ocean in one single leap. But then there is no Jambavant to tell India how to become a superpower in the military sense.

Soon after Independence, we adopted the policy of the permit licence raj. Though we set up a number of ordnance factories, we failed to develop a military industrial complex as in the United States. As a result, there are complaints that our ordnance factories have never developed a competitive edge. Many a time, we did not develop crucial defence equipments. We have a huge DRDO set up but we are also dependent on imports. So long as the Cold War lasted we were de facto in the Russian camp and our dependence on the Russian equipments is very high. The collapse of the Soviet Union has created a dangerous vacuum so far as the defence equipment sector is concerned. Throughout these 50 years, we never consciously allowed an Indian arms industry to develop. We could not even produce an effective pistol or an effective gun. On the other hand, countries like the United States, France, Britain and Germany, which were great powers before the Second World War had a tradition of developing the arms industry. When it comes to the economics of the arms industry, one important business reality is the compulsion and pressure for exports. The United States arms industry, perhaps, has to export 30% of its production to be financial viable. Probably, in France, the exports required may be to the extent of 60% of production. These countries, therefore, not only have a vigorous indigenous arms industry but are also competing in the global market by exporting of arms. Countries like Sweden, South Africa or Israel are also emerging as effective suppliers of arms.

On the other hand, in India, we never allowed the civil side to be actively involved in the arms production. We did not have a policy of exports of arms till recently. As a result, our system is dependent on critical imports. Along with imports come all the wheeling-dealing of middlemen and the scope for corruption. The net result is that instead of being superpower like China, which has a vigorous military industrial complex and which has been able to meet its arms requirements and also export arms to the Middle-East or Pakistan, for example, we are dependent on imports for our critical defence requirements.

Israel, which is a small country and which practically from day one, faced hostilities and fought three wars for existence in the last 50 years, has been able to develop a vigorous arms industry. It is true that the geo-political factors may be different but Israel must be given credit for developing its own strategic electronic industry and emerging as an effective supplier of equipment in that field. I wonder whether, in India, we can take a 50 year perspective and examine whether we can ever be self-reliant in arms and also become an arms exporting country so that we can match the other superpowers in the world at least by the year 2050. Unless such a long-range strategic thinking is done, what is likely to happen is that we will become a great importer of weapons and thereby encourage the arms industry in countries like Israel, South Africa and Sweden apart from France and the United States but will never be in a position to have a capacity to resist sanctions and denial regimes which may become increasingly important as we go along in the 21st century. Where there is no vision, people perish. Will we have a vision for developing a vigorous Indian arms industry, which will also become a new significant exporter of arms? We must build an India, which is not only an economic superpower but also a military superpower.

There is a reason why we must have become a nation with aspiration deficit. So long as the permit licence raj existed, what was focused was the domestic market and there were severe limitations on the capacities. It is only an exception like Reliance, which built up world scale capacity plants, whereas most other industries had to be satisfied with a culture of limited capacity. As a result, what was found was that the Indian industry was very small and pygmies by global standards and could not take on the competition. Added to that was a culture of conscious or unconscious anti-technology policies.

After Pokhran-II in 1998, science and technology for a brief time, came back on the political radar screen. Along with 'Jai Jawan-Jai Kisan', the then Prime Minister Atal Bihari Vajpayee has added a new slogan 'Jai Vigyan'. The development of technology can take place only if we are able to encourage scientific research and link it with industry. In fact, in the last 50 years, the only areas of technology where India has made breakthroughs and proven itself are strategic technologies like missile technology, atomic energy and space. These are technologies which we cannot buy or get easily from outside. We had to develop these technologies in the interests of national security. Necessary was literally the mother of invention in these areas of technology. However, when it comes to technologies, which are dominant and important in the world of business and industry, we have been content to take a back seat.

As I look back on the approach to technology we adopted in the past, I find a distinct two-pronged pattern. The first prong relates to sensitive and strategic technologies – atomic energy, space and missile – where Government provided adequate funds and scientists were relatively free to operate. They, in turn, produced technologies, which are operational and make us all proud. On the other hand, when it comes to industrial research and development, we followed either consciously or unconsciously an anti-technology policy. This was the second prong. In the context of ensuring that India emerges as an economic superpower in this age of technology, it is necessary that we correct our mistakes and take appropriate action.

The Patent Act generally is expected to provide a sense of assured return and profit to the inventor of the intellectual property. But our Patent Act, by providing, in the area of Pharmaceuticals for process technology patenting and not products, enabled our pharmaceutical industries to copy the molecules invested elsewhere and produce drugs cheaply. Perhaps, there can be a social justification that in a poor country, such a policy of legally permitting what in a stricter regime would be considered as stealing of intellectual property. Nevertheless, the long-term impact of that approach has been to devalue the worth of intellectual property for the Indian inventor. He did not get attractive returns as he would have got under a stricter intellectual property rights regime. Also, he did not enjoy the protection for a longer time.

The stunted growth of India in commercial technologies is due not only to the Patent Act but also policies followed by the government in other areas. For example, the set of policies regarding foreign exchange discouraged the inflow of technology and the development of indigenous industrial technology. There were strict limits of 3% and 5% on payment of royalties and the maximum 8% was permitted if there were exports. Restricting the royalty payments reduced the scope for flexibility for the Indian companies to get better technologies and upgrade the technological level of the industries. In fact, one of the worst conditions by which technological obsolescence was perpetuated for nearly four decades is the condition that there should be outright purchase of technology. This was again because of our perennial shortage of foreign exchange. Technology is like fish. It does not keep for a long time. In view of the financial returns under the patent regime prevailing in the developed countries, the newer technologies got better returns. When Government insisted that the Indian companies should go for outright purchase of technology, the Indian entrepreneurs were driven to buying only obsolete and third-rate technologies.

The problem about royalty and outright purchase of technologies could have been solved if we had adopted a liberal approach so far as foreign investment is concerned. Here again, because of FERA, the foreign equity was restricted to 40% and the foreign collaborator did not have interest in providing the latest technologies. The anti-technology bias in the FERA, as well as the foreign collaboration regime was further strengthened, by removing the incentive for domestic research under the permit licence regime where plant capacities were severely restricted. Thanks to high tariff falls, a seller's market was provided for the industry. This ensured that the Indian industry and entrepreneur did not have any incentive for innovation or go in for the latest technology because even with old matured technologies, he could still make a killing in the domestic market.

Coming to think of it, the perennial organisational problem in government is that different aspects of policies that affect a sector or an issue are handled in different departments and ministries. These departments and ministries have their own tunnel vision. Although inter-ministerial groups and efforts at coordination through machinery's like the Committee of Secretaries are used and as the overall anti-technology policy package of the permit licence raj still shows, the net effect of policies may be sub-optimal at best or counterproductive at worst. As we face the technology driven economy of the future, it is necessary for us to avoid this tunnel vision trap of departments.

The path to hell is paved with good intentions. Perhaps for each of the policies, which in practice turned out to be anti-technology, there might have been social and financial justifications like our perennial shortage of foreign exchange etc. But, now that we are entering a new era where India is expected to emerge as an IT superpower and take its rightful place in the comity of technologically advanced nations, should we not learn from our past mistakes? Apart from the amendment to the Indian Patent Act to bring it in tune with the TRIPS requirement, I think we will have to look at every policy especially relating to investments by foreign companies, joint ventures between Indian companies and foreign companies, as well as issues like royalty from the point of view of whether this would be in the long-term interest of India emerging as a technological power. A more liberal approach, which will create an environment by which India is able to build on technologies accessible from the rest of the world, is called for. In fact, we can make a beginning by identifying all the policy areas, which have a bearing on India developing indigenous technologies which will be world class and then follow a coherent approach. This will ensure that what we gain, for example under the Patent Act is not lost in the policies we adopt under the Companies Act, FERA, Income Tax Act and Customs Act.

As a result, therefore, when liberalisation was introduced in 1991, the Indian industry found that they could not compete globally because of having no world scale plants and the plants we had were technologically outdated. The liberalisation process gave an opportunity for overcoming this culture of building up global sized plants as well as accessing new technology.

However, when it comes to technology, we should develop a culture of being proud of Indian technology. Here again, we find that there is a tendency not to take pride in domestic technology. It is interesting that Sir Ashutosh Mukherjee, long before India became independent, realised the need for developing a sense of pride in our being Indians. He also realised the need for education as a tool for development.

Sir Ashutosh was one of the greatest sons of India. Deshbandhu Chittaranjan Das said in his tribute to Sir Ashutosh: "He was a great judge but his greatness was greater far greater than the greatness merely of a great judge. I doubt whether you can come across a greater educationalist than Sir Ashutosh, but here again, he was for greater than merely a great educationalist. His heart was with the nation. He was a great builder, to build the great Indian nation". Sir Ashutosh achieved distinction in many fields, particularly as a famous judge, an eminent and visionary Vice-Chancellor of Calcutta University and also a great mathematician. In fact, Sir CV Raman once lamented: "Bengal is gaining a brilliant judge and a great vice-chancellor but lost in Sir Ashutosh a still greater mathematician". As I was searching for a theme for paying homage to Sir Ashutosh in the form of a memorial lecture, I came across an interesting observation made by Purnendu

Kumar Banerjee in his book *Sir Ashutosh: Our Grandfather*. He narrates an encounter between Deshbandhu Chittaranjan Das and Sir Ashutosh.

> "Mr CR Das came to see him one morning. Instead of receiving CR Das in his office, he took CR Das upstairs for privacy and discussion. My grandfather's assistants told me about CR Das, I was as usual curious. I went upstairs and they were having serious discussions. When my grandfather saw me, he called me (interrupting their discussion) to introduce me to CR Das. Das asked me what I wanted to be when I grew up. I knew my grandfather was a great lawyer, I was told earlier that CR Das was also a great lawyer and a well-known nationalist; so in reply I told him that I wanted to be a lawyer. They both laughed. That night I asked my grandfather as to what was that important meeting he had with CR Das. He explained that both he and CR Das were determined to make India free, strong and great. He believed that it should be done through the education of the people. Education was the foundation of freedom while CR Das believed through public agitation and popular boycott of the British Government. It was said later that CR Das and my grandfather agreed that my grandfather should join politics, after his retirement, and seek election to the Legislature as the Leader of the new political party to be called "Independent Liberal".

As we look at the 21st century that lies ahead of us, we can draw inspiration from the life of Sir Ashutosh Mukherjee and in the areas where he distinguished himself to see how we can build a great India and make this century the Indian century. We got independence politically 67 years ago but we are still to become economically independent as a developed country. With a population of one billion and a rich tradition, India must be able to emerge as a great superpower in the 21st century and can be the Indian century. If we reflect deeply on the attitude and approach of Sir Ashutosh, we will find that we can evolve, inspired by him, a strategy which will be relevant in the 21st century and which will show us the way to make India regain its glory in a real sense.

The first requirement for achieving success is that we must regain our pride as Indians. Sir Ashutosh was proud of being an Indian. He took pride in the Indian dress and traditions. Purnendu Kumar Banerjee in his book mentioned above relates this interesting anecdote.

Lord Curzon extended an invitation to him to attend the Coronation Ceremony of King Edward VII in London. When Sir Ashutosh informed Lord Curzon that due to the disapproval of his mother, he was unable to accept Lord Curzon's invitation, Lord Curzon said, "Tell your mother that the Viceroy and Governor-General of India commands her son to go to England." Ashutosh replied, "Then I will tell the Viceroy and Governor-General that Ashutosh Mukherjee refuses to be commanded by any person except his mother, be he the Viceroy or be he somebody higher than him."

It was not only with Lord Curzon, the highest authority that Sir Ashutosh could assert his sense of pride as an Indian. In the same book, there are also two stories about how Sir Ashutosh wore the Indian dress with pride when we were still a colony and wearing a western dress was considered a sign of authority.

> "I was told about an interesting situation. My grandfather was then a member of Viceroy's Imperial – Legislative Council. In that connection, he was visiting Shimla. An 'Indian Sahib' who was a high official, heard about my grandfather's presence in Shimla and decided to call on him. He went and knocked on the door of the house where my grandfather was staying. As the servants were somewhere else, my grandfather went and opened the door. He was as usual dressed in his dhoti and long coat. The Indian Sahib not expecting my grandfather in 'native clothes', said, curtly ignoring my grandfather's 'Namaste', that he wanted to

> meet Dr Ashutosh Mukherjee. Whereupon my grandfather took him to the living (drawing) room, offered a chair to him, pulled another chair and sat down facing the Sahib, who, because of my grandfather's Bengali clothes took him as a domestic servant or assistant. When he realised his stupidity, he was so embarrassed that he took considerable time to recover his tongue to offer his apologies. My grandfather, of course, was enjoying the situation in silence only with a mischievous twinkle in his eyes!
>
> My grandfather's dress, like that of many other leaders in India, was one of the various manifestations of his ardent nationalism. On another occasion, he was visiting Mysore State to deliver the Convocation Address in the University there. My father Pramathnath and uncle Syama Prasad were with him. After the meetings, that particular evening, the Maharaja was hosting a reception in his palace, where he was invited. In the afternoon, a message was delivered that all guests attending the reception were required to wear western dress. He was upset and annoyed. He immediately ordered his special railway carriage to be ready as he decided to leave Mysore that evening. The news reached the Maharaja. He was angry and recommended that the 'overzealous official' be suitably reprimanded. He sent his minister to my grandfather to express regret and to extend a warm welcome to the reception that evening. My grandfather attended the reception, greeted the Maharaja with respect, but proudly dressed in his Bengali dress!"

When we read such incidents from the life of Sir Ashuṭosh Mukherjee, automatically we feel proud of being Indians. This sense of pride of Indians can also help us to take on the challenges of the emerging global scene and evolve a strategy so that India becomes an economic and military superpower.

At the time of Sir Ashutosh, India was not independent. He felt strongly that education was the route by which we should try to build our nation. His focus on education is particularly relevant because now we are living in, what has been called, the knowledge economy. We are in the age of information technology. Thanks to information technology, the world has become a global village. There have also been other developments of the world becoming a global market because of the tariff barriers coming down.

Sir Ashutosh focused on research and post-graduate education as he built the Calcutta University. As a great mathematician and educationist, Sir Ashutosh Mukherjee's focus was always on education and developing the human capital we have. In the age of technology, therefore, India must be able to take full advantage of the emerging scene. Our economy in these days is dominated by information technology. Information technology is nothing but the synthesis of computers and communication. Fortunately, in information technology, India seems to be in an advantageous position especially in software. This is because for generations, we Indians have been accustomed to abstract thinking. Mathematics, therefore, is one of the excellent examples of the reach of the Indian mind. India contributed to the world of mathematics – the concept of *'shunya'* or zero. We have also produced geniuses in mathematics like Ramanujam. Sir Ashutosh Mukherjee himself was a great mathematician and as Sir CV Raman bemoaned by Sir Ashutosh becoming a great judge and a great vice-chancellor: "probably India lost a great mathematician."

Dr Homi Bhabha was asked when he was planning for India's nuclear energy programme in the '50s, where will India find the nuclear engineers and technocrats. Dr Bhabha is reported to have replied: "Do not forget that for 5,000 years, what we Indians have done is to sit on our bottom and contemplate the infinite." Abstract thinking therefore, comes naturally to Indians and when India has its nuclear power programme or nuclear energy programme, it will not have to look for engineers and technocrats from abroad. The confidence of Dr Bhabha in the Indian brainpower and tradition has been fully vindicated not only by Pokhran blasts but also by the nuclear power programme, the missile programme, the space programme where Indian scientists have shown that even in spite of denial regimes and sanctions, India can master technology. In this context, it is worth noting a point made by Narendra Krishna Sinha in his biography of Sir Ashutosh. Sir Ashutosh's achievements as mathematician and his interest in science are well-known.

It is said that in 1919, Ernest Rutherford, famous for his atomic research, could not attend a meeting of experts which was to advise the British government on defence against German submarines. He was censured for his non-appearance. He retorted, "Talk softly please. I have been engaged in experiments which suggest that the atom can be artificially disintegrated. If it is true, it is of far greater importance than a war". Ashutosh Mukherjee could also speak in this strain that his nation-building activity in the University of Calcutta was perhaps more important than other forms of nationalistic activity.

In one of hearty tete-a-tetes with rising young men, he is said to have remarked, *"Ekso desro bachar age amader thakurdadara ki karto Jam's? Tara du pata Pharsi pa'rto ar kharam paye diye berto. Eito chilo sekale amader daur?"*

"Do you know what our fathers and grandfathers used to do a hundred or a hundred and fifty years ago? They used to read two pages of Persian and used to walk with wooden sandals. This was all that they did in those times." In his address at Mysore he said, "we cannot sit on the lovely snow capped peaks of the Himalayas absorbed in contemplation of our glorious past. We cannot waste precious time and strength in defence of theories and systems which however valuable in their own days, have been swept away by the irresistible avalanche of world-wide changes. We can live neither in nor by our defeated past and if we would live in the conquering future, we must dedicate our whole strength to shape its course ... let us raise an emphatic protest against all suicidal policy of isolation and stagnation." In higher teaching and research, he followed the western model."

It is a tragic fact that while education is the root for success, India still has about 40% of the population as illiterates. We must find some method of ensuring that we fight this disease of illiteracy effectively and make India totally literate as fast as possible. In this context, I would suggest that we should think of even declaring an education emergency.

We Indians are great in thinking analysis contemplation and debate. When it comes to action, we are nowhere. We will examine at some length this culture of action-shyness later. "The Indian administration is action-shy," said Paul Appleby, the expert engaged by Jawaharlal Nehru in the early fifties to study the functioning of our government. There is, however, an exception. If there is a crisis or an emergency, we act because there is no other alternative. The dramatic introduction of economic liberalization by the Narasimha Rao government is an example of the government acting fast in a crisis. Another example is what happened in 1975-77 when Indira Gandhi imposed emergency. Suddenly, the government babus came to the office on time, trains became punctual and railway wagons were available. The Central Government also resorts to emergency under Article 356 when President's rule has to be introduced in a state. We have also resorted to emergency recruitment to the army, the IAS and other services. I recall one of my friend's commenting about such an emergency recruit, "My god! It must have been hell of an emergency if Mr so and so was to be recruited!"

In their report on "Human development in South Asia in 1998", Dr Mehboob ul Haq and Ms Khadija Haq highlighted the pathetic condition of literacy in South Asia. Statistics reveal that in South Asia, one in two adults is illiterate and one in three primary stage children is not attending school. With the adult literacy at only 36% lowest in the world, South Asia is entering the 21st century with 243 million illiterate women who represent two-thirds of the total adult female population. India has the dubious distinction of having the world's largest illiterate population of 424 million. We will need to enrol an additional 44 million in school to achieve universal primary education in the next five years. The report suggests declaring an education emergency in the sub continent.

Desperate situations call for desperate remedies. So far we have been tackling the problem of education only through the beaten track of setting up committees and commissions. These operate leisurely and the processing of the recommendations is a slow process. Education is low in the pecking order so far as the finances are concerned. We hardly spend 3% of the plan funds on education as against at least 6%, which is expected. For the IAS officers, education is not a glamour sector. I know officers who have been posted in the education department as a form of punishment.

Can we think of a new approach? We can use the concept of emergency to solve our problems on the educational front as we are perennially short of funds. The emergency concept will not strain our financial resources but still achieve our goal of improvement in education right across the spectrum from primary education to higher education. We must declare an education emergency and implement the following strategy:

The key element of the emergency strategy is to allow experimentation in the education system. Unfortunately as the government supports the entire budget of educational institutions, there are rigid rules about all aspects of educational administration starting with the recruitment. We have the social obligation of reservation in the recruitment of teachers. We have single teacher schools in villages where the teachers may not be present at all or even if they are present, they may not be teaching.

On the strength of the declaration of education emergency, we may fully authorize pilot schemes, irrespective of the rules and regulations governing recruitment. The local authorities, be it the collector or the assistant collector or the district education officer or the local panchayat, must be permitted to experiment with recruitment on a contract basis of teachers who can teach. The funds under the various programmes like the IRDP, Prime Minister's Rozgar Yojana, Jawahar Rozgar Yojana can be diverted as well for employing such teachers and paying their salaries.

In higher education, I understand that because of reservations, many a time, large number of posts are vacant even though teachers from the non-reserved communities are available. Why not under the education emergency authorise the authorities of the educational institutions to recruit against these vacancies on a contract basis teachers who are available so that we do not have the pathetic situation of posts not being filled and as a result, the quality of education suffering?

Another idea under the education emergency should be to remove the concept of retirement age of teachers at least in key areas where we are not getting enough teachers. In the case of higher education, this may include specialised subjects where teachers are not available. In primary or secondary education, the non-availability of the teachers may relate to remote locations where fully qualified teachers are not available or unwilling to serve. So why not employ retired teachers who are willing to fill in such slots and carry on?

One factor, which affects the quality of education particularly at higher level, is the syllabus. Under the education emergency, the institutions may be permitted to experiment with new subjects and have them included for credits in degrees or diplomas. This will give a direct benefit to the students in terms of getting suitable jobs. Perhaps industries, which are the employers, may be able to suggest the content of the syllabus. These new and modified subjects must be given full recognition as regularly approved subjects so that the career prospects of the students are not affected. It is a sad and surprising fact that even though so much noise is made about computer education, in most of our secondary education systems, computer science is not a subject, which carries credit for being considered for admission in the twelfth standard. The same is true for admission from twelfth standard to the degree courses because computer science is not a subject in the 12th standard duly approved by the educational authorities. Under the education emergency, this defect must be rectified.

Another aspect of the education emergency must be to employ massively the unemployed youth to produce the education materials in computer readable form as well as CD ROM and videotapes using the funds now being spent for rural development programmes and the Rozgar Yojanas. This will ensure that the quality of education right from the primary and secondary level can be substantially enhanced. It will be ideal to have computers in every school so that with CD ROM and videotapes, uniformly rich multimedia CD ROM libraries in the local languages can supplement the library books. This, if undertaken on a massive scale in the next two or three years, will provide a paradigm shift for the better in our education.

The very idea of emergency means that action must be the watchword. Incidentally, in their classic management book *In Search of Excellence*, Peters and Waterman identified "bias for action" as the first characteristic of excellent companies. The drill must be not "aim already and shoot" but "ready shoot and aim".

Yet another aspect about the Indian work culture that has been commented upon by some observers is that we lack what has been called a killer instinct. Countries like Japan perhaps could synergise their effort between government and industry and take on the competition and grab market share. Such alignment hardly takes place in India. The only exception has perhaps been the software industry where the Indian success shows that if there is alignment and synergy between the policy makers in government and the industry, India can be globally competitive.

One of the reasons for the lack of killer instinct may go deeper to the Hindu sense of tolerance. As I have mentioned earlier it is this tolerance, which makes us put up with shoddy goods and third rate services. It is the same reason why we do not go for quality do not bother about cleanliness of environment or develop a sense of national pride. We can hope that with the economic liberalisation policies being introduced, this culture may change. This is because out of necessity, the Indian industry will have to develop competitiveness and the Indian mindset will have to change. As we have seen in the case of software industry, the mindset can change if right from the beginning, the environment in which the Indian industry has to compete is a global one.

There is, however one aspect about the various negative perceptions about the Indian work culture. They are all curable. They can be remedied, in fact for each one of them there could be exceptions, which can be pointed out. This only shows that given the right type of leadership in an enterprise, there traditional negative aspects of the Indian work culture can be overcome. But then what is the reason for our present unsatisfactory work culture? One of the main reasons in India is a multi-speed country. India is a snake whose head is in the 21st century and the tail in the 17th century. Alvin Toffler talked about the three waves – the agricultural wave, the industrial wave and the post-industrial wave. In India, we find that all the three waves exist. Along with 3 each wave comes a certain mindset.

The mindset is an agricultural wave era where the rural and pastoral life is dominant, leading to certain values. Perhaps this leads to an easy attitude towards the value of time except being sensitive to the seasonal changes. When it comes to the industrial era, the culture of productivity could not grow in India because of the permit licence raj. Secondly, the feudal culture also prevailed because majority of the industry were in the private sector hands where the family concepts and family loyalties were probably as dominant and important as business strategy. This was also coincided with the activist role played by the government under the rigid philosophies from 1947. What has happened is that the organised labour, which constitutes hardly 8% of the total labour force in the country has been pampered. Therefore, there is a high degree of labour rigidity in the Indian work culture. This goes directly against any effort at bringing in a more effective reward and punishment system.

After the process of liberalisation, promises were made for example, by the Finance Minister in the budget speech for 2001-2002 that labour flexibility will be introduced by amending Part VB of the Industrial Disputes Act but this policy has not yet been implemented. Equally important had been a loss like the Contract Labour Abolition Act. According to this Act, any work of a perennial nature has to be performed only by labour on regular employment and not by contract labour. This led to a ridiculous situation like for example, in the Gujarat State Fertiliser Company at Baroda where 90 contract sweepers were regularised. Once they were made permanent, they stopped sweeping. The actual work of sweeping was done by hiring 60 contract labourers and the 90 permanent sweepers were supervising the work of the 60 contract sweepers. In recent times, the Supreme Court also has indicated that a more flexible approach can be adopted in a Contract Labour Abolition Act. But, as of now, the rigidity of the labour laws remain and this is perhaps one of the reasons why Indian industry cannot improve in productivity or competitiveness. Again where managements have shown more imagination and persuasion as well as perseverance, better work culture has been brought about. What I am saying applies to the general run of industries and enterprises in the country.

The general perceptions about the negative aspects of the Indian work culture we have seen above can be corrected and overcome by proper leadership in management if it is committed and has vision. Does this mean that the Indian work culture does not have any positive aspects? There are many positive aspects.

Perhaps the most important feature of the Indian work culture is the Indian spirit of entrepreneurship. The remarkable success is the Indian Diaspora is a standing proof of this fact. Indians can succeed if there is the right environment to permit entrepreneurship. Unfortunately, India has a feudal culture and a high regulatory approach to the economy which stifles the Indian spirit of enterprise. The four decades of the rigid approach has so conditioned the mindset of the babus and netas that one decade of liberalisation has not resulted in any major change. Let us hope in another decade at least it changes. It was rightly commented upon by Dr Manmohan Singh when he presented his first budget in 1991 ushering the reform process that he wanted the animal spirits of the Indian enterprise to be given full reign.

The second important feature of Indian work culture is that by and large, Indians work very hard. They have distinguished themselves by their hard work when they went abroad. Many Indians with hardly any resources have gone abroad, done well and risen to high positions in countries like the United States and elsewhere. This is because of the Indian culture of hard work.

Equally important I think is the third positive aspect of the Indian culture. This is the Indian ethos centred on the family spirit. For example, when the Gujaratis migrated from Uganda in the '60s and '70s to Britain they were able to emerge with very strong presence in the real estate business. The Gujaratis in America have so dominated the Motels that people think that Patel is the Gujarati word for motel. Behind every successful chain of motels, you will find the hard work of the entire family to achieve success, in India also at the level of artisans and small-scale industry the entire family pitches in to make their contribution. So it is not that Indians are not hard working. What has happened is that because of the overall environment of regulation and legislative systems especially relating to labour combined with the pampered organised labour is low in productivity. This combined with the overall culture of corruption has made Indian industry not competitive in the global market.

One of the reasons given for ineffectiveness of Indian organisation is that they operate on a culture of mistrust. The blame is placed on the legacy of the colonial rule which developed a series of checks and balances with the result that people became more audit minded and the scope for initiative was lost. Is it necessary even after 70 years of independence that we should be under the same situation? The series of scams have shown that perhaps while an element of trust is good in principle, we have also to ensure that there is a proper check maintained. We have explored the issue of corruption elsewhere in this book. There is need for monitoring and at the same time the challenge is to strike a balance, which will provide enough scope for initiative. This can perhaps be done by building systems which are transparent and where the leader of the organisation can operate on the principle of trust. I have generally trusted people and I have not been let down. If there is any breach of trust, prompt action must be taken so that the message goes that while people may be trusted, if they misuse the trust, punishment will be severe. Especially in the Indian context, the scope for corruption can be reduced if we do outsourcing of business and this itself can provide the competition which will be the basis on which efficiency will grow.

Another reason why we are not successful is because we do not focus on productivity. We have discussed how the problem of productivity can be overcome. A third aspect is that we do not celebrate success. We have explored in another chapter the success stories in India and the rules for success. Attempts must be made to replicate the success stories.

How does extreme concern for value of time gets translated into motivation for getting things done? From my experience, I found that my concern for the value of time has translated itself into a tendency to fix time limits even when no time limits or deadlines are imposed from outside.

Throughout my career, I had set for myself time limits and what is more, announced them openly. By making announcement of time limit, one's ego gets committed and it becomes a starting point for working back the steps to be taken so that the objectives could be achieved within the stated time limit. Even from my days as Collector, I adopted the practice of telling members of the public especially that their matters will be settled within a particular time limit of say, 10 days, 15 days or so, and then I used to follow it up. How does one follow the various time limits? If one is not true to his word, then one becomes a man of promises rather than a man of promise. This means that I have to keep the record of the various time limits given and the various requests so that they could be monitored effectively. Once I started using the Dictaphone from 1982 onwards, it became relatively easy for me because I used to record in real time the various decisions including the time limit decisions. I have always been fortunate to have stenographers and assistants who would keep records faithfully and remind me. This sort of self-monitoring comes from an extreme commitment towards the value of time. This technique also helped me twice to move my offices to new buildings resulting in increasing efficiency. The first was when I was Secretary, Department of Electronics and the second was when I was Central Vigilance Commissioner.

When I became Secretary, Department of Electronics in June 1990 the office of the Department of Electronics was located in eight different offices with the main office at Lok Nayak Bhavan. A separate building, named subsequently as Electronics Niketan was under construction. I pursued the matter of construction with the CPWD vigorously and visited frequently the construction site and reviewed the progress with the engineers of the CPWD. The building was ready in late 1991 and still there was a last minute hitch because the fire service clearances had not been given. A slum had come up in the area near to the building and the municipal authorities took the stand that there was no easy access for the fire tender in the case of fire. This was the reason for holding back the fire clearance certificate. I felt it was odd that ₹20 crore building was kept unoccupied because of this certificate. The irony was greater because we continued to work from the Lok Nayak Bhavan, which was also not considered safe from the fire hazards point of view as declared by a big red board at the entrance to my office! I, therefore, decided that we would shift to the Electronics Niketan on 31st January 1992 (31st January is my birthday). This fixing of the time limit was again one more example of my technique, which I have already mentioned. There was, however, one major difference in my fixing the time limit and my willingness to shift to the building. Traditionally, while moving into new buildings, in government organisations, the senior officials move when the new offices have been effectively 'colonised' by the junior officers who move in first and rough out the initial problems like lack of adequate telephone facilities, canteen facilities, transport facilities etc. In my case, I decided to shift myself first whether others followed or not. This, in the hierarchy ridden Government of India, had a good impact because it sent out the message right through the organisation that the Secretary was serious about shifting to the new building and the problem about the fire service would be overcome. One of my officers had a feeling that we may be violating the law by moving into a building, which was not properly certified. After all, Delhi is a city where everybody is violating the law. I felt that the balance of convenience in a situation where ₹20 crore building would remain unoccupied and thereby waste government investment and the risk of occupying the building by committing a technical irregularity especially when we are committing an irregularity in the Lok Nayak Bhavan itself was clearly in favour of moving into the new building. In fact, on 31st January 1992, I shifted to the new building and thereafter the entire department shifted.

The same technique I adopted when I became the Central Vigilance Commissioner. I found when I took over in September 1998 as CVC that the CVC was sitting in an old building called Jaisalmer House. The attraction of the building was that it was located in Lutyens' Delhi and shifting to the Satarkta Bhavan which was near the INA Market and next to DDA was considered as perhaps leaving the prestigious location. Between prestige and convenience, I adopted for convenience because the CVC was scattered in four buildings. The Chief Technical Examiner (CTE) organisation was in the Satarkta Bhavan occupying a small part of the building, the Secretary, CVC was sitting in Bikaner House and the Commissioner for Departmental Inquiries operated from Jamnagar House. Again I chose 31st January 1999 as the date for shifting. This time I had an energetic Additional Secretary, R Ashok who ensured that the shifting took place on time. The technique of fixing time limits and the carrying out the work is one secret of getting things done in India. Here the main motivation is that of the boss himself. When the boss himself is motivated, the entire organisation gets galvanised. Perhaps one of the big challenges I took which later on went waste was my experience in setting up the Gujarat Narmada Auto Company when I was MD, GNFC. We took the sick unit of Girnar Scooters set up by Gujarat Small Steel Industry Association from Ahmedabad to a location near GNFC Headquarters at Narmada Nagar in Bharuch. We chose Valia as the place. I had an excellent team of young engineers and a dedicated manager in the late Shri Kanakbhai Trivedi who was able to galvanise his team to come up with a 28,000 sq metre building for manufacturing 50,000 scooter plant in 144 days! Unfortunately, after I was transferred in April 1987, the project was mishandled and was ultimately closed down. The time limit within which the entire task was done was again an example of how fixing a time limit sometimes even nearly impossible is a method of getting things done.

In the book, *Managing Radical Change*, Sumantra Ghoshal, Gita Piramal and Christopher Bartlett have drawn attention to the case wherein Patalganga where the managers of Reliance company were able to bring a factory into operation in 11 days when experts predicted that it will take at least two months to complete the task. This only shows that strong motivation and commitment especially from the top provides a tremendous opportunity for compressing time and getting things done.

CHAPTER 6

INTERESTING ENCOUNTERS

(i) POLITICAL LEADERS

One important aspect of the life of a civil servant is the relation with the political leaders. In fact, politics is ultimately an exercise in grabbing power and using the power ideally for public good. In the case of the civil servant, the basic objective is to act as an important arm of the system of governance. It is therefore, natural that the civil servants and the political leaders have to work in close association in any system of governance.

Our Constitution, modelled on the British system, visualises the political leader to be the main instrument for governance reflecting as it does the collected will of the people. The political leaders in our system get elected directly to the Lok Sabha or the State Assembly or indirectly to the Rajya Sabha or the Legislative Councils where they exist at the State. As democracy is the government of the people, by the people and for the people, elected representatives of the people perhaps play the most crucial role in the governance of the country. But the Constitution also provides checks and balances as is well-known to any person familiar with our Indian Constitution and the system of governance.

The role of the civil servant as I see has been to work closely with the political leaders and help in ensuring the good governance of the country. I joined IAS in 1960 and finally stepped down from the office as Central Vigilance Commissioner in 2002. Out of these 42 years, I spent 24 years in Gujarat including three years as Officer on deputation to the Ministry of Commerce in the Government of India as Development Commissioner, Kandla Free Trade Zone, 1974-77 and the remaining 18 years in the Government of India, two years in Mumbai as the Additional Secretary, Department of Atomic Energy and the rest in Delhi, first as the Under-Secretary, 1965-68 in the Ministry of Home Affairs, Political Division and the last 12 years, 1990 to 2002 as Secretary to the Department of Electronics and Telecommunication as well as Chairman, Public Enterprises Selection Board and Central Vigilance Commissioner.

Looking back, I have had interesting experience with political leaders and I can see with the 20/20 hindsight of experience how my attitude towards political leaders has undergone a subtle change over the years. When I joined the IAS, I shared perhaps with many of my colleagues at that time, a sense of mild hostility, if not a sense of distance so far as the political leaders were concerned. I was greatly impressed by the legendary stories about the ICS, I have heard and how they were independent and could tell the political bosses where the line was drawn. There was an officer, Raghevender Kaiwar, of the ICS belonging to the old Madras Presidency who is supposed to have told the first Chief Minister of Tamil Nadu, Omandur Ramasamy Reddiar, the following:

> "Remember Mr Chief Minister, I can resign from the post, contest election and become the Chief Minister, but you can never become an ICS Officer."

Such stories were also reported about different officers of the ICS. One matter of value for me was basically ensuring the independence of the civil servant. It was much later I realised that the ICS represented the zenith of what has been called civil absolutism and a totally different mental attitude is needed for working in a democracy. I can see how green I was and wet behind the ears in those early days as a supernumerary Assistant Collector in Godhra and Panchmahal districts in Gujarat.

Supernumerary Assistant Collector is the designation given to an IAS officer under training. This was the old Bombay Presidency designation. Gujarat has just been formed on 1st May 1960 when I joined the IAS on 16th May 1960. I landed in Godhra in May 1961 and as the practice was that time, after one year's training at the National Academy of Administration, later on named as Lal Bahadur Shastri National Academy of Administration (LBSNAA). I was all keen to absorb experiences and learn the language and understand the basics of the district administration. After passing the Revenue Lower Standard examination after 6 months training, I was given charge of one taluka, Halol and the leading politician there was Dr Jeevan Lal. He was a medical doctor and I used to look upon him as a person who somehow was trying to challenge my authority. I was perhaps, too conscious of difference between permanent civil service and politician. I always therefore kept a distance and my reaction I can realise now were generally distant formal and with my lifelong experience today, I can say, I need not have been hostile. The leading political leaders of Panchmahal district were two great names, one was Dayabhai Nayak who was the son-in-law of Thakkar Bapa, a close associate of Mahatma Gandhi. Dayabhai Nayak himself had earned a great reputation for the pioneering work he did among tribals in Panchmahal.

The other was Maneklal Gandhi, from Kalol. He was more an avuncular and affectionate person. He has naturally commanded the respect of all people. Later on he became the Minister for Panchayats. For a long time the political leaders were all from the freedom movement, who were by and large honest and at the same time genuinely concerned with serving the people. On the other hand Dayabhai Nayak, somehow appeared to be a very stern person and a disciplinarian and almost a junior version of Morarjibhai Desai, who was well-known for his record as a very strict and firm officer, who was to resign from the post of Deputy Collector of the Bombay Presidency and who became the great leader of the freedom movement in Gujarat ultimately getting a title of 'Sarvochcha [supreme] Neta'. The rigid attitude taken by Morarjibhai on many issues made him a controversial figure and he had many devoted admirers. Naturally, there were also at the same time leaders who were hostile to him. Morarjibhai I used to admire for the sense of discipline he maintained in many matters and his firm commitment to the cause of prohibition. Incidentally, he was posted as deputy collector in Godhra when a communal riot took place. He was accused of being sympathetic to the Hindus and he had to resign from service. Many times he was ridiculed by his opponents particularly critics like Russi Karanjia, the editor of *Blitz* who called him as Moralji Desai. The auto urine therapy he advocated and which became very prominently discussed in the media when he became Prime Minister at the ripe age of 81 is well-known. One aspect of Morarjibhai which we always admired was his sense of extreme pragmatism. I remember in Tagore Hall in Ahmedabad, on the banks of Sabarmati, he had come to inaugurate a painting exhibition. He came on time and he said, this is an exhibition, where we have to see things and admire them and there is no need for a talk. He promptly went on to cut the tape and that was that. The Disciplinary manner he radiated in every moment of his was something which very few political leaders today are able to observe. Perhaps it was the reflection of the era in which he grew and it was something of his unique personality which made him a centre of endless stories and legends about him.

Coming back to my interactions with political leaders, when I became Collector of Sabarkantha, I was just 4 years into service and I have described elsewhere the first confrontation I had with political leaders. This was about a religious discourse or awasis which one Muslim preacher was to deliver in a village. My district Superintendent of Police KDSP Jha told me that Deobandis and Barelvis the two sects in the village may enter into clashes if the Muslim preacher was allowed to preach. Before I took over in 1964, my predecessor Mr CC Doctor had given an assurance that when he visits the second time after six months or so, he would be permitted to deliver his lecture and this was the commitment and the programme was fixed but, at the last moment, I had to invoke Section 144 in the village and hence the programme could not take place. The leader of the district panchayat at that time was Gopalbhai Patel and he directly contacted the then Home Minister Hitendrabhai Desai, who later on became the Chief Minister of the State. Jivrajbhai Mehta was the Chief Minister at that time and Gopalbhai's pressure worked and I got a call from the Home Minister, whether I could reconsider the proposal. I said, as a man on the spot, my judgement was the programme must not be permitted. Ultimately, that Muslim leader had to go without delivering the talk. This caused annoyance to Hitendrabhai. who mentioned about this when I participated in the Collector's conference held a few months later. Nevertheless, my action was further justified when after couple of months the same Muslim preacher went to another district, whereafter his talk there were clashes between Barelvis and Deobandis and Ankleswarya who was Principal Secretary to the Chief Minister at that time, told me that in retrospect Home Minister also felt that perhaps I had taken the right decision at the right time. Apart from this little incident with which I began my career as Collector, less than a year I spent in Sabarkantha as Collector, my relations with Gopalbhai Patel who was Jila Panchayat President were always on edge. I still remember, he once complained about the condition of availability of the foodgrains in the villages in a district supply meeting. I used to also travel extensively and I told him that I was also travelling in the villages and the situation was not as bad as he represented. Perhaps that annoyed him. This was the time when the panchayat raj has been introduced and Gujarat was one of the earliest states to introduce Panchayat Raj in 1963. This was not surprising because the famous Balvantrai Mehta Committee which articulated the concept of democratic decentralisation which was the precursor of the Panchayat Raj was from Bhavnagar in Gujarat. Incidentally after Jivrajbhai, Balvantrai became the Chief Minister. Tragically he was shot dead along with his wife when he took the unnecessary risk of flying into the war zone in 1965 when Ayub Khan's Pakistan raided Kutch on the issue of border. So far as Jivrajbhai as first Chief Minister of Gujarat was concerned, my relations were very pleasant. After all, he was a famous doctor who earned great reputation in the erstwhile Baroda state and was also the finance minister in bilingual Bombay when BG Kher was the Chief Minister. I had to interact with him closely when my first posting after completing my training was as Controller of Accommodation and Under-Secretary, PWD in the Secretariat which was in those days located in the Ambavadi area in a building called polytechnic. There was one particularly a nasty case where we were trying to evict a person who used to approach CM along with his family every time we threatened action. Ultimately I had to implement it and Jivrajbhai was quite understanding about my dilemma and I still remember his mischievous smile with a twinkle when from the post of Under-Secretary (Political) I was promoted to my first posting as Collector Sabarkantha in 1964.

The politician whom I came to know very closely in those days as Under-Secretary PWD was the then Minister of State for Revenue, Madhavsinh Solanki. He had a beautiful hand and very fine taste. In fact, Madhavsinh Solanki was one of the most sophisticated and at the same time pleasant political leaders I have come across. He had a wide interest in reading particularly poetry both in Gujarati and Urdu. He was a journalist and he was the only political leader I have come across whom one can meet in the bookshops in the Relief Road in Ahmedabad. There was a small shop called Pocket Book Centre in Relief Road and as Controller of Accommodation I used to go to the bookshop and buy things, I used to run in to Mr Madhavsinh Solanki there many times. I have described in different chapters in this book, my interaction with him in different stages. One thing I always admired was his interest in reading and what is more sharing books. He has gifted me many books and in those days, Japanese management styles were in fashion and written about. After his visit to Japan, he sent me a couple of books on Japan and it was always a pleasure to interact with him and he had a very pleasant smile and most of the time he was unruffled and maintained his poise. I remember that when I got married, he was one of the first ministers to visit our district after I took over as Collector. As was the tradition in those days, I invited him for lunch at my house and my wife had described in her book of how she entertained Madhavsinh Solanki and he was so polite as to come to the kitchen and not only appreciate her cooking but also thank immensely for the Spartan lunch we had provided. Such was Madhavsinh Solanki.

I could never understand how when he became the External Affairs Minister in the Indira Gandhi government in the 1980s he had to lay down office and ultimately gradually fade from public life.

Ghanshyambhai Oza was the Chief Minister of Gujarat from 1970 to 1973. He was a clean and affectionate leader. My meetings with him were always pleasant and smooth.

Another powerful leader in those days in Gujarat was Chimanbhai Patel. He succeeded Ghanshyambhai as CM in 1973. Starting as a professor in Economics, he was a very powerful person who was one of the earliest to challenge the authority of Indira Gandhi and his rise is an example of a rise of a regional leader in the Congress regime where Indira Gandhi had established her authority after the death of Jawaharlal Nehru over the first generation leaders like Kamaraj by splitting the Congress Party in 1969.

In the Congress Party, Chimanbhai Patel acquired a reputation of being a very tough leader who could show extraordinary organisation skill to the extent of even managing to form a government and becoming the Chief Minister of the State in defiance of the Indira Gandhi's central leadership in the Congress party. He left the party for some time and formed his own regional party called KIMLOP (Kisan Mazdoor Lok Paksh) and came back to Congress and died as Chief Minister of Gujarat. This was in 1994. The last occasion I remember meeting him was 1994 February when I was Chairman, Telecom Commission along with my Minister Sukh Ram, we went to inaugurate the Electronic Exchange at Mehsana. Shri Chimanbhai Patel, Sukh Ram and myself were in the Helicopter ride from Gandhinagar to Mehsana and back and the total command of Chimanbhai over the whole situation was indeed remarkable.

Chimanbhai became part of the history of the post-freedom India especially when in 1973, the Navnirman movement started in Gujarat against Chief Minister on the ground of corruption. In fact, the students of LD Engineering College started the agitation on the ground of poor quality of the food being served in the hostel and this combined with the rise in the prices of groundnut oil, the hostility of Morarji Desai to Chimanbhai and a lot of other factors combined to make the Navnirman movement the first popular agitation against the corrupt Chief Minister and perhaps first time in India, a Chief Minister was forced to leave office on the grounds of corruption. It is probably also a reflection of the twist and turns of the Indian politics that the same Chimanbhai came back to the Congress and became Chief Minister again and died in 1994 because of renal failure. It happened soon after within a month of my last ride to Mehsana along with Sukh Ram.

Even today there is an overbridge in Sabarmati called Chimanbhai Patel Bridge. Chimanbhai was known for his intelligence and sharp wit and I found that he had a tremendous capacity to judge people and approach them in a most persuasive way. I was Director, Geology and Mining and one of the officers was his erstwhile student and he was very polite at that time, he was Deputy Chief Minister in the Ghanshyambhai Oza cabinet and told me, "Vittal, if it is as per the rules, I know you will transfer him where he wants, but I am requesting you to consider his transfer because he happens to be my student." I greatly appreciate his sense of politeness in talking to me personally like this. Of course, cynics may say that being an extremely practical and competent politician, he knew how to handle people and I was just being used by him. But I thought that he showed how politicians keep themselves informed and one lesson I have learnt is that the politicians get information from number of sources and no officer can think that he can do something by which he can take action away from the gaze of his political master. Even the ever polite Madhavsinh Solanki had this skill being a successful politician and I remember that I was close with one of my friends who had a different image and once he asked me, "I am thinking of putting this officer as your deputy in the Gujarat Narmada Valley Fertilizers where I was the Managing Director." I told him, "Sir, I would not like to take him because he is very close friend of mine. But I know him." Thereafter, Madhavsinh did not press the issue and he was all the time trying to probe me. I once remember a flight in which we were together and he asked me, "Why are you vegetarian?" I said, "Sir, I am a Brahmin and orthodoxy I got this and therefore I struck to vegetarianism." I said, "I am a teetotaller, so I have not tried drinking." Gujarat of course is a state where prohibition exists and many officers used to drink outside the state but I was always a teetotaller. Then he asked me, "Why are you a teetotaller?" I said, "I come from a family where nobody drinks and I maintain this because I am the eldest son. They are supposed to be conservative and following the tradition." Next is, he was always probing and as one realises, a politician has a much tougher job to do than a civil servant. A civil servant has only to point out the rules and that is that. Whereas, in the case of the politician, he has to satisfy the lot of demands, most of the time, which may be illegal or not strictly according to rules. Unless they satisfy their loyal co-workers, they cannot win elections. I think a mature civil servant understands the political compulsion which was carried forward to a ridicule extreme in the UPA-II when the Prime Minister had to justify many of the scams on the ground of 'coalition dharma'.

Perhaps the most pleasant recollection I had with the political leader and so far as Gujarat is with Mr Manoharsinh Jadeja. He was the Prince of Rajkot and definitely had a very noble princely qualities and I was Secretary, Civil Supplies in 1980. The Congress won the election after a brief period of President's rule and came to power. But in the internal fractions of Congress, he was opposed to the then Chief Minister Amarsinh Chaudhary, who was a tribal leader in the Madhavsinh ministry. Amarsinh was the Irrigation Minister and Manoharsinh Jadeja was the Civil Supplies Minister.

I was Secretary, Civil Supplies and I had a very smart and very strict Director of Civil Supplies in CJ Jose who was sure that all the black market cement was coming from the irrigation department only. This was the period of extreme shortage of cement where the famous scandal involving the Antulay on the cement scandal where the Trust was started in the name of Indira Gandhi and cement was sold to the Trust and the political parties. There was the Act for controlling black market called Prevention of Black Marketing Act under which preventive detention of the holders and black marketers could be done. In fact, we went to the extent of in one case, preventively detaining an executive engineer of the Irrigation Department, this was around Deepavali time in 1980. The issue became quite sensitive because, for the irrigation department it was a matter of prestige and for my Minister Manoharsinh Jadeja, Civil Supplies, it was equally a matter of prestige because I do not think it is common anywhere for the officers of one department detaining the officers of another department. The provision was there in the Prevention of Black Marketing Act that within 3 weeks or so, the case will be reviewed by a District Judge and if the Judge upholds the detention only the detention will continue, failing which the detenue will have to be released. Madhavsinh as the Chief Minister called a meeting and asked me that you have created an embarrassing situation where the two departments have done the unprecedented situation of detaining a senior Class-I officer of the Irrigation department. Imagine the embarrassment if in the judicial review of the action as required under the Act, the detenue is released. I presented the facts to him that whatever our Director, Civil Supplies had collected and evidence available on record, there is a very strong evidence to detain the officer concerned and we stood our ground. To my great relief, the detention was also upheld. I recall in retrospect the embarrassment that would have been caused to the government if the detention was not upheld and in such situation, my minister fully supported me.

Another charming aspect of Manoharsinh Jadeja was that he was absolutely unassuming, though he was a Prince, will not mind dropping in my room to get clarification anything he wanted that and many a time in the airports used common facilities available at the airport and not the VIP lounge.

One of the most pleasant recollections I had of Madhavsinh Jadeja was that I described elsewhere that I have prepared a 23 point note of action to be taken, a new blueprint for the department of Civil Supplies in Gujarat and gave it to him as soon as he became the Minister after election in 1980. He kept with him for a week and told me, "Vittal, I have gone through your note and we can implement it." And within one year we implemented practically all the ideas including the starting of the Civil Supplies Corporation in Gujarat and a single licensing system for the multiple licences that used to be issued as that was the practice earlier. Perhaps, the case of Minister and the Civil Servant thinking on the same wave length but for a good purpose, so that good governance could be realised by combining both the political as well as the bureaucratic initiative. The type of incidents like action against the department of irrigation which was the source of black market supply of cement in the market would not have been possible perhaps but for this type of cooperation and understanding and the vision of the political leaders.

In our context, no improvement is possible, unless at political level we have leaders of vision and pragmatic persons like Manoharsinh Jadeja. Unfortunately, in his political career

Mr Manoharsinh Jadeja could not raise further but if fate unveiled, otherwise would have become one of the memorable leaders of this country.

An out and out Gandhian was Babubhai Jashbhai Patel, who was CM in 1977. He was the most simple and unassuming leader I have come across in my life. He had a great vision. He ensured that Gujarat had adequate power to become an engine for industrial growth.

Babubhai was a sincere Swaminarayanite. He lived up to the great ideals of Swami Sahajanand the follower of Ramanujacharya. He observed the strict discipline of the Shikshapatri. He was perhaps the most honest and sincere political leader I have come across.

Interestingly, like Mahatma Gandhi, his tiffin was also a handful of groundnuts.

It is thanks to him that right from the beginning of the plan era one third of Gujarat's plan funds were ear marked for power generation. This vision played a great role to help Gujarat emerge as a vibrant state in later years.

Among the ministers in the Central Government with whom I worked, perhaps, the most affectionate and most vigorous was Rangarajan Kumaramangalam. He used to say, "From the day we met [when I was Secretary, Electronics and he became my Minister] we got on like a house of fire." In fact, he was a very active trade union leader and coming from a political family combining the best of Tamil Nadu and Bengal politics, Kumaramangalam was a person who can charm anyone within 5 minutes. He was very actively associated with Narasimha Rao who was the Prime Minister in the handling of the delicate matter relating to the Ayodhya Movement. He used to say that thanks to his short stature, he could easily mingle with the crowd and get lost and that itself was his greatest security for him. He was fluent in many languages and can immediately interact with different political leaders across the wide spectrum of Indian politics. He could therefore, after having a spell in the Congress government lead by Narasimha Rao, do equally well in the BJP led government of Atal Bihari Vajpayee.

Electronics was the sunrise sector and as a young person who also was catching up with the technology, he was always a few steps ahead of me, so far as my ideas are concerned. It is a great pity that he died at the young age of 48 or 49. Those whom god loves, said the Greek, die young. Rangarajan Kumaramangalam was a rising star in the political firmament of India and would have played a very active role but the fate willed otherwise.

Equally gentle and quietly cheerful was Eduardo Faleiro who became also my Minister in the Department of Electronics for some time. I still remember the visits I had along with him to Goa in 1994-96 especially after my innings as Chairman, Telecom Commission and I came up with the idea of how to use the MPLAD funds for improving electronics in every MPs seat. I recall once he entertained us to a dinner of purely Goanese dishes. Once we had a dinner in El Coquero, the famous [notorious?] restaurant from where Charles Sobhraj escaped. What moved me more was that when my mother was sick, he came quietly one afternoon to our house in Tilak Marg to wish her well. Eduardo Faleiro represents the best of the Goanese culture and what is called Christian charity.

Among the Prime Ministers, perhaps, having worked with Narasimha Rao, I am his great fan. I think he was the most underrated Prime Minister who did a lot of good for the country. My friend, PVRK Prasad who closely worked with him had brought out his role especially during the controversial Ayodhya Movement in his book *Wheels Behind the Veil* and one lasting proof of his integrity, in spite of so many allegations of corruption against his children and especially his son is the fact that to pay off his lawyers' bill, he had to sell his house at Hyderabad which work was entrusted to PVRK Prasad. The depth wisdom and knowledge PV Narasimha Rao displayed has to be experienced. When I was Secretary, Electronics, there used to be a frequent question about one project in which we were trying to promote Sanskrit research to see whether it can be used as a computer language. Panini in his grammar is so perfect and so logical that Sanskrit can be used as a computer language for man machine interface and so on. Narasimha Rao always would like to listen to Ramanujam who was an expert in this language and working in Tirupati lastly on the Sanskrit language.

Margaret Alva, who happened to be a college mate of my wife Gita, from Mt Carmel Bangalore was another person though active in politics was also a charming hostess and very informal. In fact, there was an association of ladies who are alumni of Mt Carmel College Bangalore, who had married the alumni of the Loyola College Chennai. Gita and I belong to this exclusive group which includes my colleagues like JC Lynn and Margaret herself. So once in a while, Margaret Alva used to give us lunch or dinner at her place in which all the favourite south Indian dishes will be provided. It was my pleasant task to brief her for Parliament questions especially on subjects of Department of Electronics and that too relating to the funding of Sanskrit projects and like a good student and an excellent debater in her college days, which she was, she used to handle the question superbly and share her joy with us after the question hour every time.

Atalji as a Prime Minister has always been a hero to me. I am one of the millions charmed by his superb Hindi, his sense of humour and his oratorical skill. It is a tragedy that by the time he became Prime Minister, his faculties were ebbing and he came to be known for the long silences. Nevertheless, I have always been impressed by Atalji's universal charm. I have seen him years ago in 1968 when I was the Under-Secretary taking notes of the group headed by Brahmananda Reddy, the then Home Minister on the issue of communalism. This was in the 1968, National Integration Conference held in Srinagar, when Indira Gandhi was the Prime Minister. Atalji was a member of the Committee and I remember that he is very persuasive interventions in the Committee put across without offending anybody and at the same time firmly expressing his point of view. I had mentioned elsewhere the story I heard about how I was chosen as the Central Vigilance Commissioner after the judgement of Justice Verma in 1997 in the Vineet Narain case. The essential wisdom of Atalji was always captivating. I think it was Sudheendra Kulkarni who said in comparative study of India's Prime Ministers that among the Prime Ministers of India, he was the most loved of all. There will be hardly any person who dislikes Atalji.

Among the political leaders, I found LK Advani, perhaps the most sincere and intellectual and above all being a bibliophile like myself, great lover of books. I have always seen Advaniji keeping up to date with the latest publications and the moral standards he set up especially when he stepped down after being wrongly accused in the Hawala scam, but he would not join the government or become the MP till his name was cleared. And he walked his talk.

I had sent my book *Ending Corruption – How to Clean-Up India* in 2012 to many political leaders. Advaniji is the only one person, who not only acknowledged this but read the book and was serious on the issue of tackling corruption. It is a pity that he never realised his dream of becoming the Prime Minister of the country. India would have had a Prime Minister of great ethical values if he had become the Prime Minister. He would have set up the standards to fence the public life to a better level.

Although I had worked with a large number of political leaders in a fairly long career, the one political leader with whom I had serious difference of opinion and against whom I had to discharge task of being a witness for the prosecution in a case of corruption is Sukh Ram. He was called Panditji hailing from Himachal Pradesh and I found that he was universally popular and respected in his state. I have seen people fall at his feet and perhaps, I was too harsh in my reacting with him. He faced the realities of a political leader and in those days, 1990s before the National Telecom Policy was announced in 1994, he was trying to see how best a Member of Parliament can retain loyalty of his followers in the state. He used to say that so far as the State Assembly is concerned, the MLAs can directly go to the Chief Minister at the State headquarters which was near and try to tackle public problems. So far as the Member of Parliament is concerned, the link is more tenuous. In those days of scarcities, the system like out of turn quota for telephone or gas cylinder allotment, where one of the very few patronages were available to Member of Parliament to retain the loyalty of his followers. I could see the logic of his argument. But where I differed with him was his resistance to bring in open transparent system and especially, privatisation, entry of private sector in the century old monopoly of the telecom sector. I have described my experience in telecom elsewhere. But unfortunately, what brought him to ruin was a raid conducted in the late 1990s, where ₹3 crore were found in his pooja room apart from money elsewhere and the CBI framed charge against him in one case where he is supposed to have favoured a company in Andhra Pradesh. In that case, I had to appear as a prosecution witness number 13 on behalf of CBI after I became CVC and he was convicted for 3 years. As luck would have it, on 25th January 2012 when I got my Padma Bhushan, the Supreme Court finally rejected his request for bail. But ultimately, I think he was granted bail on the ground of his advance age of 86 and his health condition.

Even Sukh Ram had nice things to say and I cherished happy memories about our spending time together. I have described the confrontation with him on the issue of the National Telecom Policy in 1994 and I had also put my conscience to test in handling practically every controversial sensitive issue, when I was Chairman, Telecom Commission, Secretary, Department of Telecommunications. I have described this experience elsewhere, but in retrospect when I see the actions he took, when he was Minister for Telecommunication and compare them with those who came afterwards, I am afraid his misdemeanours appear to have been on a very much smaller scale. Ethically, however, his fault is no less.

In short, my journey through life which this book recall finds the politicians form a very interesting and important part of it and they have their individual difference. But ultimately, I realised that if the civil servant can explain his point of view and put up clearly in writing and giving clear choices and indicating his own choice also then one can have frictionless governance.

As the Prime Minister, Deve Gowda was very harshly rated. But I came to know about him through Mr Meenakshi Sundaram when he gave a talk in the Centre for Advanced Studies in Bangalore, describing different Prime Ministers. I was the Chairman, Public Enterprise Selection Board when Deva Gowda was the Prime Minister. One great thing I noticed was that he strictly went by the choice made by the PESB and candidates who were listed at Rank No 1 was universally selected and appointed. The one exception was Ram Vilas Paswan, as Minister for Railways made a change selecting the person who was recommended as No 3 to a post. With that exception, Deve Gowda's record as Prime Minister, I think from the civil servants point of view has been spotless. He chose excellent officers to be his aides arising from his practical experience as Chief Minister of Karnataka and ensured that during his time no deviations from the norms of propriety so far as management of civil servants are concerned was committed.

Inder Kumar Gujral as Prime Minister was the same intellectual whom we used to meet in the Saturday Club of the India International Centre. His views and doctrine so far as Pakistan is concerned may be considered by many as too soft. But he had as a person hailing from Lahore perhaps his own rationale for the attitude he adopted.

Among the Prime Ministers, I could see Jawaharlal Nehru only once at close quarters soon after my joining service. This was when we probationers were taken to meet him in a group on 14th August 1960 at Teen Murti House.

Ultimately, interaction with people be it seniors or political leaders, is a matter of human chemistry. As we grow old in life we become more mature and are able to see others point of view.

Especially if you are aided by a *dharmapatni* like my wife Gita, then you are forced to think all the time about the other person's point of view. One thing is clear any person who wants to lead a happy and productive life cannot afford to be like the Englishman who went to France for a holiday in spite of his poor command of French. When he was asked on return whether he had any difficulty with his French. He said, "I had no difficulty with my French but the Frenchmen had."

(ii) CIVIL SERVANT AS AN AUTHOR

I have always had a general feeling of admiration tainted with a dose of envy for the bureaucrats who wielded the pen in arenas other than files. *TIME*, the American magazine once came up with a write up on Arthur Schlesinger Jr with the title 'Historian as Participant'. Part of the glamour of the Kennedy era of whiz kids was due to the excellent articulation of the participants. In short, the participants made excellent historians. Even if the final verdict of history on the Kennedy presidency is that it was one of promise rather than performance, for me it shall always remain a glorious Twentieth Century Cameo.

There are those who question the very idea of a bureaucrat writing. LP Singh (ICS), who retired as Governor of Assam and who has held a variety of assignments in a long career in the Indian Civil Service is reported to have rejected the idea of writing his memoirs. He was one of the perfectionists in file craft I have ever known and perhaps a memoir may not pass muster with a perfectionist. Perhaps, all the notes which he recorded can be scanned for *'bon mots'*, which make interesting reading. Although formidable in appearance with a perpetual frown, he could make wry jokes on files. In one file regarding whether a VIP (a Judge of the Supreme Court) should be entitled to get four berths in a first class railway compartment to keep up with his status when he travelled on duty. Singh is supposed to have remarked that when he himself went by train, he found one berth adequate for accommodating his body as well as his ego!

There are many bureaucrats who can write well and if they could publish their point of views from their ringside seat of government, it could help a great deal to clear the common perception of the bureaucrat as a faceless non-entity buried behind files collecting dust.

On the other hand, the bureaucrat who rushes to print faces a lot of danger there is always the Official Secrets Act which can catch him tripping. Years of circumspection, caution, "on the one hand and on the other hand" style of submitting facts of a given problem, may have drained whatever originality be might have possessed once. Then again, the tribe of administrators is divided into the Yogis and the Commissars. My colleague BS Raghavan, who has a high sense of humour, once introduced a person as 'a man of thought and thought alone'. There are the administrators who once decide on action, do not want to be confused with facts. My sympathies are with the latter because it is this category which 'delivers the goods' whatever the goods may mean.

In actual administration, the Yogis many a time act as brakes and revel in what one of my American friends called "a system of sequential obstructionism". Nevertheless, it is the Yogis who may tend to write memoirs or publish articles, which is useful to posterity.

There is another danger when a bureaucrat writes. He is likely to be eminently dull. The classic perhaps is Shri CD Deshmukh's autobiography. Here was a person who achieved so much but recorded it so badly.

Other motives also intrude. There is the tendency to justify one's action, or the action of colleagues. I suppose we shall have to permit this as every person is entitled to put his best case forward.

Being a bureaucrat myself, I have always tried to had whatever a fellow tribesman may have written. It has been my good fortune to know quite a few of them.

One of the earliest writers in the Administrative Service I admired and knew was S Santi. He was Under-Secretary in the political division of the Ministry of Home Affairs. This was a desk which gave full rein to save to display his love for English and poetry. Even in a routine submission of a paper, he could bring a touch of fun. Once he wrote, "The Deputy Secretary may see in Dak and throw light". Another pithy sentence of his while describing government's policy about a political leader was this: "An iron hand in a velvet glove may be the right policy in certain circumstances. A velvet hand in a velvet glove may indicate either extreme weakness or extreme affection."

Santi's contribution was in poetry. He published collections of his poems from time to time. The titles are evocative: 'Whisper Near the Niagara', 'Lamplight in the Sun' and 'Arangetral'. The titles indicate the delicate and sensitive person that Santi was. I was shocked to learn that he had an attack of cerebral haemorrhage.

Dr Ram K Vepa represents an entirely different approach to writing. He could easily become the Samuel Pepys of the Indian Administrative Service. Vepa literally bubbles with energy and what is more, it is all controlled and well directed energy. My first encounter with him was when he was the Development Commissioner for Small Scale Industries in the Government of India. His predecessor i e Puri used to be a serious, clever person, although helpful. Vepa, on the other hand, radiated easy familiarity and a hail fellow well met approach. He is easily one of the lively and constantly cheerful persons I have come across.

It is Vepa's technique of practically recording everything that happens systematically and publishing articles and books that is inspiring. Like Somerset Maugham, he believed in building a body of works so that posterity can judge him better in a proper perspective like Hemmingway, he had a strict sense of discipline when it came to writing. Rain or sunshine, at home or abroad, he must put in his ninety minutes of writing. Such consistency is indeed remarkable.

In 1978 October, Vepa and I went to the People's Republic of China on an ESCAP Seminar while we all gathered at Hong Kong railway station. Mrs Abid Hussain, wife of Abid Hussain, who was the co-ordinator of the team from ESCAP joked that Vepa's book will be ready on China even before we landed home and unpacked our suit cases. Well, she was proved true. Promptly on return came Vepa's book on China *Behind the Bamboo Curtains?*

I find in Vepa's style of living and writing a partial explanation of Socrates' observation that the unexamined life is not worth living. Life is a parabola between birth and death. What we observe depends on what we choose to observe. What we record depends on what we choose to record. If one regards the life in a generalist's service like Indian Administrative Service as one long peregrination from one point to another, there is hardly any great variety. At the same time, each job brings its own challenges and contributes to enrichment of experience. Instant replay by way of records like Vepa has the advantage of preserving the richness of detail. Quiet reflection over a distance of time may add depth of perspective.

In an entirely different class of bureaucrat writers I know Mahadevan. He had developed professional expertise in the Indus Valley culture of Mohenjo-daro and Harappa. He took two years off to study and decipher the Indus Valley script. I was fortunate when he landed at Ahmedabad one day in 1979 on some official duty. He asked me whether I could arrange to take him to Lothal, the site of Harappan culture 45 kms from Ahmedabad. "You will have the best guide on the subject," he said with cheerful bravado.

I had never been to Lothal either. We arranged to leave the next day morning at 7 AM and when we arrived at the village Lothal, day was just dawning. Mahadevan was transformed. He started talking enthusiastically how it must have been years and years ago. "In my earlier birth, I must have been a Harappan. That is why this interest," he said. It was a unique experience to set eyes at dawn on the 4,000 year old sway and peer down the lanes and by lanes of Lothal's acropolis. I was indeed fortunate to have Mahadevan with me during my first visit to Lothal.

To run life on two if nor more parallel likes of professional interest is a feat. I admire. Mahadevan belongs to the tradition of Principe who was a member of the Indian Civil Service and contributed to the growth of epigraphy and numismatics. Principe lived in a leisurely era but Mahadevan living in the midst of the frenetic pace of the twentieth century bureaucratic life contributing in the field of history is indeed remarkable.

Even since joining the service, I have been also trying to read every scrap of writing by civil servants. Philip Woodruff's *The Men Who Ruled India: The Founders* and *The Men Who Ruled India: The Guardians* evoke memories of what life must have been in the two centuries when the British established their rule in India. KPS Menon (ICS) is another writer who has combined a charming sense of humour with a easy flow of anecdotes in his books. The Bharatiya Vidya Bhavan brought out in the early sixties a collection of reminiscences by the civil servants of the ICS. Barakataki who became the Chairman of the Assam Public Service Commission wrote the humorous book *Escapades of a Magistrate* and *The Great Panjandrum*. Noronha's *Tale Told by an Idiot* is full of intelligence and sensitive appreciation of the tribals of Madhya Pradesh. Chettoor's book retails what must be the best collection of service anecdotes from the old Madras Presidency.

Is any classification possible of the type of bureaucratic writing? There is a Chinese proverb to this proverb which is helpful. According to this proverb, there are three types of conversations. The highest class is that which involves a discussion on ideas. The middle class is one where incidents are discussed. The lowest class is a talk which is a gossip about the other people coming to think of it. Writing can be visualised as a form of stylised conversation of the author with the readers. One can easily apply the Chinese classification of conversation to writings also.

I will begin with the lowest class. Gossip is the spice of life. For most of us, interesting titbits of personal life of the great and the not so great always have an enduring fascination. Perhaps this explains the increasing popularity of film magazines with their endless columns of gossip and innuendo. At a higher level, speaking of journals, magazines like *TIME* and *Newsweek* highlight the focus on the newsmakers who happen to wield the power or hold the attention for the time being. In McLuhan's 'Global Village', personalised journalism that peers deeper and probes farther into the personal life of individuals have become staples of television and the news media.

When it came to gossip, the bureaucrat has an edge. He is the one, who though faceless to the people at large is sniffing at the helms of power. He is the valet to the policy makers and power brokers and there are no heroes for him. He can therefore tell the truth and write about people with 'warts and all'.

In addition to the wielders of power, there are always one's colleagues and friends. Any one, with an eye for detail and a flair for anecdotes can collect a lot of material that makes interesting reading.

In most of the writings by bureaucrats, be it Philip Woodruff or Chettoor or Barakataki or Noronha, there is a wealth of little anecdotes giving brief glimpses of men who ruled this country and helped the men who did so.

I am always struck by the individuality and eccentricities of the men described. I wonder whether in the twentieth century with its accent on mass production and growth, individualism has taken a beating. Drab uniformity seems to be the order of the day. Perhaps, the earlier times were less structured and hence provided a ready opportunity for the individual to improvise, develop his personality and leave a stamp of it on the events and institutions. Is individuality and originality at a discount today? I hope not.

The second level of conversations according to the Chinese system would be incidents or description of incidents. In other words, history itself is a prolonged conversation of this type. In recent times, VP Menon's *Transfer of Power* describing the historic integration of the country is a classic example of this type of writing. Most of the autobiographies and biographies fall in this category.

The third type of conversation – that of ideas is difficult. Administration is managing people to get the desired results and a whole bunch of administrative journals, institutes and organisations have sprung up. I have been associated with such institutions somewhat and I know their weakness. Every entrant to government service passes through a training institution and in the course of his career he is subjected to repeated training programmes. The question is, how effective is training? If it is a question of merely imparting knowledge in a given subject like law or quantitative techniques or procedural drills, it is fairly easy. It is when we step into the arena of behaviour and management of organisations that we encounter fascinating uncertainties. I once asked a psychology professor whether a study of the subject will help me to perform better through a better understanding of the minds of the people. He could not give a definite reply.

It is in the field of administrative conceptualisation, I have yet to come across a book which makes an original contribution. There are many number of writings by administrators applying western models and concepts to Indian situations. This is perhaps typical of our approach. I understand that bulk of the scientific work in the laboratories in this country involves repetition of work done elsewhere by changing a few parameters. The same situation applies more or less in writings on administration.

In the West, in the recent years, men like Peter Drucker and Parkinson have been able to provide penetrating insights into the working of executives and organisations. Their observations may be valid in Indian conditions also. Why is it we have not yet produced contributors of this calibre?

While we wait for this, we must be thankful at least for the writers of the first and second type of books. As regards the absence of the third, it is likely that such a contribution can come from only one who is outside the bureaucratic jungle. We might as well therefore enjoy what we have!

(iii) CIVIL SERVICE CREATIVITY

Can life in administration be creative? The commonly held idea of the bureaucratic stereotype will immediately prompt a negative reply. Bureaucracy can be a great dehumanising instrument. 'Statesman' once called the mandarins of the Government of India, 'the faceless non-entities of the South Block'. The 'sun-dried bureaucrat' was a well-known figure from the British times. In a similar context, Lamb talked of the wood having entered his soul.

Why is this so? Bureaucracy functions within a broad framework of rules and regulations. In a way, rules are the very basis of the system in which myriad people with a wide diversity of talents and inclinations functions. In absence of a set of rules, any organisation can be reduced an anarchic free for all.

Unfortunately, the very rules which are evolved for better and objective functioning of the system became many a time the cause for paralysing the system. Practically in every organisation, rules can be quoted which have long outlived their use or relevance. A periodic weeding out of obsolete rules itself can be a good starting point for creativity development within a bureaucratic organisation.

Getting rules out of the way may not be always as easy as it sounds. Every rule or convention or regulation makes its own little contribution to the mythology of administration. As an organisation grows in sizes, the basic objectives and goals are blurred. Many a time, these are perceived by only the people generally at the top. It is interesting that generally rules are framed to achieve some objectives, which the administration wants. If the objectives are the quintessence of the bureaucratic religion, rules and procedures are the theology of it. As in the case of religion, while in its infancy, the basic tenets are emphasised, as the organisation grows old, theology wraps the place. It is almost axiomatic that older the organisation, the more rule bound it is.

In its anxiety to ensure uniformity in performance, administration favours mediocrity. The maverick or eccentric or the one who likes to take initiative runs always the risk of jealousy of the pack when he is successful and sanctimonious retribution when he slips.

Sometimes, I wonder that the rules are like microbes in the air. So long as one is healthy and powerful, there is no harm. Once, one falls sick or the body lowers its immunisation guard, a multitude of microbes can attack the body. An away of diseases follows. Same is the case with rules and the creative administrator. So long as one is successful, there is no harm; same failure and the army of mediocrities wearing the granny glasses of hindsight pick sides with glee in every act of commission and omission.

Another inhibiting factor when it comes to creativity in administration is the fear of audit. Perhaps, this is an overrated factor. We do need an organisational check especially to ensure that the canons of financial propriety are followed. Bulk of the problems with audit arises perhaps because of inadequate recording of reasons for a cause of action. In fact, it is an useful practice to adopt the role of Devil's Advocate when examining every proposal, however attractive it may be. I have found it useful in examining every action to consider all possible means by which the action could be criticised or misrepresented and record detailed notes. Human memory is fickle and prompt recording of reason is a safeguard for any creative administrator.

The reverence with which rules are held varies from place to place. It largely depends on the local culture. We have the feudal culture where the holders of power can do what they like so long as they wield power. The king can do no wrong. Perhaps, in such places, the question of my colleagues Chandramouli "What is the use of power, if you cannot misuse it", has more than a ring of relevance.

We have at the other end administrations where the era of civil altruism still lingers on. Rules are apotheosized. Especially if a general approach of cooperation is lacking, rules tend to become the arbiters or the weapons in the skirmishes and battles of bureaucracy.

We also have administrations where there is an overall atmosphere of cooperation and the approach is pragmatic. Perhaps, this is the best climate for creativeness to flourish on a long term basis.

The question that then arises is whether if the chances of success of a creative administrator are dependent on the environment, a person cannot be creative at all if the environment is not alright. The answer is that creating a limited environment, however limited even in a small organisation must be worth the effort.

Another general issue that is related to creativity in administration is whether the scope is the same in a regulatory and a developmental organisation. The earliest type of organisations that evolved was regulatory ones. It is with the onset of Independence, we have launched massive developmental efforts. Government is entering a wide variety of areas especially in economic and industrial development. Certainly, these new areas offer wide scope for creativity, but are regulatory administration less conducive to creativity?

I hold that this need not be so at all. Perhaps every single regulatory function today has a developmental angle. Without law and order, there will be no peace on which economic development could be built. Prison administration can lead to experiments in social development and better management of prisons. The basic land revenue administration can be linked with the whole series of efforts at rural development. The regulatory functions for managing the distribution of essential commodities and scarce resources, with some imagination can turn into exiting efforts at building modern marketing systems. The list can go on. The challenge to the creative administrator is to find the areas of challenge, innovation modernisation and rationalisation.

Any creative endeavour in administration need not always be an isolated individual effort. It could be a collective search for excellence. How to initiate this search? Here of course, the creative administrator has to play Pygmalion or Professor Higgins to his organisation. In fact, given excellent human material, perhaps without even a modicum of effort results could be achieved. Alas, one does not always have the choice of choosing one's subordinates and colleagues all the time. Again, civil service may promote mediocrity and by prolonged operation of the Peter principle, many organisations are full of people who have reached their level of incompetence. One is reminded of the joke in the United States where it was suggested that the Vanguard rocket fizzling on the pad after a period of brief upward shudder (in 1957 when the first American attempt to launch a space satellite failed) that it should be called "'Civil Servant', it won't work and Yen can't fire it."

I have found out one method which has been useful in kindling interest even in dead organisation. It is possible to set imagination on fire and the long extinguished embers of enthusiasm could be kindled. This is the technique which I call the 'McNamara Questionnaire method'.

Way back in 1969, I came across an interesting passage in Arthur Schlesinger Jr's *A Thousand Days: John F Kennedy in the White House*. It described how when McNamara took charge of the Defence portfolio, he shot off questionnaires asking for specific information by a specific date from the Generals and his senior staff. Some of them were so sharply worded, said Schlesinger, that if a Japanese General had received them, he would have committed hara-kiri.

This set me thinking. When an administrator, especially a generalist takes charge of a new department or organisation, he is generally ignorant of its ways, culture and problem. The standard method is to settle down first and then start functioning. Caution and circumspection is the watchword. My experience is that pussyfooted cautious men have generally the negative achievement of avoiding same problems, very rarely have they broken new ground and progressed. I am not giving a call for all the fools of the world to rush where angels fear to tread. I certainly believe that a certain modicum of risk taking, breaking of convention, willingness to experiment and commit mistakes is necessary if one is to achieve any breakthroughs in bureaucracy or achieve the satisfaction of a creative approach to work. My esteemed senior colleague SM Ghosh who is such a master in minting memorable phrases once said that to achieve results, one should have the quality of 'responsible intransigence'. It is an attractive, though unorthodox concept not found in standard books on administration or the sermons of the pundits on management.

So, making a break from tradition, I thought it will be worthwhile to try the McNamara questionnaire experiment immediately on taking over charge of a new department. The very ignorance is a fertile ground for generating new ideas. There is a honeymoon period in every organisation which a new boss can successfully exploit.

Back in 1969, therefore, when I was given charge of the Directorate of Accounts and Treasuries in Gujarat, I tried the McNamara method. It was immensely successful. In my questionnaire addressed to all the officers, I asked questions like the following:

- What are your problems and what are your suggested solutions to them?
- What is the work we are doing, which we need not to do?
- What is the work we should be doing but are not?
- Do you have adequate staff and equipment support?
- What are the powers that could be delegated?

I shot off the questionnaire to all the officers and gave them a time limit of 15 days for reply. It had a number of beneficial results.

Firstly, it gave me a ready mechanism to identify the really intelligent and competent officers irrespective of their status who given a time limit can deliver the goods.

Secondly, starting from scratch, I had a sheaf of ideas on which action could be taken. Especially in a huge organisation, there is many a time no sense of direction. It is like a huge mass of slowly drifting river. Distilling the suggestions can give a readymade programme to give a sense of purpose and direction to the organisation.

Thirdly, there is an electrifying effect of participation from the members of the organisation. Men who have spent years in service, have ideas which have never been tapped. It improves the morale tremendously.

Fourthly, visible tangible palpable improvements can be effected right from the first month itself.

There democratising of the process of improvement is a highly satisfying creative experience. It is as if a chain reaction of enthusiasm has been set and the results should be seen to be believed.

In the last more than 12 years or so, in department after department, I have adopted McNamara method with success. It has helped to revive a dead or almost dead organisation like the Kandla Free Trade Zone in 1974, inject a greater degree of dynamism in industrial administration in the office of the Industries Commissioner in 1977, radically give a different developmental turf to a traditionally regulatory and fire fighting department like the Food and Civil Supplies department in 1980. Helped to tap the professional skills more effectively of a technical organisation like the Directorate of Geology and Mining in 1970.

How lasting are the effects? It depends on a number of factors. Procedural improvements can help to sustain the momentum for a larger time. Physical tasks completed within a given time can outlive the officer who initiated them. Morale, however is fickle and unless there is sustained efforts to tap the creative potential, the initial enthusiasm may look like more a flash in the pan.

How to sustain this sense of creativity? An intuitive understanding of the basic objectives of the organisation is the main requirement. As intuitive skills may not be uniform, the objectives may be identified by any process like brain storming, long tete or tetes with one's colleagues or a formal target setting in an exercise like Management by objectives.

The questionnaire method is better than the normal methods because it avoids the standard pitfalls of commitology. It has been well said that a camel is a horse put up by a Committee. The standard method of appointing committees to study problems, considering them on file or even in an empowered committee and taking decisions is less fulfilling on two counts – delay and lack of any personal involvement. On the other hand, the McNamara questionnaire method is speedy and there is maximum participation of people who are immediately affected by the decisions.

Is the questionnaire the only tool the creative administrator can have? Certainly not. The very concept of creativeness involves a wide variety of techniques and approaches depending on the skill of the administrator.

Another technique is that of developing maximum options by exploring the possibility of any of the following:

(a) Eliminate
(b) Combine
(c) Change the sequence
(d) Modify
(e) Replace with an alternative
(f) Reverse etc

When any problem is examined through this set of choices, a variety of options is thrown out the creative administrator can then make his own choice.

A third method is to identify the objective clearly and start eliminating all the obstructions. In an organisation, which generally consists of a few workers and a lot of malingering passengers, the administrator is all the time faced with a problem of getting things done. The more incompetent a person, the more fertile is he with alibis for non-performance. It is a useful technique to take care of all the alibis in the beginning itself and create a situation where the work gets done because, there is no option but to do it even for the most lazy workers.

All along, we have been examining the problems and techniques of creativeness in administration as if it is a desirable quality. One comes across many people who take just the cynical view and question whether one needs to be creative at all. After all, we are all birds of passage. Nothing is permanent or immutable. Even the empires of the past have long since vanished. Why be so egoistic and try to be creative at all?

Perhaps there is a lot of validity in this view. In India, we have a long tradition of venerating people who renounced the material world. Unfortunately, management and administration of people cannot be built on philosophies of renunciation. Such problems cannot be tackled today by superimposing on them the mental framework devised for the hereafter and the great beyond.

Administration, in the ultimate analysis is a network of egos. Every great institution has been the shadow of a man. It is the highly motivated creative individual who has given life and shape to many an organisation and movement.

We have another set of people who advance the argument of frequent transfers which are unexpected as an argument to support the thesis that no creative effort is worthwhile in an atmosphere of uncertainty. If one craves for certainty, even life is essentially uncertain. In fact, it is the glorious uncertainties, as in cricket, which add a spice of excitement to life. If everything was predictable there will be no fun left in life; no motivation for people to strive and make good.

Coming specifically to administration, I have adopted and will advocate the 'cricket views' of administration. Administration is as unpredictable, especially where postings and transfers are concerned, as cricket. You never know when you will be out of your present post. As in cricket, you may be bowled, run out, caught behind, get out by hitting your own wicket and so on. A batsman so long as he is at the crease should try to score as much as he can. If he is an opening batsman, that is an administrator setting a new organisation, he may have to wear out the new ball attack. If he is a bowler he must try to get as many wickets as he can.

In short, there may be a case for viewing administration as a game. This may not sound so unusual especially after transactional analysis and Eric Berne's *Games People Play: The Psychology of Human Relationships*. There are also books viewing business as a game. The game theory in decision making is well-known. Perhaps, such a mental framework is conducive for promoting creativity in work.

While one has to be serious a sanctimonious approach leads to the ossification of imagination. One of my friends once described a senior official as looking like a 'Constipated Cockroach'. It is a colourful expression. The cockroach is the arch symbol for survival. It had preceded man by many millions of years and can survive an atomic holocaust, but that is perhaps the only field where the cockroach gets the better of the multi talented creative man. In the administrative race, there are cockroaches who merely survive. A creative administrator can retain his humanity till the end.

For, when the day of retirement comes, if one is asked what has one done in all the decades of paper shuffling and file pushing, the creative administrator can honestly feel a sense of fulfilment. He no doubt will realise that many of his micro and mini bureaucratic triumphs may no longer be relevant. It is like battles fought long ago. The din and excitement had died down, but the memories of a positive sense of participation can help to keep warm against the cold setting of age.

An American friend of mine (Hawkins) once called our system as one built on the principle of 'sequential obstructionism'. He was connected with setting up a major fertiliser plant in the cooperative sector and the various hurdles the project had to cross before it became a reality had perhaps made him a cynical and embittered man.

In any administration or society there have to be checks and balances. It is desirable that instead of acting in haste, any decision that has wider financial, social, ecological and political implications is examined in all aspects before it is implemented. Obstructions and obstacles for any project can be viewed as forming a framework of screening. What my friend was objecting was our method of arranging the obstacles in sequence which has a decisive flow. It causes enormous delay and time is one resource which cannot be retrieved or recycled or renewed. In the present context of almost continuous inflation, delay also means cost – enormous escalation in project costs. However, many of the obstacles have since been removed by the present government.

Operation of Parkinson's Law and the expanding bureaucracy is a very strong factor helping the votaries of sequential obstructionism. As three people start doing the work which was being done by one, there is a dilution of vision and direct boost to tunnel vision. As each has to justify his existence, he has to raise an objection or at least contribute by way of delay because till he clears the papers, the decision has to wait.

There is another psychological factor operating to encourage people in the bureaucracy more negative in their approach. In any hierarchy, the degree of discretion increases as one goes up the ladder. For the man occupying the lower rungs, there is not much discretion left. At the same time he is part of a huge organisation or bureaucracy. As he is deprived of the power to say 'yes' to a proposal he works overtime to develop skills to say 'no'. Dr Dwyer (*Your Erroneous Zones*) in his book *Pulling Your Own Strings* has brought out clearly how petty bureaucrats became victimisers, ever ready to make the citizens a victim.

There is a sense of power involved in saying 'no'. It was Parkinson who coined the phrase about the existence of the 'Abominable No Man' who exists in every organisation. The psychological pay off in exercising negative power may partly compensate for a poor pay packet. One can work out one's frustrations in saying 'no' – it could be an act of revenge against the society at large which has kept the petty official at his low office, it could be a way of creating an embarrassing position to the boss who may like to oblige a person but does not have the courage to overrule his recalcitrant and defiant subordinate. Of course, the power to say 'no' can be a catalyst to get bribes.

We have stumbled on to the idea of 'speed money'. Just as stagnant pools breed mosquitoes, stagnant papers breed corruption. One of the important factors that has scuttled the efforts of reforms in administration is the vested interests of corrupt elements in a complicated system. Many a time changes introduced with the best of intentions can themselves become breeding grounds for corruption. Shakespeare with the unerring instinct of the poet identified this in his play.

While corruption is pillar supporting delay in any system, there is another factor which contributes equally to this. This is the tribe of sincere devotees of perfection. I think it was SG Bawa, LK Jha (ICS) one of the most disguised civil servants who said that in our country the better is the enemy of the Good. If a person comes up with a reasonably good suggestion, immediately, it is pounced upon for microscopic analysis by the brilliant mandarins in the bureaucracy for detecting flaws or come up with a better suggestion or improve upon it. I believe that with man being imperfect, it is impossible to come up with a perfect solution. Anyway, in the search of the Holy Grail of perfection, an enormous time is lost.

The fancy for perfection is perhaps due to our Hindu tradition of excessive exegesis. We revel in abstract logical analysis, display of knowledge and literally believe that if a problem is clearly identified and analysed, we have already solved it.

If one takes a general view of our present administrative system, one finds that it is essentially a large bureaucratic maze which is fascinated most of the time by its own internal processes. A vast army of knowledge workers chip away at smaller and smaller set of problems endlessly examining and re-examining issues. If at all anything substantial or new gets done, it is due most of time to factors which are mainly external.

It is interesting that although the bureaucratic juggernaut moves at snail pace most of the time, in times of real crisis or emergency it can really rise for the occasion. Events like floods, accidents, drought and earthquakes, have a momentum of their own. Here the time horizon is compressed and objectives stand out in stark relief. Rules and procedures take secondary place. These are seen as merely as means to an end rather an end in themselves.

It is well to remember that not all bureaucrats behave in this fashion. For instance, after the Sicilian earthquake in 1979 in Italy, aid for the victim flared massively but according to press reports, they did not reach the victims in time or in a large measure.

My main point is this. In administration, there are two forces acting constantly – the force for perfection and the force for speed. Most of the time, the perfectionists have the day because it helps to make the bureaucrat feel important. Wage intellectual battle on fine points of administrative theology, help breed corruption or at least give the perfectionist the feeling that he is doing something worthwhile. The force for speed is weak most of the time. It gets a boost in times of crisis where the time constraint makes speed a condition for survival and not one of the many options.

If administration is to become effective and result oriented, there should be a conscious attempt to encourage the force of speed in administration. Any amount of lip service is given in circular exhorting delegation of powers and assurances that bonafide mistakes will not be punished. The insiders in administration know most of the time that there are pious platitudes. If there is a conscious policy of encouraging speed and the votaries of speed encouraged. We can perhaps make a break in the present culture. Spiro Agnew used the colourful expression of the "pussyfooted pusillanimity of the nattering no lobs of negativism." Such negativist nabobs should be discouraged.

This is easier said than done. Even a policy of encouraging speed has limitations because vested interests outside government who thrive on delay will be a powerful force. Still, such a re-orientation in outlook will galvanise the administrative machinery into action.

At the individual level, each official must develop the mental framework of fixing a time limit targets for every action. This should be followed closely by a systematic approach in implementation. One of the most competent executives with a methodical approach to work I know is Harish Chandra Sarin (ICS) who was twice Adviser to the Government of Gujarat in 1974 and 1980, and who has held varied posts in the Government of India. He had a system of using the phone and the telex instead of the letter. Systematic and total follow up of problems – however big or small by noting meticulously in a dual diary system. One for daily engagements and one for items needing follow-up.

Such techniques really help in choosing the follow up action and impart a certain degree of speed to the disposal of work. In practice, I have found that it is easy to adopt these techniques. The only precondition is that one should be willing to work. As Tagore observed, it is only a lighted candle that can set light to another. It is only an administration with a commitment to speed who can impart speed to the organisation.

Another method that can be considered is the adoption of the gadgets and instruments which save time in office work. Newton's first law of inertia operates with a vengeance in bureaucratic organisations. Every procedure continues its state of rest or motive till set aside by an external force. Same is the case with introduction of time saving and labour saving gadgets.

I find this is somewhat intriguing. It was long after the ball point pens came into use that they were considered proper for official use. When I was Director of Accounts and Treasuries, a treasury officer did not accept a cheque written on a cheque writing machine with perforations; he insisted on the cheque being written in indelible ink made at Calcutta. How many government offices have photocopying machines? How many use electric typewriters? Are the electronic calculators common in government offices? How many use intercoms?

I feel that some conscious effort at continuous modernisation of office equipment is necessary. In every office there should be an officer earmarked whose job will be to constantly search means for mechanically reducing clerical work. A case can perhaps be made against this on the ground that we must adopt the manually most intensive method. This will be wrong because more people there are, more confusion and office politics result. It is better to have lean productive organisations rather than vast ponderous unproductive bureaucracies.

Another idea that can be adopted in the interests of speedy and effective organisational structure is designing offices which are lean but can depend upon or draw on a reserve of manpower to meet sudden bursts of work. The vast number of unemployed in our midst provides ideal material for such reserve forces. The Chinese 'human sea' tactics can be adopted to get vide of accumulated routine work but on a permanent basis the organisations have to be kept lean and active.

Another approach to ensure speed is the tactics of removing all alibis for non performance. Once a goal is defined if all the ifs and buts coming in the way are cleared, there is no alternative left but to achieve the goal.

A continuous application of O&M concepts to all procedures is one method of ensuring that the organisation does not become set in its ways. There is always a better way.

In short, an alert questioning attitude especially at the top levels can go a long way in helping setting the right preconditions for a speed and result oriented administration instead of a procedure ridden perfectionist and paralysed bureaucracy.

(iv) HUMOUR IN CIVIL SERVICE

Humour is anathema to the serious business of administration. In fact, in the first and practical look on administration, I read when I joined the service – *Assistant Collector's Manual* by Lely (ICS) an old hand of the Bombay province – there was a distinct injunction against attempting humour in official correspondence. Very correctly it was argued that the temperaments vary and one cannot be sure that humour will be appreciated. For a young officer to attempt humour is to a risky proposition. He was bound to be misunderstood at best as a flippant person with a lack of seriousness in approach or a deliberate scallywag thumbing his nose at authority for which severe bureaucratic retribution should be the proper treatment. One man's joke is another man's insult.

No wonder, you find most of the senior administrators generally with a serious outlook and grave mien. After all, administration of the largest democracy in the world is a grave responsibility and one cannot be smiling while groaning under the heavy burden of one's responsibilities.

I have a faint suspicion that there is a direct correlation between the serious look which an official wears and his level of self-confidence. Greater the self-confidence, greater the degree of relaxation. A person can relax in his work and enjoy a joke. In fact, I suspect that the less confident civil servant wears his serious outlook like a chastity belt to ward off potential threats to his administrative hollowness.

The reverse is equally true. The more confident an officer, the more ready is he if smile. He can afford to crack jokes and place the job in proper perspective.

Two of my colleagues with an almost impressible sense of humour are RV Chandramouli and HR Patankar. Chandramouli is quiet and extremely quick on the repartee. Patankar likes to clown and is an excellent raconteur of anecdotes.

I had just joined service and had come to Assistant Collector's seminar in 1962. AS Gill who was in charge of the seminar and training, in his suave, gentle and polished manner had organised that we must call on the senior secretaries to government at their houses. It was to be a sort of meet the people programme for the young officers.

V Iswaran (ICS) was the Chief Secretary. He had a formidable reputation. Many were the tales told of how he used to tick off even senior secretaries and keep them in check. One story doing the rounds was that he had called GL Sheth (ICS, who later on rose to became the Secretary to Government of India in the department of Defence Production) for discussing a file. Apparently, Iswaran's point was not understood by Sheth, whereupon Iswaran was reported to have said, "I shall give it in writing. You go to your room and read it and read it again. Then you may understand it". Predictably, another senior officer used to say that when Iswaran wrote on a file 'Please speak', it really mean 'please listen'.

We called on Iswaran and he was pleasant to us, tyros in administration. He was living along those days at Ahmedabad. As Gill introduced us and we quietly took our places – Iswaran's opening observation was: "My nephew was here but he has just gone out" of course, later on, there was some polite conversation and we took out leave – feeling relieved that we had furnished a social call by and large unsheathed.

Later in the evening, I met Chandramouli. "How was your meeting with CS?", he asked. I said that it went off well and gave him almost a verbatim account. When I mentioned about the nephew and said this was a mystery to me, Chandramouli cracked, "well, I suppose it is a sort of joke. Perhaps it was too subtle for you chaps!" We all had a hearty laugh.

Iswaran perhaps did have a sense of humour. He had a tough look and a round bald head, but perhaps behind that severe external mien there lurked a sense of humour. A file from the legal department was put up to him once with a request for additional chairs because the officers and staff did not have adequate furniture. Came the curt final order of the CS on the proposal: "Rejected.. Why should the legal department need chairs when in any case they are sitting on the files?"

English is a tricky language and unsure hold on the language can lead to many a bureaucratic slips providing totally unintended humour. R Bharat, a think sensitive intellectual had strayed in to the world of administration (1957) and was Under Secretary in the finance department for some time. He had a subtle sense of humour though the cautious and tentative manner of his speech led one to believe that here was a person who was the epitome of nervousness and quiet anxiety.

There was a proposal of the Forest department to purchase elephants which were required for hauling logs. The file had gone through the usual process of prolonged scrutiny and vetting and journeyed up to Bharat. He cleared the proposal but added a note of caution with a mild fun: "Proposals for purchase of elephants accepted. I hope they do not turn out to be white elephants!". Promptly when the Government Resolution was drafted, the caution of the Under-Secretary Finance was immortalised thus: "The proposal to purchase elephants accepted but on the condition that they are not white in colour!"

One of my early Collectors under whom I received training was BD Desai. Unfortunately, he died young. He had just been promoted to the IAS from the State Civil Service and naturally look to his enhanced responsibilities with the proverbial vigour of the new broom. It was February 1962 and the financial year was to end on 31st March. The ideas of March galvanise even the most somnolent of government department to action as their financial and budgetary fortunes hinge upon their performance before the critical annual Day of Judgement.

The Small Savings Drive to reach the targets handed out by the government was also in its annual feverish pitch. Desai called a meeting of officers where he observed: "Well, we should popularise small savings so that they become thrifty. In fact, they must become so thrift minded that ultimately they should be all spendthrifts!" The seriousness with which this was mentioned convinced me that here was a linguistic banana peel: The traditions at the district level where authority is held in reverence is such that no one laughed.

Lack of knowledge of English meaning can also lead to save genuine situations of unintended humour. In Gujarat, in the Industries Department, Industrial Commissioner and the Chief executives of the public sector enterprises had formed an informal co-ordination group called Industrial Extension Team. It was known by the acronym 'INDEXT'. Nevertheless, one of my ministers in charge of Industry genuinely felt it was only 'Index'. In meeting after meeting, inauguration after inauguration, seminar after seminar – the industries department has them by scores – he will hold forth on the concept of 'Index'. Just as in a book the Index gives you all information at one place the Index of officials was to help the prospective industrialists and entrepreneurs in Gujarat to find their way to success. Well, it was certainly an index of my minister understanding of the situation. When you came to think of it, perhaps he even had a convincing case.

Chandramouli can come up with prompt slogans tinged with humour. I was Secretary in charge of Civil Supplies and in April/ May 1981 the situation became sensitive. The State was recovering from a prolonged bout of agitation on the issue of reservation in government posts and medical colleges. The opposition parties were planning a new agitation on the issue of price rise and inadequate supply of essential commodities. The Chief Minister Madhavsinh Solanki suggested that I should bring out a weekly bulletin to educate people on the realities of the situation and how government was trying to cope up with the situation. We thought that the bulletin should be called 'Supply News' (Puravatha Samachar).

I told the idea casually to Chandramouli, who incidentally had held that charge with distinction years ago in 1974. He smiled and said: "Vittal! I can give you two slogans which will be just right. The first: *'Maal Nahi Male, Pan Mahitu Malshe'* (supplies will not be available but information will be: Supply: 'No', Information: 'Yes'). The second: *'Maal ma Belsel Hoi, Pan Mahiti chokki'* (there may be adulteration in supplies but our information is unadulterated). Well, ultimately, there was no 'Puravatha Samachar' but we had a hearty laugh.

He then related how in civil supplies one is reduced to giving explanations which at times could be ridiculous. 1973-74 was a bad year and prices kept on rising. Chandramouli's minister (Sanot Mehta) in the House once gave the explanation that price rise was a universal phenomenon. He then went on to explain that the election of Nixon in the US elections may have something to do with this. On this, one of the opposition MLAs, Motibhai Choudhary came with the prompt repartee in Gujarati: *"As to Gadhedane Taar Aave Aavi vat che"* (this is a case which can make a donkey get fever). The explanation was laughed out.

Promotions and reversions sometime can follow in quick succession. In 1963-64, there was an Under-Secretary BD Desai who used to get promoted in leave vacancies and got reverted when the vacancy ceased to exist. This happened so frequently, that Chandramouli suggested that like the flexible "In-Out" Boards to indicate the presence or absence of an officer, for BD Desai there could be a 'Under/Deputy' flexible board which could be used at enormous savings to government!

One of Chandramouli's grievances was that his original and sure fire slogan to popularise family planning was not accepted by the government and he was not rewarded. He said that around the time of Emergency, when family planning was in full swing, he came across a report which said that contrary to the fears being entertained about the loss of virility after Vasectomy, there was medical proof that it improved and made sex life more enjoyable. Chandramouli suggested to the Health department that the new family planning slogan should be "Have Vasectomy and enjoy more vitality in sex!" Of course, government was too much of a puritan.

Aditya Nath Jha (ICS), who was the Director of the National Academy of Administration when I joined the service and went for training was a man who thoroughly enjoyed humour. A giant of a man he was huge. He was every inch a good-hearted jolly person and he had many inches of it. He hardly gave any lectures. He gave, I remember only two talks in the entire year. One was on the nonsense rhymes of Edward Lear and I forget the other, which was on an equally off blandish subject.

He however used to meet us in the lawns of the lovely 'Clarabelle' where the Academy was located. His huge rotund figure constantly clutching a pipe and with his little dog around was a sight which was as common as the tall coniferous trees of the campus.

I never liked horse riding. I am told the Prime Minister Indira Gandhi believes that if a man can control a horse, he can control a district. Thank God, they do not apply this test rigidly. Many are the tenors of the riding school that I still recall. Once Jha came to take a test of my riding. When the horse was to canter, I lost my grip. I somehow maintained myself, but Jha shouted: *"Saab ko grip nahi hai"*. I shouted back, "Sir, I have the grip of fear!" He had a hearty laugh.

That night we had one of our weekly dinners where the local talent of the IAS probationers was displayed. I had been silent member all along. I was once a member of a group of Gujarat cadre officer (six of us) who sang a boatman song. It went so badly and off key that if a poor boatman went by our song he will sink out of the sheer cacophony!

Anyway, this was the best such programme, T Padmanabhan, a close friend of mine who was a singer with a classical touch and

I decided to give a 'Ragamalika' in the programme. It was disaster. Wodehouse would have enjoyed it and would have easily fitted into any of his Bettie Wooster escapades. If I had a Jeeves, I am sure he would have advised against such musical adventure.

Well, there it was. As we started, I found that I was becoming loud and clear and Padmanabhan's ass voice was at ground level. I soared, he was far below. It was a parody of classical music – MS Subbulakshmi who had rendered that song, 'Malai Pozudinile' would have rushed to her grave hearing us. Anyway, we never gave up. We went our discordant way and finished the long song. When we ended, there were prolonged catcalls and cheers.

Jha came up to me. He said, "Vittal! Don't worry! For that song, I will pass you in the riding test." To this day, I wonder whether I got through the riding test due to my equestrian skill or the musical!

Well, there was an earlier exchange with Jha on riding also. He asked me "Vittal! Why are you worried? These are after all mares". I shot back, "Sir, they may be mares to you but to me, they are nothing short of night mares!"

When I left the Academy in April 1961, I almost saw the last of my riding in life barring one horrible incident absolutely nightmarish when I was Assistant Collector Dabhoi. In the book of parting remarks by probationers, V Venkatesan whose name preceded me in the alphabetical order had commented. "Riding was great fun." When my turn came, I had one last parting kick: "Riding was great fun – I also wrote – and added: for the horses!"

In our Academy days the probationer's world was divided between the born equestrians and the congenital non-equestrians like me. Horse was a popular subject in the social gatherings. I remember a probationer singing to the tune of the Hindu film song hit from 'Shree 420' – *"Pyar Hua Ekrar Hua"* these words:

"Banna Hai Rider, Bachna Hai Mushkil
Ghode se phir kyon dartha Hai Dil!"

Jha himself had couple of equestrian anecdotes to narrate. Even when he joined the service, he conceded, he was quite fat, like all fat men, Jha had carried his weight around lightly all these years. Perhaps all that sense of humour added an element of buoyancy to counteract the force of gravity on his massive body.

On his first day in the riding grounds, the coach had one look at young fat Jha and asked "young man, don't you think you will have a problem in riding?" Jha's reply was as prompt at it was innocent: "Why should I? The horse might have a problem!" The coach was naturally shunned! Even after years when he delivered that punch line, Jha used to have a healthy belly laugh (should I say, paunch laugh)

R Natarajan (1952) when I met years later when he was Chairman of the Tamil Nadu Civil Supplies Corporation had another story about horse riding in his days. In those days, the IAS training school was at Metcalfe House, Delhi.

The system in those days, Natarajan said was to earmark specific horses to each probationer. The south Indian probationers, being weak in body and strong in cleverness, adopted, according to Natarajan, a clever strategy. They saved the sweets served to them in the mess and fed them to their chosen horses. As a result, the horses displaying sound horse sense were very docile. Thus, while probationers from other parts of the country had their full measure of the rough and tumble of horse riding, the south Indian gang was coasting along easily.

One day, somehow the secret was out and the riding instructor was briefed. The next day, when the usual riding session started the riding instructor announced that with immediate effect the old system of earmarking was scrapped. It was going to be a system of random selection of horses for every session. Many a south Indian probationers fell off his horse at this mere announcement itself!

I shall revert to a couple of Jha stories which throw light on his basic philosophy of administration. As our director, he hardly gave any lectures but took occasionally what were called tutorial sessions. This was nothing but a friendly meeting over a cup of tea with a group of probationers. At one such session, one of the probationers asked him: "Sir, we hardly see you taking any classes for us. What exactly is your role here Sir?" It was a bold question and were expecting some nasty remark. We thought the probationer was also going to be penalised for such impertinence.

Far from it, Jha kept his cool. He had a long pull at his pipe and said: "Have you been on a ship and seen what the Captain does? If you find the Captain relaxing and doing nothing in particular, you can be sure that all is well. If the Captain is rushing about, it means that there is some trouble. Well, I am the Captain here!" He then let out a hearty Ha-ha-ha laughter.

HKL Capoor told me another version of Jha's approach to administration. According to Jha, he believed that a top level administrator should be like the 'Teli' in charge of the old oil grannies. There he sits smoking his hookah and the bulls go round quietly pressing the oil out of the Til or any oilseed. The ideal paradigm of an well-oiled organisation running smoothly with the routine work being taken care of by the lower ranks and the top level manager concerned only with major and non-routing issues.

The other incident of Jha was told to me by S Krishnaswamy who rose to be Secretary Chemicals and Fertilisers and rated as one of the most distinguished civil servants. He had worked as Deputy Secretary in the Ministry of Defence (Department of Defence Production) when Jha was the Secretary, PVR Rao was the Defence Secretary. This was in 1962-63 after the Chinese aggression when defence had become a very critical ministry.

PVR Rao was known to be an activist eager bearer and was always hustling people around, making statements and making his presence felt. Jha was cool as ever. Krishnaswamy noticed that Rao was making statements regarding matters falling within the jurisdiction of the Department of Defence Production. Krishnaswamy being an equally alert expert in bureaucratic infighting felt that this was an issue of 'turf' and unless checked, very soon, the department will become a mere appendage of the defence department. He told Jha of the various incursions of the bureaucratic turf taking place. Jha kept his cool.

The last straw for Krishnaswamy was a statement made by PVR Rao at Bangalore on some matters relating to Hindustan Aeronautics Limited (HAL). This was a case squarely within the jurisdiction of the Department of Defence Production. Krishnaswamy rushed to Jha and once again pleaded with him to check this constant erosion of department's turf.

Jha at last be stirred himself. He casually walked over to Rao. He talked amicable for half an hour on all matters other than that on hands, cracked jokes and so on. Just while he was about to leave, he said: "Rao! I find that you have made some statement about HAL at Bangalore. Well, I don't mind your making this but remember, all along I have followed one principle in life. If I find some idol doing my dirty job, I let him keep it!"

Rao was stunned. From that day, there were no more incursions in the turf of the Department of Defence Production.

Humour in files is rare. When BS Raghavan (1952 WB) was Deputy Secretary in the political division of the Home Ministry and S Santi (1957 Karnataka) was the Under-Secretary, the notings in the file occasionally had flashes of humour. I recall one case in which Santi had put up some proposal which would have meant the ministry taking up cudgels against some other ministry, Raghavan wrote: "Let us hump it." Santi sent up the file with the remark: "If we hump this, we will look as ridiculous as a double humped camel!" Well, Raghavan humped that! Another of Santi's file was marked: "Not all immediate". This was a humorous piece written in the Wodehousian style about the civil servants writing memoirs and the need to permit consulting files for this purpose. Even the clever LP liked it.

LP Singh's humour had a wry ring about it. Once, Gopi Arora and I were hauled up to his presence. There has been some news item and we had been rather slow in reacting to it. The political division those days was performing partly the function of second guessing the Intelligence Bureau, doing endless analysis like an anonymous institute of political affairs and generally acting as a rag bag for all the left over work in the Ministry. Long hours were the rule rather than the exception.

We used to have endless jokes about the hours and working methods of the political division. TP Issar used to say that the political division is like a brothel. It starts functioning only after 6 PM!

There was a manpower division in the Home Ministry which could afford to bask in the luxury of academic work lesser working hours and no tension. Issar used to say: "If you go to Manpower division, you can retain yours. If you come to political division, you shall lost it!"

Well, back to LP Singh. He berated us for our lapse and added, "Years ago, an ICS officer in Bihar was given a KBE for his cool and unflappability. There was an earthquake and hundreds of people died, but this officer who was the divisional commissioner did absolutely nothing. He displayed commendable sang frail indeed! It is a good story but was not very happy occasion to hear it."

BS Raghavan, a great admirer of LP Singh and interpreter of his moods is an excellent raconteur. He had his own sense of humour. The day I joined the political division in the Home Ministry, Raghavan gave me an excellent briefing on the predatory world of the Central Secretariat.

"There are two types of Under Secretaries", he began, and added perhaps, "there are basically two types in any sphere of human activity. The first is the lazy man's Under-Secretary. This is the chap who 'bites' into the file and ferrets out all the facts and put up notes which are so self-contained that there is hardly any need for the Deputy Secretary to bestir himself. The second category – yes, you have guessed – is the lazy man Under-Secretary! I hope you will be of the first type."

Raghavan had his own set of put downs. The political division with its penchant for endless analysis during the time I was there gave excellent scope to Raghavan to play with English. He was once discussing a communal exception in a state and said, "Well, it is time that law and order is the responsibility of the state but we in the Home Ministry are supposed to give at least advice. They are saying that the Central Government is vicious, well, let it be at least advisories!"

On another occasion he introduced an old friend of his thus: "Mr So and so had in his academic career never stood second (In fact was always somewhere the bottom, he added in an aside!)

There was a time when he met a gentleman who said he was 35 years old. Well, said Raghavan "you don't look 35 at all! In fact, you look not a day older than 45!"

Raghavan had a flair for writing. In 1968, he went to US on a course and one day I was surprised to read an article by him in *The Statesman*. The article was critical of Lyndon Johnson, the then President. I thought that Raghavan, who was ever to careful, had goofed. I thought the Ministry of External Affairs and the Home Ministry's own vigilance services division will haul him over the codes of conduct rules. Surprisingly, nothing of the sort happened.

I was curious. When he came back, I asked him about the article, and how it had escaped bureaucratic retribution. Raghavan's reply was breezy: "Well! It was a coup. No coup is ever according to rules. If it succeeds, you are safe. Otherwise, you had it!"

Raghavan met LP Singh and repeated that everything had gone on well in the US trip. Jha's only problem was that he was thought to be much younger than what he was. LP's reply was: "Well, it could be an advantage after 6 PM!"

Another of Raghavan's escapades was reported to me by R Natarajan, his batch mate. In one of his subsequent US visits, Raghavan had been to a shop in New York in the Fifth Avenue. He wanted to have a look at a stereo. Raghavan told the Jewish shopkeeper that he only wanted to see the stereo. The shopkeeper's response was unusual: "Sir, you need not look at it. You may take it as a gift!"

Raghavan was bowled by such unexpected generosity for which he was not prepared. He looked stupefied. The shopkeeper added, "You Indians do not have the money to buy the piece but you insist on seeing all the models. I spent half an hour and do no business. I have therefore adopted the practice of gifting the first piece itself and save my time!"

I still do not know how far this story is true.

R Tirumalai who was my boss when I was Development Commissioner of the Kandla Free Trade Zone was another person with a sense of humour. I had just taken charge and made what I claimed to be some improvements in the Zone in the first few months. In one of the meetings of the Board, a member said with reference to a problem, "Well, we were told that Kandla Free Trade Zone had turned the corner. Then why should this problem exist?" Thirumalai, in his deliberately slow way said, "Yes, the Zone has turned a corner but it has many a corner to turn!" The problem was dissolved in laughter.

Raghavan and Santi used to trade jokes occasionally in the otherwise sterile noting of the files of the political division. One exchange went like this:

There was some proposal and Santi had suggested an activist approach. Raghavan felt that the best course was to keep mum. He wrote, "Let us hump it." Santi shot back, "If we hump this, we shall look as ridiculous as a double humped camel!"

Patankar's humour is not of the type confined to the files. He is an excellent raconteur and he has developed the technique of injecting the comic angle at the most unexpected moments.

This helps him to retain the initiative with him all the time and keep those dealing with him off balance.

He was the Managing Director of Gujarat Industrial Development Corporation and had gone to consult the legal luminary Nani Palkhivala for some work. Here is what he said: "We had gone for over appointment and were waiting in the ante room. A girl entered. We took her to be the Secretary of Palkhivala. We inquired from her whether Mr Palkhivala would be busy or will be able to see us for the appointment.

The reaction of the girl was very odd. She frowned and kept coldly silent. The mystery was clarified soon. She was no advisory girl. She was Jaya Bhaduri, the up and coming star of the Hindi film!"

Patankar's theory of administration was derived from practical experience, tinged always with the comic angle. While long faced professors spun boring theories about the relationship between the civil servant and the minister, Patankar had his own theory to describe the different stages of the emerging relationship.

At the bottom or elementary state of the relationship is the file based relationship. The civil servant puts up long notes arguing the pros and cons of a situation and the minister gives the orders.

At the next stage, the file is still the medium, but before putting up the note, the civil servant sounds and assesses the minister's views and then puts up the note.

The third stage is of 'chits' or 'slips'. The minister issues slips, which convey his wishes. These are executed by the officer.

The fourth stage is the telephonic stage. Issues are settled on phone. The file is only for the record.

The fifth and the ultimate stage is the musical stage. At this stage, the civil servant is turned to the final tonal variations of the minister's voice. A mere 'Hmm' may convey different meaning in different cases. It may be an affirmative in one: negative in another and a question in the third!

Patankar believed that only those civil servants in the musical stage scaled the higher reaches of the career pyramid.

A minor variation of the same story is the different meanings of the Gujarati 'Jojo' (have a look) which the minister may utter to the civil servant. A short urgent toned 'Jojo' meant that the work had to be done immediately. A sing song 'Jojo' made it a stalling device to keep the applicant hanging on the tenterhooks of doubt. A carelessly uttered 'Jojo' meant that the case may be decided on merits.

I think a well-developed sense of humour is a great aid in maintaining one's sanity in a long career. A readiness to see the ridiculous side of any situation helps one to keep a sense of proportion and develop a sense of detachment. I have always found those civil servants who lacked a sense of humour ultimately mean, vindictive and utterly forgettable in the long run.

The logic is simple. If a person has a sense of humour, he can realise at times that functions which appear so serious, after some time look utterly harmless and transient in the eye of history. This at once brings an approach that is more broad-based. Against his wider perspective, a civil servant can always operate with a greater degree of maturity. However, if this vision of the antic is lacking, every little issue becomes a matter affecting the ego. No wonder meanness is the result.

A ready wit and fine sense of humour is a valuable asset in a civil servant's tool kit of skills.

The Civil Servant is no longer the faceless non-entity hiding behind a curtain of files. At least in the Indian Administrative Service, the way it is constituted and the way the officer learn the ropes, there is a lot of exposure to the public. After all, the officer is a public servant and his relations with the public are an important aspect of his everyday life.

As I look back over the more than twenty one years, I have spent in the service(?), I can find that many of the ideas I had started with so far as the relations with the public are concerned have changed. Sometimes, I hesitate to record my views as they have evolved now because, in a few more years, I may be adopting a different set of norms. Nevertheless, I feel it is worthwhile to record one's evolution of ideas because, there are certain principles which I hope I will not give up and an analysis of their evolution would by itself be of some value.

I come from a family background of government officials. My parental grandfather was a district *munsiff* (civil judge) and my father an Assistant Public Prosecutor. My maternal grandfather was a chief engineer in the native State of Travancore. I do not think this background as such did have any influence on my ideas of public relations.

In Tamil Nadu, an IAS officer is a highly respected person. He is invariably visualised as a know all and even the man in the street has an idea of what IAS stands for. In Gujarat, on the other hand, it is money power and business acumen that are rated high. Religious leaders also have a good following but an IAS officer is not a well-known prototype. Part of the reason is also that British India and the ICS tradition covered only a small part of the state: Saurashtra and Kutch were mainly a potpourri of federal states.

I am very much aware that if instead of being posted in Gujarat, I had been posted in Tamil Nadu or Punjab, my ideas of public relations may have evolved in an entirely different direction. Nevertheless, the first principle of public relations of a civil servant is clear. It is that PR is essentially dependent on the median in which it is practised. An approach which is successful in one state may fail utterly in another.

As a civil servant is entrusted with the task of achieving results that signify the implementation of government policy, a first prerequisite is an intelligent awareness of the median in which one is functioning. PR is an interpersonal skill and a civil servant can choose from an awry of skills to arrive at a successful formula.

Perhaps, the first point that confronts us is the degree of accessibility that one wants to accord to one's subordinates, colleagues and the member of the public who deal with the department. On the one end we have absolute hermits, who would require even their nearest colleagues to have an appointment to discuss even the most pressing problems. At the other extreme are the popularity seekers, those of the back slapping, hail fellow, well met type. In the service, I find that the later are any day a preferable lot than the former.

Nevertheless, the image I have of the normal run of the mile or garden variety of government servant is not very flattering. He is generally not business like. In the case of counter clerks and the like who deal with the public day in and day out, there is a dyspeptic churlishness. It may be one in a hundred clerk who has a cheerful smile or even the hope of uttering polite words.

Corruption is another endemic feature of our system. One can become the poor pay scales, the universal scarcity of items, the labyrinthine set of rules and regulations or the plain greed to get rich quick, but petty corruption is the rule rather than the exception.

Bacon said that accessibility could be one means of reducing corruption. In our bureaucratic system, I believe that every officer should be as accessible as possible to the public dealing with the department. This is one method of reducing the scope of corruption in the department. Surely, the middle and lower rungs of officials will be not very happy. In fact, they may take a pleasure in passing the luck to you.

There are a number of drawbacks. Your time may be swallowed by public whose problems could be solved by a lower level functionary. You may be killing the initiative of the middle and lower level officers. The management pundits may tell you that higher level officials should practice management by exception. He should budget his time following the principles of Peter Drucker.

In practice, I found that these fears are exaggerated. Firstly, your time especially after meetings and tours and so on is so limited that even the adoption of a free access policy will not swamp you with visitors. Secondly, if the middle level executives are doing their jobs properly, when any complaint is received, they will be able to answer effectively. An easy access policy, I find helps you to monitor the small and big problems confronting the department. You can feel the pulse of the department and the public's reaction to it. It thus provides a solid realistic framework of reference on which to ease your policies and caress of administrative action. I have therefore found this to be a useful technique.

Another principle or rather a technique which I have found useful in dealing with the public is that of openly declared time limits for solution. You will come across many wise and experienced administrators who can wax eloquent on being non-committal. One of my colleagues Chandramouli used to joke that the index of an officer's seniority and maturity in his capacity for being "talkative without being communicative".

I have found that if one had to be effective, it was better to be communicative but not necessarily talkative. I operated on the assumption that even though from the comfortable perspective of the civil servant who was not affected by the consequences, most of the time, one can lay down priority, for the member of the public who comes to you, it is a priority problem. Hence, it is best to fix time targets and openly confront the same.

This has two advantages. A time target by itself gears up the machinery to action, and the open commitment provides the requisite investment in ego to provide the thrust needed to achieve the goal. Certainly, this adds to the work load of the officer but it ensures that the results are achieved. The credibility of the officer in the eyes of the public grows.

I know of officers who take the cosmic view of administration. After all, as one of them said we are not taking earth shaking decisions. We are here today and gone tomorrow. In the long run all of us are dead, in the short run all of us are transferred. If you have a suspicious boss, every initiative you take is viewed with suspicion, if you have an insecure boss, for every achievement of yours, he will take credit. In fact, one can build up a logically convincing case for taking the path of least resistance and doing the just minimum on the job. The great principle is: "Do not rock the boat."

Perhaps, happiness and sense of fulfilment may not be always logical. For all the analyses of men being rational, I have the feeling that real breakthroughs have come through short bursts of enthusiasm unrelated to logic. Russell may form at the pleasures of unreason but it was Russell again who wrote of the pleasures of useless knowledge in his 'Sceptical Essays'.

Well, placing a time limit has the excellent advantage of placing the issue on a sharp focus. You can easily spot the key factors and make the choice. The standard technique of endless cleansing of cud at umpteen levels generally contributes only to delay.

The one common complaint against bureaucracy is delay and red tapes. If one can cut down delay, one can perhaps hope to have reduced if not eliminated a constant irritant in public relations.

The second advantage of a time targeted approach is relations because clear and business like. Delay, like stagnant waters breeding mosquitoes, breed corruption. At least when the person approaching you gets a clear reply – yes or no – in a time limit, he has the option of pursuing his case elsewhere if he is dissatisfied.

To the officer, such an approach keeps the mind clear and uncluttered. One can easily develop an objective and detached approach and can give a better performance. One does not carry any excess mental baggage or feeling of guilt.

I think, it was Walter Lippmann who defined diplomacy as saying what you want in terms of what the other person wants. I always found this principle an excellent guide in handling people. Of course, this perception, I have developed over years.

Straight from the Academy, when I came to the district of Panchamahal in Gujarat in 1961, my ideals were of those executive who were rigid. It is time that even today I admire the principled approach of the legendary Visweswarayya, who it is said used his own candle (those were the pre electric bulb days to write his private letters and the government issued candle for doing his official work. I try to follow this in practice even today.

But, an excessive obsession with what is proper and what is improper is a great hindrance to an easy rapport with people. Integrity in a civil servant is a vitally important virtue. In fact, it is what distinguishes him from others who are mere time servers. Nevertheless, one should guard against this obsession with integrity becoming a form of negative snobbery or a Howard Huges type of social phobia making one into a recluse.

When I was the Development Commissioner, Kandla Free Trade Zone, I had agreed for a dinner to be given by the Industrialists Association to my boss. However, when he landed, he did not agree to join. His point was that I should have consulted him before I agreed for the dinner on his behalf. He did not join the dinner. In such a situation, I would have readily joined the dinner.

Another aspect of the delicate network of human relations is helping one's subordinates. When I was Assistant Collector Dabhoi (Baroda district), I had a peon who used to bring my food and polish my shoes and what not. He was in fact my Treves. One day, he made a small request. His son was applying for a job in the local municipal office. Can I put in a word to the Municipal President?

I rejected his request. I was a young principled Assistant Collector and I would not compromise my position in making such recommendations. The peon did not say anything to me but I learnt indirectly that he told one of my clerks that the Saheb whose shoes he cleared everyday could not do such a simple thing for his son.

This incident has haunted me. Ours is a poor country and in the mad scramble for jobs, what is wrong if one puts in a word? I know of so many principled and honest officers who would not lift their little finger to help anyone within their own area of activity, but would unhesitatingly ask you to do things out of the way. I have nothing but contempt for such persons and as a matter of practice I refuse to help in such cases.

Nevertheless, when it comes to helping the lower paid employees, after the Dabhoi experience, I have adopted a consistently positive approach. There is so much unfairness and injustice in this world. It is better to help persons to the extent one can. I also try to follow Dr Hudson's technique of not remembering whom I have helped.

Such an approach, I find is generally helpful in creating an atmosphere of friendliness and co-operation in an organisation.

However, in our society, goodness is many a time mistaken for weakness. If you are good and kind-hearted, the subordinates perhaps think that you are so because (a) you want cheap popularity, (b) you are not strong, and (c) you are a weak and timid person. Just to counter this image, I have found it necessary from time to time to take harsh measures or unpopular decisions. At a subliminal level this practice, I feel is also a good antidote to one's moral fibre for decaying.

It is a curious fact that people respect strengths and toughness even though they may oppose you. A strategy of combining a generally helpful and positive approach with occasional flashes of toughness is what I have adopted over most of these years.

Another aspect, I have generally found wanting in many government offices is lack of imagination when it comes to public relations.

Nirad Chaudhuri, the gadfly of Indian writers in English observes somewhere that unless you like dirt or are comfortable in shabby surroundings, you cannot appreciate India. While we Hindus carry the concept of personal and ritual cleanliness to an extreme, when it comes to public places we cannot care less so far as cleanliness is concerned.

This cultural undertow pervaded over government offices. It is almost axiomatic that the clerks and other denizens of the office should sit in broken chairs and have heaps of files all around them with heaps of dust on them. Just as a person gets accustomed to the silver lines of slums life and gets with the main job of keeping body and soul alive, most of our offices are slums of paper where the paper shuffles eke out a livelihood by a process of professional non-performance.

Slovenly surroundings breed slovenly behaviour. The environment in most of the offices is totally unconducive to polite behaviour. Cleanliness in offices is therefore one aspect I have repeatedly tried to emphasis. This was perhaps due to my personal matter of taste. It was also an indirect effort to improve the morale of the organisation. When I took over as Industries Commissioner in 1977, I sent away sixteen truck load of records to a place away in New Mental Hospital, Ahmedabad (by a curious coincidence, the building meant for mental patients was being used for housing government offices – the Director of Education, the Inspector General of Police and of course the Industries Commissioner's store purchase wing) When in 1980, I took over as Food and Civil Supplies Secretary, I was appalled, to see the food controller's office suffocating under old records. My remedy was to dump these in the godowns so that at least the staff and the public may breathe in slightly better surroundings.

To brighten the offices, I found that selection of bright and cheerful coloured curtains are helpful. I borrowed the paintings lying in the Education Directors godown to decorate the Industries Commissioner's office at practically no cost.

I am citing that instances at length because in my perception of better public relations elegant office atmosphere is very vital. I feel that in every office there should be one person with a sense of appreciation for matter of interior decoration whose job must be to ensure elegance in office. An elegant office will take an almost imperceptible fragrance induce people to behave more gently and decorously. Perhaps, one day such a dream can come true.

Another instance of lack of imagination is in the field of communications. In how many departments are the rules and regulations which affect the public readily and freely available? In fact, in many offices, even the staff are not aware of the latest orders. It is a case of the corrupt or the half-baked misleading or exploiting the public most of the time. I always try to make the administration as open as possible. When I was Industries Commissioner, for example, I permitted the Chambers of Commerce to publish the industries subsidy manual. I started the system of sending press notes and copies of gazette notifications to the trade associations in the Civil Supplies department. In fact, my success in the Kandla Free Trade Zone was mainly due to achieving better communications. Of course, it was a situation involving promotional work and I evolved a multimedia publicity campaign. The package included cinema slides, advertisements in the press, pamphlets and booklets, advertisements in the Vividh Bharati, meeting with the Chambers of Commerce and above all individual regular tete-a-tete with the prospective industrialists. This communication was very helpful in removing lot of misunderstandings about the zone, modifying procedures to attract more investments and finally attract industries to the zone.

An important aspect of public relations is relations with ministers, non-officials, MLAs, MPs and so on. In the training school, one is taught (at least in my time) that the civil servant is concerned with execution and policy making is in the realm of the politicians especially the ministers. However, in the field the situation is more complex.

In reality it is the individual cases in which many are interested. General policy is too abstract for money to grasp and appreciate. At the cutting edge, it is the limited powers of the petty official – the talati or the constable which symbolises influence and power. Unless a political or social worker can affect that decision, his credibility as a power at the local level is not established.

When I became a Collector at a comparatively young age of 25 in 1964, I was still under the influence of the theoreticians of administration. Being a democrat by temperament I felt that every individual whether he is a MLA or not, will get the same treatment. It was fine in theory but in practice, I must have appeared brash when Hitendra Desai who was the Chief Minister visited my district and advised that I may take the local MLAs and social workers into confidence.

I consulted Shri SK Gangopadhyay who was my Collector at Baroda and one of the very few officers who had unimpeachable integrity both moral and intellectual and for whom I have abiding respect. His reply was simple. He said that you should act according to the rules and if the MLA wanted something not in the rules, you may politely point out that they may get the rules changed.

In my years as Collector, I was still perhaps too much aloof. I did visit the villages, met the people and held tent camps. Sometimes in meetings, a simple observation can become a source of irritation. In a supply advisory committee meeting, the District Panchayat President one Gopalbhai Patel made some grave observations about the availability of foodgrains in a village. Somehow, I had also visited the village. When I began my reply with the remark that I also went to the villages – Shri Gopalbhai flew into a rage. In retrospect, I realise, I was questioning his first charge of right with the people as a social worker. After all, I was only a paid government servant!

Years have perhaps mellowed me. After 1965, I never went to a district as a collector. I was mostly head of various departments but with greater exposure to the problems of handling people, I have realised that in the first instance, it is better to adopt the 'Yes, but' stance rather than a blunt 'No' approach. The 'Yes, but' approach has the advantage of not immediately annoying the person who is making a request, order or suggestion. One can prepare the ground and then came with a polite 'no' for an answer.

I have also realised that in our democracy, an MLA as a representative of the people, deserves a greater attention from and also an effort at better communication by the civil servant. A generally pleasant approach to them is better than an official stand offish one. At the same time, one need not be obsequious.

Just the other day, I read in *The Economic Times* of 17th October 1981 an article by KK Khanna that bureaucrat in our system is an 'actor'. In the field of public relations, are skills of an actor needed? Perhaps to some extent thespian skills are needed. However, administration of a department is more serious than mere play acting. However, consummate the actor, the audience knows that he is only acting. An actor entertains. An administrator has to deliver goods – resolve problems, render assistance and maintain order where necessary when the chips are down, I do not think there is any substitute for hard work. Mere plodding is of no use. One should work smartly also.

Another technique that has helped me in public relations is to issue orders in writing in front of the party. Whenever a person comes with a problem, I not only explain the position and give my decision. I also in most cases call the stenographer and dictate it on the spot. This has the advantage of ensuring that memory does not play tricks, nothing is lost sight of and a confidence in the applicant that he has been heard effectively. This calls for a sense of commitment on the part of the civil servant.

In short, the cardinal principle in public relations is open communication based on mutual trust. It is better to be polite, clear, committed to time targets. It helps to have a nice and pleasant environment, up to date information to that assistance rendered is effective. Finally, a positive approach of helpfulness makes all the difference. When I began as Controller of Accommodation, my favourite line was that I would better be more accommodating than controlling. In civil supplies, my approach was that one should not be uncivil and non-supplying. It is really surprising how a positive way of looking at a problem throws up an entirely new set of options.

These are the principles that have guided me these 30 years. Will they change in the future? Time only can tell.

"Experience is a comb that nature gives to a man when he becomes bold," says a Thai proverb. A member of the Indian Administrative Service gets posted from one job to another in the course of a long career. Is he a mere rolling stone, gathering no mess? If at all he gains any experience is it not only one of simple survival?

These days one of the popular methods by which any one in power can show dynamism is by orders the transfer of officials. The papers publicise this as a shake-up, which is supposed to revitalise the administration. Although this is a populist measure, it also adds an element of glorious uncertainty to the cricket of administration.

In the ultimate analysis, the experience an officer gains depends on a number of factors – the capacity of the officer himself, his attitude and approach to work. The experience has a private or individual aspect and a public one. We are here concerned with the latter.

An officer who moves from one department to another, soon learns that certain aspects are common to all organisations. The housekeeping functions like service matters, standard procedures for financial clearance etc are matters of this type. These are also matters which get least attention generally although they could be the main problem areas in some cases. Knowledge gained in one department is useful in another.

The second aspect is that of cross fertilisation of ideas. As one moves from one department to another, one can see scope for using techniques which were successful in one can succeed in another also.

(v) REFLECTIONS ON DRIVERS

I do not know whether you have ever wondered that the modern day philosophers may come, not out of any *ashrams* or meditation centres, but from the tribe of staff car drivers or chauffeurs. In the nearly three decades I have spent in government service, I had the opportunity to entrust my life to a succession of chauffeurs. I had held jobs which involved practically continuous touring. My wife used to say that my address was C/o National Highway No 81.

When you travel so much and spend so much time in the company of your chauffeurs, you cannot but got impressed with the totally different perception of life they have.

Or look at the graffiti on the trucks in the highways, as you drive. Perhaps lorry truck driver is a poet and philosopher. In fact, one can write a whole hook on the highways philosophy of the modern Indian truck driver.

I cannot resist the temptation to digress here and give you some of the gems:

"Chandni chand se hoti hai, sitaron se nahin
Mohabbat ek se hoti hai, hazaaron se nahin!"

Apparently this driver is a choosy lover.

And here is the hymn of the eternal traveller constantly on the move; arising somewhere and sleeping somewhere else:

"Main musafir hoon, meri subaha kahin, meri sham kahin!"

Loyalty is a very highly priced value in the tribe of drivers, but they do not want you to become toddy of anyone. It is surprising that in our semi-feudal culture steeped in the 'sijarish' syndrome, the truck driver holds out:

"Dost bano, dushman bano
But, chamcha mat bano!"

Of course, there is pride in driving a fully loaded truck:

"Saleem sala bharka chala
Dekh ke Anarkali ka Dil jala!"

The driver is ever wary of the evil eye:

"Buri nazar wale tera munh kala!"

Is perhaps the most popular graffiti among the drivers!

Let me get back to my chauffer. Perhaps the most memorable is Hiralal who was my chauffeur when I was Industries Commissioner. Chubby and eternally smiling, Hiralal was known as a chatter box (*'Vatudio'* in Gujarati).

Hiralal was no ordinary driver. One day, during a long drive, I discovered that he had a direct access to the Industries Minister Jaswant Mehta. I was intrigued. Then came, in the course of Hiralal's glandulous talk, his interesting story.

Goa was a Portuguese Colony and remained so far nearly 14 years after India became independent in 1947. Jaswant Mehta was one of the political leaders who participated in the liberation struggle. Hiralal had been driving the cars of the leaders who were connected with the agitation.

In one of these missions, Hiralal was also rounded up by the Portuguese authorities. He was shipped along with others to Portugal. He spent a few days in the prison at Lisben. Then as suddenly as he was rounded up, Hiralal found that the Portuguese brought him back to India and released him!

No wonder, Hiralal was no ordinary driver. He had been a freedom fighter! But, by now, he had discovered the secret of a secured life. His advice was:

> *"Service karo to Sarkari*
> *Sadhu bano to Swaminarayan!"*

In other words, if you want to take up a life of service, become a government servant. You are not likely to be sacked. You enjoy total security of tenure. On the other hand, if you want to become a Sadhu and give up all this worldly life, become a Swaminarayan Saint. This is a well organised cadre of saints which is doing a very useful service to society. Apparently, the Saints are also well taken care of!

I think the professional responsibilities of a driver are so designed that it gives him an excellent opportunity to ruminate and think of the life as a sweeping and ever changing panorama.

Manubhai, who was my driver when I was Additional Chief Secretary in the Home Department, was a potential historian. He had long memories and was a keen observer of life, especially of his bosses. One of my friends warned me: "Beware of Manubhai, he is a spy!"

Anyway, I found that Manubhai could give you an update on all developments past or present. He would comment on the working style of my predecessors, who was good in disposal, who was effective and who was not. (As I write this, I am sure Manubhai would be entertaining my successor in office, if they lend him their ears, about me and my style of work also!)

Listening to Manubhai, you got an idea of the continuity and manage in the working of the departments, the challenges and issues of the past and gave you the philosophic perspective how temporary was your "power and glory" – "*Sic transit Gloria*". Manubhai could be a mini Edward Gibbon commenting on the decline and fall of Secretaries!

As the drivers have plenty of leisure time, they become active in other fields. In most organisations and companies, I am not surprised to find that drivers are the active unionists. When I was Health Secretary, Haribhai Patel was my driver. He was not the very glamorous type like Hiralal. Imagine my surprise when he told me laconically one day that he has been elected president of the state level drivers Union! Silent drivers run deep.

Some drivers are so driven (fun unintended!) that they want to quit the drivers' profession and grow in another career. Young Ramu, one of the gentle and well behaved drivers I had when I was Managing Director of GNFC wanted to get out of the driver syndrome. He came from a family in Gadkol village of Bharuch and his uncles were Sarpanches. He was the first to take advantage when I introduced a scheme to train drivers on technical skills to become operators in the plant.

A driver wants his children to come up if he himself cannot make it. Ashok Waghmare, my youngish driver in the Industries

Commissionerate, was of this type. He also had some pride in his family history. From him, I learnt that the great Shivaji, the Maratha Chief, used to award the title 'Wagh Mare' to those of his men who caught the tigers haunting the Maratha countryside and brought them to him. Those who killed the tigers, became the holders of 'Wagh Mare'. The grandfather of Ashok was the charioteer of the great maharaja of Banda Sayaji Rao. Of course, being my modern charioteer was a great care doom! But Ashok was ensuring that his son will not be a driver. He was educating him in the English medium. The boy was shaping well. I wished Ashok's son all the best of luck!

Philosophers, spies, historians or young super achievers, I found quite a few drivers have a strong sense of loyalty to their boss. If you are a little kind and gentle, they will give their life for you. Sheikh, my driver when I was Secretary of Civil Supplies got married on my birthday in 1981. I attended his marriage and he was so thrilled! Whenever I meet him, there is always the beaming smile and he keeps me up-to-date on his growing family! My wife calls him my 'Hanuman'.

Some of my drivers have been true professionals. They have an immense and quiet pride in their dexterity in driving and mastery of motor mechanics. Paryani, my driver in Kandla Free Trade Zone was a tall fair handsome man. He had initiative also. He was instrumental in breaking the conspiracy of the taxi drivers in Kandla who had promoted the idea that three wheel auto rickshaws were unsafe in the highly windy Kandla. As part of my effort to improve the transport infrastructure in Kandla, I wanted to introduce three wheel auto rickshaws in Kandla. Paryani came forward and I arranged a loan to his brother in law, who became one of the early auto rickshaw drivers in Kandla. I think Paryani also drove the auto rickshaw when he was free.

In my thirty years in government, I have seen many drivers. Quite a few of them have same common values. For example, if you advise the driver to take enough petrol before or during a journey, I find that they mildly resist the idea. It appears every driver wants to challenge his vehicle and see to what extent he can get the best mileage out of the petrol already in the vehicle. Sometimes, this exercise used to give me anxious moment but somehow in the ultimate analysis, the drivers managed to reach me home safely.

Pattatroya Pawar, my driver when I was Additional Secretary in the Department of Atomic Energy, I am afraid should have become a race car driver. Speed was his passion, my predecessor in office perhaps wanted to make the best out of his time and kept only a minimum time to race to the airport. It seems that practically every trip to the airport was a test in race car type driving. Pawar had developed techniques for beating the red lights and weaving his way through the maddening Bombay traffic. The only problem was that if you do not have nerves of steel, you were likely to be briefly rattled by the time you reached the airport.

I am a cautious person who provides a large cushion of time in my travel plans. In the early days, I found that Pawar literally felt that I was a great care down. In a way, I will not be surprised if he felt that I have compromised my position and brought down the status of the Additional Secretary's office itself! After all, in our country, status is inversely proportional to punctuality. Pawar also had a fertile brain and I was all the time wondering whether he was telling the truth. For him, the Bombay policeman was the villain and he was always within inches of rubbing the Bombay policeman on the wrong side.

Variety is the spice of life. I have also had very sober and phlegmatic drivers who were literally unflappable. Barnare my driver when I was Director of Geology and Mining was of this type. Affectionately called 'Dada' Barnare was the strong silent type.

I can go on and on. I hope have given you an idea of the rich variety of life you can witness in the drivers. Perhaps, this is true of any group of people. And that is what makes life so interesting.

CHAPTER 7

GOLDEN SUNSET

I write this in May 2014 and this is the 13th year of my retirement from active service in Delhi. One key decision every civil servant has to take is where to settle down. In my case, I had three choices. One was Chennai from where I hailed and where my closest relatives live. I have two brothers and lot of cousins who are Chennai based. As one grows old and in the evening of life, it is the close relatives who come to your help and can provide psychological and moral support. As I had been in IAS and spent three decades I had two more choices. One of course was to settle down in Gujarat. I had two houses, one in Ahmedabad and one in Gandhinagar. The third choice was to settle down in Delhi itself. The question of settling down in Chennai was the most attractive option for me. The most important reason was not only my relatives were there but my daughter, son-in-law and grand daughter were settled there.

The greatest blessing Gita and I enjoy in our retired life is the proximity of our daughter and her family. This is perhaps the greatest satisfaction one gets and it is a guarantee for our happy golden sunset years.

I was very clear that I will never settle down in Delhi. Delhi is a *matlabi* city. In fact, my friend, Dr P Rama Rao, Secretary, Department of Science and Technology used to say that he was told "when you go to Delhi, if you want to have a genuine friend, buy yourself a dog."

My friend and batchmate Bhaskar Ghose has written in his autobiography *The Service of the State: The IAS Reconsidered*, about the rat race that goes on among the retired civil servants settled in Delhi for finding some sort of a sinecure. I did not want to settle down in Gandhinagar because the attraction of being in Chennai with my daughter's family was more overwhelming. At the same time, I have decided not to sell off my house in Gandhinagar because my entire career coincided with the formation of Gujarat as separate state. I spent 24 of my 42 years service in Gujarat and that attachment continues. In spite of strong suggestions from Gita that I should sell off that house, I am not going to do that.

Once having decided to settle down in Chennai, the question was about a residence in Chennai. It is perhaps a classic example of my lack of worldly wisdom that I had never taken any concrete action to have a house in Chennai. Living only on my salary, which in those days was ₹17,000, I had not saved enough nor could afford to save more to invest in down payments for a new house. But here again, as mentioned in the earlier chapters, the grace of Lord Venkateswara intervened. I was to finally lay down the office of the CVC on 2nd September 2002. In the 2002 Independence Day evening Rashtrapati Bhawan party, my colleague GS Rajamani of the Indian Postal Service asked me where I was going to settle down and when I told him Chennai, he asked me whether I had a house. I told him that I had no house and I had to go and buy one after selling my house in Ahmedabad. He made a graceful offer. He said his new flat at Raja Annamalaipuram was ready and as he would be retiring only in 2003, for a year if I was interested, I can have his flat on rent. I jumped at his offer and I thought that it was a direct signal from the Lord that he was shepherding me smoothly into retirement. Promptly I made the necessary arrangements and retired on 2nd September 2002. On 22nd September 2002 I was the tenant of Rajamani in Chennai. That is how smoothly the transition took place.

The subsequent years in Chennai, the decade of retirement, had some interesting events. The most significant one were my annual medical emergencies. As the member of IAS, I had seen in the state level of Gujarat and the Government of India, practically the entire spectrum of departments. In fact, after retirement, I have seen practically the entire spectrum of the various medical specialities in Apollo Hospital Chennai, Cardiology, Nephrology, Urology, Orthopaedics, Physiotherapy and you name it, I had been to every specialist in that division. Thanks to the generosity and friendliness of Dr Prathap Reddy, Chairman of the Apollo Hospitals and by the grace of God, I have been able to overcome every medical emergency I faced regularly and I have lived so far to tell the tale. I am an example of the survival of the un-fittest exact opposite of Darwin's theory of evolution of life.

Looking back over the years, the years 2012 and 2013 represented the best and the worst in my life. January 25, 2012 was the one of the most unforgettable moments in my life. It was noon and I was in my car approaching the stationery shop. I got a call from the Ministry of Home Affairs that the President of India had decided to confer on me the Padma Bhushan and whether I would accept it. I thought somebody was pulling my legs and I said, "I hope this is not a prank call." I said it would be great honour for me to accept the Padma Bhushan. I was told it was an officer calling from the MHA and it was not a prank call. I was also asked to keep the information to myself till the official announcement was made by the government. Within two hours of my getting the call around 12 o'clock, the message was flashed all over the media. For the next two days, our phone never stopped ringing and I was literally bombarded with the congratulatory messages 24 × 7. What gave me great satisfaction was that this was a public recognition of whatever contribution I have made in the civil service and as Dr Manmohan Singh graciously mentioned after the award function on 4th of April 2012, Vittal you should have got this long ago. Perhaps, as the old Hindi proverb goes: *"Samay se pehle aur bhagya se jyada kisi ko kuch nahin milta"* (before its time and beyond ones destiny nothing happens).

I received a flood of message of congratulations and e-mails, they included political leaders, captains of industry, business executives and of course colleagues and relatives. Just as a sample, I reproduce below the comments received from Ratan Tata, SM Krishna, Bharat Doshi of Mahindra & Mahindra.

1. Letter from Ratan Tata

Dear Mr Vittal,

I was delighted to learn that you have been awarded Padma Bhushan. Please accept my congratulations on this richly deserved recognition.

Let me take this opportunity to wish you further successes in your future endeavours.

With regards,

Yours sincerely
Ratan N Tata

2. Letter from SM Krishna

Dear Shri Vittal

I felt very happy to learn about you being awarded the 'Padma Bhushan' for your distinguished service of high order in the field of Civil Service. I wish to congratulate you on this occasion.

In your distinguished career as a civil servant, you have enriched the lives of the common people in the country. It is my sincere hope that you would continue to contribute for the benefit of the country as well as the people in future too.

I wish you all the best in your future endeavours.

With regards,

Yours sincerely
SM Krishna

3. Letter from Bharat Doshi

Sir,

You may recall, I am the younger brother of late Lalit Doshi (IAS), in whose memory you had delivered the seventh Lalit Doshi Memorial Lecture on 'Corruption in Public Life: Have We Become Immune?' in the year 2001.

I take this opportunity to convey to you my heartiest congratulations on being conferred with the PADMA BHUSHAN by the President of India.

The country's prestigious civilian honour bestowed upon you by the Government of India is a tribute to your exceptional and distinguished contribution to the Indian Civil Service for many decades.

I feel very happy and wish to convey my best wishes to you on this occasion.

With warm regards,

Yours sincerely
Bharat

Among this flood of congratulations, there was a different note struck by a retired Reserve Bank of India officer by name Chandramouleeswaran. He sent an email, I promptly replied and he appreciated my stand. I reproduce below the email exchanged.

4. Email from A Chandramouleeswaran

27th January 2012

Dear Shri Vittal,

Let me introduce myself before I intrude on your time and say what I wish to say. I was in the service of the RBI and retired as an Executive Director in October 2000. I am one of your admirers for your ability, bold suggestions and above all unimpeachable integrity. It was only during your tenure that the post of CVC came to notice and prominence. I used to attend your lectures in Mumbai and Chennai whenever possible, the latest being the lecture when you shared the platform with Shri Arun Shourie on the 2G scam. When I was at the fag end of my service, I was so keen to meet you that I sought an appointment with you and met you briefly in the RBI VIP Guest House in Napean Sea Road.

Before I make my suggestion in all humility, let me convey my heartiest congratulations on your being chosen for the Padma Bhushan award. There can be no two opinions on your richly deserving the award. Even then, I am of the view that you should politely decline the award even while thanking the Government as it has come from a Government which has not acted, even after almost a decade, on your suggestions for the enactment of three legislations which would prevent the corrupt from enjoying the ill-gotten wealth from their corrupt deeds. Furthermore, this Government's stand on creating an Independent Investigation Agency (in response to the debate on Jan Lokpal) raises serious doubts on their willingness to tackle corruption. I have taken the liberty of making this unsolicited (perhaps unwarranted too!) suggestion from my brief interaction with you I have gained the impression that you would not take me amiss. I find that your birthday would fall in a few days (Jan 31st) and you would complete 74 years of age. Let me wish you many more years of healthy life so that public discourses would get enriched from your contributions.

I have your residential telephone number and if you have no objection, I would also like to speak to you at your convenience.

Warm regards,

A Chandramouleeswaran

5. My Email Reply to A Chandramouleeswaran

28th January 2012

Dear Mr Chandramouleeswaran,

I thank you very much for your kind message of greetings on my birthday and thoughtful comments on the Padma Bhushan award.

I have carefully considered your sincere suggestion.

A long innings of 42 years in the IAS has made me realise that there is a Lakshman Rekha between the role of a civil servant and that of the political leader. It is the Civil Servant's job to generate policy options and suggest the most optimum option. It is the duty of the political leader to decide what will fly politically and decide. If the civil servant were to insist like a popular leader or a politician, and start competing with his minister, then he must leave the service and become a real live politician. That is the best rational solution. I am very proud of my batchmate in the 1960 batch of the IAS Yashwant Sinha. After 26 years in service he felt strongly about the conditions of the poor in his state and cadre of Bihar, joined politics and became an excellent political leader. I did not follow this path.

In my long career in every office I held, I was able to innovate and bring about changes for the better.

But I could not succeed in every initiative. The politician's sense of timing is uncanny. Ideas I mooted like the reorganisation of the geology and mining department in Gujarat, corporatisation of DoT, reserving a fixed percentage of the budget of every department for computerisation of that department are some of my many ideas that were implemented by the government.

I am therefore afraid that I am not able to accept your sincere suggestion.

I hope you will be able to appreciate my point of view.

After all, the award is a recognition of my track record as a civil servant. Not as self appointed guru on government policies for today.

Regards,
Vittal

6. Email Reply of A Chandramouleeswaran

28th January 2012

Dear Shri Vittal

I appreciate your detailed comments and must thank you for them as after all, you could have dismissed my suggestion just like that. Please accept the recognition which is richly deserved.

With warm regards and best wishes,

Chandramouleeswaran

The Padma Bhushan moment was one of the happiest points in life and adding to the happiness was the comments I received from many friends and others who had made better contribution for the development of the country.

December 2012 also was another month which was a combination of the best and worst. As the famous first sentence of the *Tale of Two Cities* of Charles Dickens begins, "It was the best of times and it was the worst of times."

On 23rd of December 2012, the CSI (Computer Society of India) invited me to receive personally their Life Time Achievement Award. In fact, they had earlier asked me to make it on 1st of December 2012 to receive it at the CSI's Annual Convention at Kolkata. As my health was not alright, I had declined the offer and finally I made it to Bangalore where a CSI programme was scheduled. But what a tragedy! In the presence of my wife, I had an attack of hypoglycaemia and literally collapsed when I went to deliver my acceptance speech. This tragedy was only a precursor of what happened in Hyderabad on 23rd December 2013. I had already mentioned it in the first chapter dealing with why this book was written and why now.

But in December 2012, that was not all. On 26th December 2012, at 2 PM suddenly I had an attack of TIA (Transient Ischemic Attack). And I just lost my power of speech. I was rushed to the hospital fortunately within an hour and thanks to the timely medical help rendered, after four days I returned home on 31st December. On 1st January 2013, I had to preside over the Aaradhana of Raghavendra Swamy in Perambur, Chennai. I had no hesitation in attributing my ability to be present and talk on that occasion as directly due to the blessings of Lord Venkateswara and Guru Raghavendra.

Apart from the story of medical records which are perhaps typical of the sunset years, there is a positive side to the decade of my retirement in Chennai. The most important is the invigorating inputs I received on the cultural and the spiritual front. Chennai is ideal for any person interested in classical Carnatic music, religious discourses and discussions about the beauty of the Tamil language. I am enjoying to my full all these three areas. I have received positive inputs of the best that the human mind in this part of the world has produced and this has helped me to add life to my years of sunset.

That is not all. There are two other sources and friends who have made my whole years of retirement as productive and meaningful. They are Mr Pankaj Saran, Vice-President of the EMPI Business School and G Suresh at present Deputy Chief Vigilance Officer of the Kandla Port Trust. Suresh has been almost like a member of my family for the last decade and a half. None of my books would have been possible but for his immense patient, commitment and cheerful follow up to see that the time targets are met and the writings see the light of day. In fact, I wrote a column for the *Mumbai Mirror* from 2005 to 2010 were met without missing a single week even though that was the period in which I had to undergo my bye-pass surgery and other medical complications. All that was possible because of Suresh.

Pankaj Saran who is just like my son and slightly younger than my son Sharan, with his idealism and vision was the person who continuously from 2002 onwards after I retired, connected me with the EMPI Business School and the various proposals we followed, starting with a Vittal Centre for Governance and Informatics ensure that we traced an exciting journey through education, industry and innovation.

Vittal Centre was to be a forum to bring the academy, industry and the government on a single platform to ensure that India derives full benefit of its advantage in the sunrise industry of IT. One major issue identified was that India will require adequate manpower to take full advantage of the demographic dividend. This in turn lead to the idea of setting up an education focused SEZ that in turn lead to the Vittal Innovation City which today is poised to launch the whole series of innovative programmes. The most significant of which is the Reserve Water Foundation as well as the association with many initiatives like the operations in the Defence production area of the Air Bus.

This association of mine with Pankaj Saran has brought a welcome twist in the basic thrust of my golden years. Instead of chewing the cud of memories and indulging in nostalgia I am active in chasing new goals and missions to build a better and brighter India.

CHAPTER 8

TARAKA MANTRAS

Many a time, we tend to forget that above all of us, there is a divine presence. For me a Hindu, it is Lord Venkateswara (Balaji). I am Madhwa and Madhwacharya, one of the three great Gurus of Hindu religion had preached that the basic fact to remember is 'Harihi Paratharaha' ie Lord Narayana (Hari) is the Supreme power. My colleague and a more spiritually evolved person in the IAS PVRK Prasad titled his experiences, especially with the Lord of Seven Hills *Naham Kartha Hari Kartha* is the ultimate reality. We do not do anything and it is Lord who performs but in our ignorance, which many call as *'maya'* we tend to think that we are the fellow who are performing things and claim credit for success. Of course, we blame others for failure because it is a universal human tendency to always blame others. When we find our shirts and pants have become tight for us because we have started putting on weight we still blame that it is the pant and shirt which have become tight. Not the other way round. Starting with that this tendency was very dramatically summarised by John F Kennedy soon after he took over as the US President. The operation to bring about a regime change in Cuba which was when under the control of Fidel Castro failed dramatically. JFK said, "success has many fathers, but failure is an orphan" and showed his qualities of leadership. When anything succeeds in life. there is many claim credit for that. There is also the basic truth that nobody succeeds only by working as an individual. It is always the team or group of people who buy into the idea which might have been provided by the leader or the visionary or the person who is under the delusion that he has achieved success, but when things fail, no one wants to accept responsibility for the failure. Therefore, failure becomes an orphan. Kennedy's greatness was to openly acknowledge that the CIA mission which ended in the Bay of Pigs disaster in 1960-61, a disaster of which as President of the United States, he took the full responsibility. The advice given by Kabir, *"Nindak niyare raakhiye, Aangan kuti chhavaay"* therefore, has to me one of the three basic mantras by which I have tried to live my life. The other two were also from saints. It is saint Tulsidas who says, *"Dukh Me Sumiran Sab Kare, Sukh Me Sumiran Kare Na Koi Sukh Me Sumiran Jo Kare, Dukh Kahe Ka hoi"*. When we are enjoying a good time, we hardly think of God. But when we are in trouble, we first think of God. The need for constantly reminding ourselves about the presence of the supreme power is something which has been my other basic mantras by which I lived my life. These mantras are supposed to be *'taraka mantras'*. Taraka means swimming or crossing the waters. In our Hindu philosophy, we look at birth and death cycle as trying to cross the ocean of Bhavasagara. To cross the ocean, one can hardly swim across the oceans but this vast ocean of birth and death can be successfully crossed and swam across only by people who realise that it is the Lord who is the supreme master and we are all only instruments.

This means that we should not become egoistic. One methods of ensuring that you do not become an egoistic, you should have a resident critic who points out all the time, wherever you fail. In my case, my wife, is an expert in providing 360 degree criticism. It may be about the cleanliness, the way of talking, the tone of the body, the failure to take in to account the other point of view, assertiveness and so on. In fact, after listening to her criticism, many a time, I felt what a nasty egoistic person I have been and how big has been my 'I' defect. This important function my wife Gita had performed, many times. I wonder she ever realised that I might have benefited not only by her advice but also realised and feel grateful to her. She was indeed my dream girl. In fact, in our among relations, I have been a typical bookworm and throughout I studied in Jesuit institutions and Christian Missionary Institutions and I didn't have the exposure of studying in a co-education institution which perhaps removes the shyness and reserved approach which those students come to such an institution enjoy. In my youth also, it was not very common for the women in the house also participate in general discussions when visitors came. Discussions will be only within the family. Practically in every household the wife of the head of the family was the dominant personality. Even Paramacharya of Kanchi Kamakoti Peetham has given a general advice to those who want to know the right path and what is the right way of observing festivals and rituals. He said that we should go by the advice of the senior most lady in the house, who has seen how different generations have observed because, each family has its own traditions and it is the lady of the house who was the head of the HUF who was the anchor and guide so far as continuing traditions of a family are concerned. Throughout my school days and college days, I have been a bookworm and I have been a model student and focusing 24 × 7 on my studies and by the grace of God, fortunately, I had a track record of standing in first throughout my school, right from the day at the age of seven I joined 4th standard in Bishop Heber School, Puttur and passed out of SSLC in 1953 and thereafter in St Joseph College, Tiruchirapalli, the 1st and 2nd University classes, known as Intermediate was again in a Christian institution and I did three more years in the BSc (Hons) course in Chemistry in Loyala College. We lived in Hostel while in the College, we in the chemistry honours course considered ourselves exclusive and a cut above others because unlike other subject there were only 20 seats so far as the Chemistry (Honours) was concerned, 10 seats in Presidency College and 10 in Loyola. So in this background, I finished my honours course at the age of 20.

The choice before me was to go for research or take a shot at the IAS. In those days, the IAS was the best opportunity available for the bright students. The idea was that it was the successor service to the Indian Civil Service, which over a century in the colonial rule had built a tremendous reputation for integrity and supreme competence so that getting into the ICS and in my time the IAS was indeed stamp of arrival and acceptance of an individual as a bright successful competent young man.

Incidentally, in our Hindu approach to life, the wife becomes ultimately, *dharmapatni*. From being the dream girl to *dharmapatni*, the transition comes through the various faces which I have gone through Gita as my life partner. It is her role in cautioning me by being a *nindhak* to ensure that I truly live up to my dharma. The dharma according to Vedanta, the essence of Vedanta summed up by Prof A Parthasarathy is: *Atmano mokshartham jagat hitaya cha*. The path to liberation comes by leading a righteous life based on dharma and dharma ultimately is as defined in our Hindu Varnashrama Dharma is to observe the codes of conduct in each phase in life – Brahmacharya, Grihastha, Vanaprastha and Sannyasa. Gita and I are in the stage of Vanaprastha and as I look back and it should be obvious as you read this book, at every stage, it is she who helped me to stick to the straight of the narrow path. In a sense, I fully realised the Taraka Mantras which our Indian cultural traditions provides. The following three mantras have been of immense value to me as a guide in my life. (i) *"Dukh men sumiran sab karen, sukh men kare na koi, sukh men sumiran jo kare, dukh kahe ko hoi"*. Remember above all the presence of the Supreme Lord, in my case Lord Venkateswara. The second is the Kabir's guidance about sticking to the dharma, *"Nindak niyare rakhiye aangan kuti chhawaye"*. It is in this aspect my dream girl Gita has become my *dharmapatni*. The third one is again from Kabir. This is a reality I have faced in my life and armed with the first two mantras, it makes my life more meaningful. What Kabir says is, *"Kabira isa sansar men sabse miliye hath na jane kis roop men Narayana mil jayen"*. Kabir says, be friendly with every person you meet, because you don't know in what form Lord Narayana will come. In fact, by nature and background and the life I have gone through, by and large, I have adopted an attitude of helpfulness to any person who comes to me with a request. I do not suspect any person who come to me skiing in my mind why is he approaching me, what is his ulterior motive. This sort of trying to help others has given me immense dividend in life especially in my last stage.

I mentioned earlier about the astrological prediction by the venerable Agnihotri from Demai village, Sabarkantha district when I was Collector way back in 1964. He said that my life is going to be one of continuous improvement from good, better, best. The better became the best because of the third principle of *"Kabira isa sansar men sabse miliye hath na jane kis roop men Narayana mil jayen"*. In this old age, the unexpected help you get from sources about which you have no idea at all when you acted and when you are in power has been brought home to me. When I took over as Secretary, Department of Electronics, it was called then and now became Department of Information Technology; one of the cases I handled was that of a complaint from the Exim Bank about the American Express Company. That company had imported duty free goods under the phased manufacturing programme. IBM System 400, which was a huge machine, like of which was used for the first time in LIC. This was for processing the requirement of the American company. The point raised by the Exim Bank was that while they had imported the IBM system, they have also entered into an agreement under capital goods scheme that they will earn the value of the duty exempted over a period of 5 years. In between, the Government of India adopted economic liberalisation process and the capital goods involving the phased manufacturing programme was abolished. The question was whether company like the American Express which had imported the system and which had only done about three of the five years covered by the guarantee. They are still to complete the remaining two years export obligation. Because I realised that once the economic liberalisation programme was introduced, the exports already done were adequate and distinction was maintained between new importers post liberalisation and old importers like American Express, it would be unfair, I issued an order in my capacity as Secretary to the Government of India and thereby responsible for the government that in order to encourage the very idea of economic liberalisation was encouraging software exports from the country and if the exporters are burdened with the phased manufacturing programme, the entire progress will be halted and what is worse there will an immediate distinction between the old importers who will be under the burden of discharging the remaining obligations of exports and the new one who did not suffer from this liability. In order to really meet the basic objectives of the liberalisation programme and more important to ensure there is a level playing field among the software exporters, I took the decision, in my power as Secretary to the Government of India under the Rules of Business, I issued a Notification that all those current exporters of software who had included the IBM computers under the capital goods scheme would be deemed to have fulfilled their requirement when the New Economic Policy was brought into operation by the Government of India. This gave a great relief to the industry and was one of the factors that helped the zooming of the software industry in my time from 100 million when it was in 1990 to 2.6 billion in January 1996 when I retired from service from IAS and the department. The Exim Bank still insisted on the letter of the law and their attitude if I can be pardoned, was that of the Shylock in the *Merchant of Venice*. So I wrote to the Exim Bank that Exim Bank should not insist on American Express fulfilling still the remaining two years export obligation and thereby put them to punishment by way of asking them to pay their entire duty on the system that imported already under the old scheme.

I therefore, recorded my decision with the above reasoning in the file. The Executive Director of the Exim Bank at that time

Ms Tarjani Patel wanted to personally come and explain the Exim Bank's stand. When she came, I heard her and repeated my decision recorded in front of her. I realised later on that I was one of the very few Secretaries and perhaps the only Secretary in the Government of India who adopted the practice of recording in the presence of the parties the minutes of the meeting in real time using Dictaphone. The standard tradition otherwise was wait for the stenographer and dictate when the stenographer was physically available. Having discovered in 1982 when I was MD, GNFC, the advantage of Dictaphone, I had become an addict to the Dictaphone, as would be seen in the relevant part of this book. One technique I adopted throughout my life is to realise the importance of time and recording decisions with full reasons in real time. When I was Collector I used to do it with a stenographer who was available even when I went on camp. Once I discovered the advantage of the Dictaphone, I started using it from 1982. In other words, from my 22nd year of service, out of my total 42 years, I had been adopting this practice of recording decisions in real time. This has helped me a lot and I have described at length this practice of mine about how one can be effective in government and also productive as well as being creative, that is much later. What is relevant at this point is the importance of consequence of what I did. As Kabir advised, when I took the decision, I had no idea of what the long time consequences are going to be. As soon as I took the decision, a few days later, Dr Prathap Reddy, Chairman of the Apollo Hospitals dropped in to my room. He introduced himself to me and said, "I have come to thank you because your this action has helped my brother-in-law a great deal from financial embracement to the extent of a few crores." I left it at that and later on I discovered that in my post retirement years, this simple decision of mine is going to give me rich dividends. Dr Prathap Reddy became a personal friend and what is more we discovered that both of us have been students of the Loyola College and I was at that time President of the Loyola Alumni Association Northern Division and we started using the hospitality of the Apollo Hospitals (Indraprastha Hospitals) Delhi every annually for holding our get together and meet all the Alumni belonging to the Loyola Alumni Association, Northern Division. This association later on became very critical especially at a time when it was the question of my life and death. I had my first heart attack, which could have led to myocardial infraction on 30th May 2006. My friend and batchmate one year junior to me, 1961 Gujarat cadre Mr Vinay Sharma who was an expert in homeopathy and who was treating my daughter died and he died suddenly. I had gone to call on his wife in their house and that night I could hardly sleep properly and I was very uneasy and complained to Pankaj Saran who was the Vice-President of the EMPI Business School, CSKM Educational Complex at about 11 PM. He rushed me to the Max Hospital which later on became Fortis for immediate relief and treatment. That was the golden hour where immediate attention is needed for saving anybody's life if he is facing myocardial infection. I was saved and the doctors advised that I should, with my background of nearly four decades of diabetes and blood pressure, I require corollary bypass and that too a quaternary corollary bypass. I was admitted and this came as a shock to my wife who was way down in Bangalore and she had to rush to Delhi and she was in a helpless condition and we had no base at that time in Delhi having shifted base to Chennai. My wife then immediately contacted Dr Prathap Reddy who was in Hyderabad and from that moment he took full charge about my medical treatment. He persuaded the management of Max Hospital, as a special case to shift me from Delhi to Apollo Hospital and flown under medical care by 6th of June 2006. I underwent quaternary bypass surgery on 8th June 2006. Subsequently, I have had serious medical problems and at every stage it was Apollo Hospital which saved my life, especially their battery of doctors. When I recall this enormous benefit I derived at a critical moment in my life, thanks to simple act of performing one's duty without expecting any favour, convinced me totally that there is enormous truth in the observation of Kabir about helping everybody one who comes across to the extent possible. My logic is very simple. The very fact that somebody approaches you with the request for help is that he entertains a hope that you will be able to help him, especially in our country whereas in perhaps many of the eastern countries, it is networking and contact that matter. In China, this is called 'juan xi'. Actually some may question, whether after retirement one can be effective. After all in government, it is the position which gives power. If we take the world of a jungle, the live lion may be the King of the forest but once the lion is dead, the living jackal is more powerful than the dead lion. Similarly, in government, a Secretary to the government who has retired is a dead lion. A lower division clerk who is in service exercises like a jackal the power much more than the dead lion. But the willingness to help a retired person, many a time finds a friendly echo and by and large, I have found that if one approaches juniors in service to the request by and large, they oblige. This spirit of helping a fellow IAS officer is extremely strong in the IAS. No wonder it has been called the strongest trade union in India is the IAS. This is but one example of what benefit I got. But there are many in my life which you will come across as you go through the book.

In the biography of Dr Prathap Reddy, *Healer: Dr Prathap Chandra Reddy and the Transformation of India*, this experience is recorded as follows:

> "One mistake that he acknowledges concerns an investment that he made in an IT company. On one of his visits to the USA, Dr Reddy had met the Senior Vice-President of Intel, who said that they would be happy to associate with Dr Reddy's group in setting up an IT company in India. Many of his friends advised Dr Reddy that this partnership with a giant like Intel would have huge potential in India and he founded a company in Madras with an investment of $8,00,000. But what Intel and Dr Reddy had not foreseen were the huge bureaucratic and regulatory delays that a

facility in the export zone had to put up with. Intel was partnering with a company in the private sector in India for the first time and it could not understand or condone these delays of several weeks for the movement of any material. This led to their disenchantment and Dr Reddy was forced to close the company. Dr Reddy feels that it was an investment ahead of its time, made well before IT became a favoured sector in India.

One of the main people whom Dr Reddy consulted before he withdrew was Nagarajan Vittal, a prominent member of the IAS, who was to become the Central Vigilance Commissioner (CVC). "He was Secretary in charge of electronics to the Government of India and interested in bringing IT and software to the country. He also was successful in introducing the electronics hardware technology park scheme to boost the manufacture of electronic hardware," Dr Reddy said:

> "Vittal could see what IT could possibly do for India. He realised what an enormous impact it could have for foreign exchange and economic growth. He saw it long before Bangalore became an IT centre and other places, like Hyderabad, followed soon after."

When I told him that I wanted to surrender my interests, he said, "Then we must have a ceremonial burial for the company." Two years after that IT improvement programmes came about and look what has happened now.

Dr Reddy added:

> "He's a very straightforward man, no ifs and buts. This was very important because he became the Central Vigilance Commissioner and his integrity was never questioned. The CVC has enormous powers and can investigate and arrest anyone for wrongdoing. He was very, very powerful and allowed no nonsense.
>
> He still comes to Apollo for his check-ups."

In short, therefore, the three principles which helps anyone to lead a clean effective, productive life are:

(i) *Dukh men simran sab karen, sukh men kare na koye jo sukh men simran kare, to dukh kahe ko hoye.*

(ii) *Kabira isa sansar men sabse miliye hath na jane kis roop mein Narayan mil jae.*

(iii) *Nindak niyare rakhiye aangan kuti chhawaye, bin sabun pani bina nirmal karat subhaye.*

If one has lived according to this principle, one realises that ultimately, the worth of a life is measured in terms of the contribution one makes to the society rather than the goods and services one has enjoyed to the full. After all, in history, the Maharajas who enjoyed themselves fully, thanks to their wealth are hardly remembered unless there are people interested in the luxury enjoyed by the Maharajas like Diwan Jarmani Dass's book *Maharaja: The Lives, Loves and Intrigues of the Maharajas of India* on the Indian kings. The contribution made by the people is only what is remembered. What is the motivation for such continuing efforts. This again arises from the above three principles. If one feels that one is responsible for all one achievement and not a *nimitta matram*, then one can develop a sense of complacency and there is no incentive to explore new horizons. On the other hand, if one realises that the value of the life is measured in terms of the contributions one make and not what one consumes or honours one gets for the services rendered, then one will seize to be productive. It has been said that those scientists who win Nobel laureates many a time seize to be productive after winning a prize and getting universal recognition which makes them celebrities and draws heavily upon their time for listening to their achievements and they hardly left with any time to continue with their research. One of the recent Indian winners of Nobel Prize like Venki (Ramachandran Venkatraman) have highlighted the fact that scientists who get the Nobel awards should continue to pursue their research and not just rest on their toes.

In short, the above Taraka Mantras I have quoted are also useful to lead the life to the full and make every moment a productive one. Or to use the cliché – This is the formula for adding life to years rather than add years to life.

INDEX